Leading Issues in ICT Evaluation

Edited by

Egon Berghout

Leading Issues in ICT Evaluation
Volume One.

Copyright © 2012 The authors
First Edition January 2012

All rights reserved. Except for the quotation of short passages for the purposes of critical review, no part of this publication may be reproduced in any material form (including photocopying or storing in any medium by electronic means and whether or not transiently or incidentally to some other use of this publication) without the written permission of the copyright holder except in accordance with the provisions of the Copyright Designs and Patents Act 1988, or under the terms of a licence issued by the Copyright Licensing Agency Ltd, Saffron House, 6-10 Kirby Street, London EC1N 8TS. Applications for the copyright holder's written permission to reproduce any part of this publication should be addressed to the publishers.

Disclaimer: While every effort has been made by the editor, authors and the publishers to ensure that all the material in this book is accurate and correct at the time of going to press, any error made by readers as a result of any of the material, formulae or other information in this book is the sole responsibility of the reader. Readers should be aware that the URLs quoted in the book may change or be damaged by malware between the time of publishing and accessing by readers.

Note to readers.
Some papers have been written by authors who use the American form of spelling and some use the British. These two different approaches have been left unchanged.

ISBN: 978-1-906638-90-0

Published by: Academic Publishing International Limited, Reading, RG4 9AY, United Kingdom, info@academic-publishing.org

Printed by Goodnewsdigitalpress in the UK.

Available from www.academic-bookshop.com

Contents

List of Contributors ii

Introduction to Leading Issues in IS Evaluation Research iii

Broadening Information Systems Evaluation Through Narratives 1
    Jonas Hedman and Andreas Borell

e-Commerce Investments from an SME perspective: Costs, Benefits
and Processes 17
    Sandra Cohen and Kallirroi Georgila

A Holistic Framework on Information Systems Evaluation with a Case
Analysis 43
    Petri Hallikainen and Lena Chen

An Interactive and Iterative Evaluation Approach for Creating
Collaborative Learning Environments... 60
    Anita Mirijamdotter, Mary M. Somerville and Marita Holst

Does ROI Matter? Insights into the True Business Value of IT 82
    A J G Silvius

Interpretative IS Evaluation: Results and Uses 105
    Jenny Lagsten and Göran Goldkuhl

Proposal of a Compact IT Value Assessment Method 126
    Przemysław Lech

When Paradigms Shift: IT Evaluation in a Brave New World.................... 145
    Frank Bannister

The Eleven Years of the European Conference on IT Evaluation:
Retrospectives and Perspectives for Possible Future Research 165
    Egon Berghout and Dan Remenyi

List of Contributors

Frank Bannister, Trinity College Dublin, Ireland

Egon Berghout, University of Groningen, The Netherlands

Andreas Borell, Tetra Pak Global IM, Sweden

Lena Chen, General Education Center, National University of Arts, Taiwan

Sandra Cohen, Athens University of Economics and Business, Greece

Kallirroi Georgila, Athens University of Economics and Business, Greece

Göran Goldkuhl, Linköping University, Linköping, Sweden

Petri Hallikainen, Information Systems Science, Helsinki School of Economics, Finland

Jonas Hedman, Copenhagen Business School, Denmark

Marita Holst, Luleå University of Technology, Social Informatics, Sweden

Jenny Lagsten, Örebro University, Örebro, Sweden

Przemysław Lech, Faculty of Management, University of Gdańsk, Poland

Anita Mirijamdotter, University of Technology, Social Informatics, Sweden

Dan Remenyi, Trinity College Dublin, Ireland

Mary M. Somerville, Dr. Martin Luther King Jr. Library, San José State University, USA

A J G Silvius, Utrecht University of Professional Education, The Netherlands

Introduction to Leading Issues in ICT Evaluation Research

It is a genuine pleasure to select 10 of the best papers of the Electronic Journal of Information System Evaluation. This selection provides an excellent opportunity to look back on so many years of excellent work. The electronic journal was started to provide expeditious and accessible access to IT Evaluation research. Its 13 years tradition confirms the success of the journal's approach. It is truly impressive to experience how many researchers throughout the world use the Electronic Journal of Information System Evaluation to discover the IT Evaluation field of research of research.

IT Evaluation research has been active since at least 1990 when the first publications addressed this issue were produced. Before that time it was generally believed that IT Evaluation was fundamentally a complex accounting problem and that it was probably too difficult and that there was no great likelihood of success in this endeavour. The early years of computing were marked by a lack of understanding of just how ubiquitous IT was to become and a general lack of appreciation of how much this technology would ultimately cost. At conferences in the last 1990s audiences were often incredulous at the research finding from the USA that in many organisations half of the total investment budget was being spent on IT. It is fair to say that some organisations proceeded somnambulantly into late 20th century and early 21st century computing. A good example of this is the awe with which we reflected on the fact that during the decade of the 1980s the world wide usage of IT had been estimated to have cost a trillion dollars. By the early years of the 21st century it was being estimated that the world wide usage of IT was more than two trillion dollars per year. No other industry has ever seen growth like this.

It was also believed that computerisation was inevitable and that organisations should just get on with it. At that time an elderly professor remarked, "Do not take doctoral research students in the field of IT Evaluation as it is just too difficult". Fortunately that advice was not listen to and the IT Evaluation research has attracted some very fine talent over the years and today we have a much greater understanding of the issues which underpinned IT Evaluation.

When we look back at research into IT Evaluation in the 1990s we can easily identify a high degree of naivety. Both the private sector including management consultancies and the public sector including quasi-government agencies spent considerable amounts of time and resources looking for a formula with which IT could be evaluated. Although good work was performed no conclusive approach was produced.

What is true is that the challenge of assessing IT investment performance, which we now generally refer to as ICT Evaluation, has at times seemed to be intractable. One of the main obstacles which we have faced is one of naivety. There is an unspoken belief that if we cannot evaluate ICT perfectly then perhaps we should admit that we are unable to do it at all. This type of thinking is a self defeating misunderstanding of the nature of business and management practice. By its very nature business and management practice, which is a social science, does not lend itself to a high degree of precise evaluation or measurement. There is simply no question of being able to measure a return on investment (ROI) to any degree of accuracy. If you are told that the ROI is 10.55% all that this signifies is that the organisation reporting this result is either unaware of the challenges in estimation cost and benefits or they are deceitful, perhaps in the hope that the reader will be gullible. Of course even if we could agree as to how to calculate the ROI on an ICT investment and it was acceptable to calculate this to the nearest few percentage points, we would still be faced with the challenge that an ROI would at best simply represent only one dimension of the impact of ICT on an organisation.

It is also worth pointing out that in the 1990s those who were interested in IT Evaluation were nearly always deeply embedded in the summative evaluation paradigm which is only helpful up to a point. Although formative evaluation was already an established technique it had not yet been adopted by the ICT fraternity.

ICT insinuates itself into the very DNA of an organisation in the western world. It not only affects processes and practices but it impacts on objectives, strategies, tactics and competitive advantage. ICT lay down the foundation for HR practices, for remote working, for the virtual office, for interactions between people at various stages of the business processes. ICT is fundamental to product development and marketing analysis. It is a key issue in product design. It is a facilitator in addressing some of the key packaging concerns. It is not possible to envisage any part of an organisation which does not draw on the facilities which are enhanced by the use of ICT.

And so we have come to realise that ICT Evaluation actually means Organisational Evaluation and thus needs to reflect the many issues which are of concern to those interested in organisational evaluation in the broadest sense of the term and this implies being aware of holistic issues.

What characterizes IT Evaluation research? First, we should conclude that IT Evaluation research is highly eclectic and thus reaches out to many fields of interests.

It includes the evaluation of successful use of information systems, either analyzed ex-post, or ex-ante. In this sentences 'success' may also refer to many target variables, such as, adding value (economics), technology acceptance (sociology), process improvements (organisational success) or technical successes (technology itself). Furthermore, IT Evaluation research refers to all industries. Healthcare and Public information systems frequently receive attention and this is probably because particularly in these areas, it is less straightforward to assess traditional financial success. In measuring this success, IT Evaluation research, because of its complexity is multidisciplinary/interdisciplinary/cross disciplinary or trans-disciplinary. This is probably, because the research is primarily driven by genuine business problems and seeks practically relevant guidelines for the successful use of information systems in organisations.

Another question which is sometimes raised is, *To what extent is IT Evaluation research different from IT Management research?* The successful use of information systems is definitely part of IT Management research, however, in IT Evaluation research one typically expects a frame of reference before the evaluation can make any sense. This frame of reference is often imprecise, such as the use of narrative in one of the papers. However, it is always there. As such, IT Evaluation research could be positioned at various points or be employed through different lenses and perhaps be located somewhere in between IT Management and IT Auditing.

But what is perhaps the most fascinating aspects of IT Evaluation is that dispute all the valuable research performed to date we still have not had any degree of consensus as to how proceed with this challenging endeavour. There are still far too many competing ideas and no were near enough consolidation of thinking. Although this is in some ways a "good thing" we are perhaps coming to a point where consolidation is essential. Perhaps the bringing together of all the ideas floating around today will be completed by someone reading this book.

In the meantime I trust you will enjoy reading these exemplary studies.

Egon Berghout
Professor of Business & ICT
University of Groningen
The Netherlands

Dan Remenyi
Visiting Professor
Trinity College Dublin
Ireland

February 2012

Broadening Information Systems Evaluation Through Narratives

Jonas Hedman[1] and Andreas Borell[2]
[1] Copenhagen Business School, Denmark
[2] Tetra Pak Global IM, Sweden
Originally Published in EJISE (2005) Volume 8: Issue 2

Editor's Comment
It is interesting to note that the concept of formative evaluation came relatively late to IT evaluators. In fact even today not everyone in the IT Evaluation community fully understands the role of formative evaluation. Formative evaluation requires much moe skill than a simple summative approach which can be really quite sterile.
In this paper J Hedman and A Borell (2005) illustrate that in IT Evaluation research, many frameworks are acceptable as frame of reference and that the application of narratives can be very successful. This is an important step in opening up the broader discussion of IT Evaluation and the application tyo this of qualitative methods of which narratives are but one example. The expression "figures never are facts" (Hoebeke, 1990) is used which can be seen as an extreme point of view and highly dependent on the definition of "facts".

Abstract: The purpose of information systems post-evaluation ought to be to improve the use of systems. The paper proposes the use of narratives as a tool in post-evaluations. The potential in narratives is that they can convey meanings, interpretations, and knowledge about the system, which may potentially lead to action. The paper offer three main suggestions: 1) evaluations should form the basis for action; 2) narratives makes evaluation more relevant; and 3) post-evaluations should be done with the aim of improving use. Narratives should be viewed as a complement to traditional evaluation methods and as a way of making evaluation more formative and thereby moving away from the more common summative perception of evaluation. The conclusion of the paper is that narratives can advance IS evaluation and provide a richer evaluation picture by conveying meanings not included in traditional evaluations.

Keywords: Narratives, information systems evaluation, measurements, measure, stories, action.

1. Introduction

The aim of this paper is to contribute to information systems evaluation by introducing narratives in the evaluation process. The potential with narratives is that they can convey meanings, interpretations, and knowledge (learning) about the system, which can be used for further action. The aim of the paper should be viewed in relation to some practical issues in IS evaluation, such as evaluations is a problematic (Irani and Love 2001) and complex process (Jones and Hughes 2001), which becomes more difficult with increased complexity of IS (Farbey, Land and Targett 1995), and the growing concern that information systems do not deliver business value (Irani and Love 2001).

The literature describes several roles for IS evaluation. Serafeimidis and Smithson (2003) described control, sense-making, learning and exploratory orientations in IS evaluation. The view taken on evaluation of information systems in this paper is pragmatic: Once a particular system has been implemented, the focus of evaluation should be on continuously improving the benefits received. The pragmatic approach is based on three assumptions about evaluation in this context.

- Firstly, evaluations should form the basis for action: do not measure if you cannot act on the measurement.
- Secondly, post evaluations ought to be carried out with the goal of improving the use of system, not only assessing the worth of a system.
- Thirdly, narratives can grasp the complexity of information systems better than traditional evaluation approaches, such as return on investment or total cost of opportunity.

The paper builds on research from interpretive research in information systems, such as Klein and Meyer (1999), Serafeimidis and Smithson(2000) and Walsham (1993; 1995; 1999); post-modern institutional theory (Meyer and Rowan 1977); and narratives in , accounting (Llewellyn 1998) knowledge management (Snowden 2002; Swap, Leomard, Shields and Abrams 2001), and requirements engineering (Jarke, Bui and Caroll 1998). The first two are primarily used as theoretical ground for the use and relevance of narratives whereas the latter is used as a source of practical and methodological inspiration. Thus, the aim of this paper is not try to improve the understanding of the evaluation process as such, which is common in interpretative research (see for instance Walsham 1993), but to provide inputs to how we conceptually can advance IS evaluation.

The paper is organised as follow. The following section addresses and discusses evaluation and role of measurement in evaluation. Following this is the theory of action and learning is described, which is the theoretical ground for improvement driven evaluation. Narratives and the use of narratives, which should be interpreted as the means for action, in evaluations are then explored and discussed. The paper ends with a discussion and conclusion on the practical implications for information systems evaluation.

2. IS evaluation and measurements

While it is reasonably easy to evaluate tangible implementation costs, e.g. software license, hardware, consultancy, and training, other intangible cost are much more difficult to measure and evaluate (e.g. productivity dip and resistance to change). As a response to these difficulties both practitioners and academics have developed a number of methods and tools to support the process of determining the costs and value of IS. These issues and others have lead to extensive research into IS evaluation. The remainder of this section highlight some research contributions, which are important to understand the role of narratives in IS evaluation.

Evaluation is not a simple and straightforward process (Jones and Hughes, 2001) and may have many purposes, e.g. control projects, govern change management, communication, improvements, resource allocation, motivation, and long term planning (Sinclair and Zairi, 1995). In addition, Remenyi and Sherwood-Smith (1999) described two practical and very relevant issues in IS evaluation. The first is the so-called evaluation gap. This occurs when the evaluator distance themselves from the project and lose sight of the business objectives. The second concerns that business objectives of the IS project, e.g. organisational change and change management, are often forgotten or superficially attended to in evaluations.

As the field of IS evaluation has matured the view of IS evaluations has changed over the past years. Today there is an increased awareness about the importance of an ongoing evaluation process. There is also a growing number of IS researchers arguing that IS evaluation should focus on how IS supports businesses – the use of system, i.e. a formative evaluation process (Remenyi and Sherwood-Smith, 1999). However, a practical issue is that the purpose of IS evaluation is often to close the project (Kumar, 1990; see also Seddon et al., 2002), with emphasis on ROI (Murphy and Simon, 2002). Hirschheim and Smithson (1998) offer an explanation for this. They claim that there is a widespread belief that IS are fundamentally a technical system. Consequently, this has lead to "a more "technical" interpretation of evaluation" (p. 402) with a focus on tools and techniques and thereby omitting the social domain. This makes it unlikely to produce a "true" or meaningful evaluation picture (Hirschheim and Smithson, 1998).

A common factor in all evaluations is the use of measurements (Venkatraman and Ramanujam, 1986). Strassman (1985, p. 100) stresses that: "You cannot measure what is not defined. You also cannot tell whether you have improved something if you have not measured its performance", i.e. the need of an operational definition. This is, however, difficult since "figures never are facts" (Hoebeke, 1990). Hoebeke (1990) made this comment in relation to a discussion regarding the use of measurements based on calculations, e.g. financial accounting. Measurements are invariably used in complex sense-making processes where both translations and interpretations take place, usually several times in different steps (figure 1). This, as Hoebeke (1990) points out, makes the concept of relevance a lot more important than objectivity - there has to be a shared meaning of the interpretations and their impacts by those who play a role in the process of collecting, translating and interpreting the measures, as well as those who act on decisions based on said measurements. Hoebeke's main point is that in organisational sense-making processes such as evaluation it is impossible to have a fit between measure and action, because of the interpretations taking place.

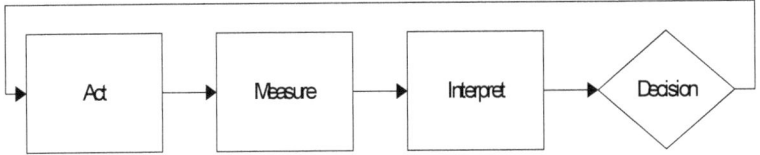

Figure 1: Chain of activities that take place in organisational sense making

Farbey et al. (1995) implicitly addressed sense-making problem. They proposed a model which is based on the perception that it is possible to stratify different types of organisational change and connecting it to different IS. Their model consists of eight levels, and while the classification is not rigid, it still implies that higher levels of change increase the potential benefits, but also increase the uncertainty of outcome. Potential benefits and level of uncertainty are both cumulative, thus systems classified on a certain level may have all the benefits (and accumulated uncertainty) from any or all the levels below. Farbey et al. (1995) conclude that for the implementation of systems on the 8th level (business transformation) "… benefits stem from the transformation as a whole. IT provides only one component of what is often a complex series of changes. It is not possible to attribute a portion of the benefits gained to any one factor" (p. 49). It would then be highly unlikely that any two implementations will have identical requirements or consequences, even if they are based on the same generic software packages. While the potential benefits might be articulated, it makes the actual benefits from implementing an IS hard to define, predict, and evaluate.

In summary, we argue that evaluation should be used as a basis for action. IS implementations are only limited in time in the most abstract sense and governed by other organisational activities; project plans, budget years, top management changes and organisational strategic decisions. Implementing a complex IS are deeply interconnected with organisational change and for the lifetime of the system, it remains a large part of the organisations formalised internal framework. Evaluation in this context should be performed continuously, combined with process reviews and organisational development, aiming to get the desired alignment and fit over time. To get the most out of a large organisation, the result of evolution has to be evaluated and new requirements formulated in an iterative process. The key to getting the most out of any IS is the use; use in this perspective is regarded in the broadest sense, including other use, miss-use, abuse and non use of system by humans and connected IS. To achieve the intended use of the system in the organisational context, organisational goals and beliefs have to be communicated to members of the organisation. Organisations use myths and narratives to make sense of equivocal situations and they are used as precedents for future actions, serving as "blue-prints" for desirable behaviour (Alvarez and Urla, 2002). The following section presents theory of action as theoretical ground and justification for the use of narratives.

3. Theory of action and narratives

Human actions are not always what they seem to be. Humans invariably employ text rich documents to propose ideas, argument cases and give verdict on actions taken. Therefore, by including narratives in the continuous IS evaluation process, we predict that business managers and IS users can increase their learning capacity and increase the value of the investment.

One source of theoretical foundation of our ideas can be founding Argyris and Schön (1974), who suggest that people act in accordance with their mental maps rather than the theories they espouse. People are not aware of the mental maps or theories they do use (Argyris 1980). One could say that there is a split between theory and action. Argyris and Schön suggest that two theories of action are involved. "When someone is asked how he would behave under certain circumstances, the answer he usually gives is his espoused theory of action for that situation. This is the theory of action to which he gives allegiance, and which, on request, he communicates to others. However, the theory that actually governs action is theory-in-use" (Argyris and Schön 1974, p. 6-7, our italics). As humans invariably think and express themselves using the full depth of language - by telling "stories" - it is therefore conceivable that unless external observations "verifies" the stories. Stories told do not reflect theory-in-use but espoused theory.

A model of the processes involved is required to appreciate fully theory-in-use. Argyris and Schön (1974) initially looked to three elements: Governing variables, Action strategies and Consequences. Argyris (1976) proposed the double loop learning theory, which concerns changing underlying values and assumptions, i.e. learning. The focus of the theory is on solving problems that are complex and ill structured and which change as problem-solving advances. Typically, interaction with others is necessary to identify the conflict. There are four basic steps in the action theory learning process: (1) discovery of espoused and theory-in-use, (2) invention of new meanings, (3) production of new actions, and (4) generalization of results. Double loop learning involves applying each of these steps to itself. In double loop learning, assumptions underlying current views are questioned and hypotheses about behaviour tested publicly. The result of double loop learning should be increased effectiveness of action and better acceptance of failures and mistakes.

Narratives are used to persuade, convince, and make people act and behave in certain ways – a tool for learning and action. The alternative in organisation for reasoning, learning, and persuading is to use numbers and calculations, including financial statements, investment calculations, and time reports (Llewellyn 1998). Clausen (1994, p. 45) states that: "Using narratives in the system development process seems to be a way in which designers will be able to come up with the kind of descriptions that are asked for." Besides everyday life narratives that are used by all people, a theoretical ground for narratives can be found in institutional theory. Meyer and Rowan (1977) suggests that 'rationalised myths' contribute to the understanding of organisations. Narratives or stories that convey myths are powerful tools that make the irrational become rational (Llewellyn, 1998).

In accounting, management, human computer interaction (HCI), knowledge management, strategic management, and software engineering narratives are common. Llewellyn (1998) discusses how narratives are best understood, constructed, and used in accounting and management research. In HCI, research narratives are used to improve the communication between end-users and developers for designing user interfaces, task modelling and prototyping, and supporting the specification of user interfaces (Bødker 2000). The role of narratives as conveyer of tacit knowledge is explored in knowledge management (Swap et al. 2001). In strategic management, scenarios are used to explore future alternatives where scenarios are "tools" in the "strategists arsenal" (Porter 1985, p. 481). Software engineering on the other hand uses narratives and scenarios to gather and validate requirements (Antón and Potts 1998; Jarke et al. 1998). It should be noted that there are different underlying philosophical reasons for the use of narratives. Llewellyn (1998), Bødker (2000), and

Clausen (Clausen 1994) represent an interpretive research tradition, whereas Porter (1985) together with Jarke et al. (1998) and Antón and Potts (1998) can be classified as belonging to a more positivistic research tradition.

In IS research narratives have also emerged as an alternative approach. Hirschheim and Newman (1991) use the concept of myth to interpret social processes during information systems projects. Clausen (1994) develops a model for how information system designers can use narratives to make descriptions of information systems that people understand, cf. traditional methods such as structured languages and formal specifications. Brown (1998) examines the use of narratives to explain and create meaning in power struggles in information systems implementations. Dube and Robey (1999) analyse stories, by competing groups in information systems development project, as symbol of organisational values or myths to gain insights into the interpretation of management styles. Alvarez and Urla (2002) describe the use of narratives in requirements specification of ERP systems. Finally, Alvarez (Alvarez 2002) examines the role of myths to construct an ERP system as an integrated system and to elaborate the existing organisational values.

Alvarez and Urla (2002) describe three sources of benefits from narratives in relation to IS. First, narratives may provide a pragmatic view of the systems, i.e. how the users perceive the system and offer insights into how the system is actually used. This may reveal institutionalised work practice, inefficiencies of the system, and how users manage those inefficiencies. This type of narratives may be used to convince consultants or managers about necessary changes in the system. Secondly, narratives functions as mediums to convey that the system is a part of the larger organisation and not an isolated thing. Thirdly, narratives are especially for complex IS, since complex IS often affect organisational function by imposing process logic on the organisation. Other large affects imposed through complex IS may also be communicated within the organisation through narratives, e.g. integration, standardisation of work processes, implementation of business rules.

4. Integrated model and discussion

In this section we present a model narrative based evaluation. The model integrates organisational sense- making and double loop learning. The model is depicted in Figure 2 and the logic of the model is the following. Organisational sense-making, which forms the overall process in evaluation consist of four iterative steps: action, narratives, interpretation and decision. Action refer to the use of IS, which can be individuals, groups, organisations, or society. The four groups of IS users are based on four out of five groups defined by Seddon et al.'s (1999). External parties, i.e. independent observers, are excluded since they are not users. The next step in the model is narrative, which refer to the task of producing and diffusion of narratives, which can be performed by any user group, stakeholder or external auditors. Note that we have replaced Hobeke's measurement with narratives. Narratives should be perceived as one tool among many others, see for instance Deschoolmeester et al.'s (2004) excellent summary of different evaluation tools and methods. The third step in the model is interpretation of narratives. Interpretation can be done by any one having decision power or potential of influencing the behaviour of IS user. It can be the individual user or the management. Decision is the last step and the beginning of a new sense-making process refers to the decisions which are guided towards changing behaviour, i.e. action.

Double loop learning is integrated into the model in two ways. First, interpretations influence an affects the narratives leading to modifications of existing narratives. Modification refers to both reflection and learning in process of making sense of narratives prior deciding on which actions to take. Second, the narratives produced include criteria of success which are used in the decision process of which actions to take. Narratives make the case that effectiveness results from developing congruence between theory-in-use and espoused theory, i.e. both the creation and interpretation of narratives. Reflection is a key tool to reveal the theory-in-use and to explore the gulf between espoused theory and theory-in-use or in bringing the later to the surface. Provided the two remain connected, and then the gap creates a dynamic for reflection and for dialogue. As humans invariably think and express themselves using the full depth of language - by telling "stories" - it is therefore conceivable that unless external observations "verifies" the narratives. Narratives told do not reflect theory-in-use but espoused theory.

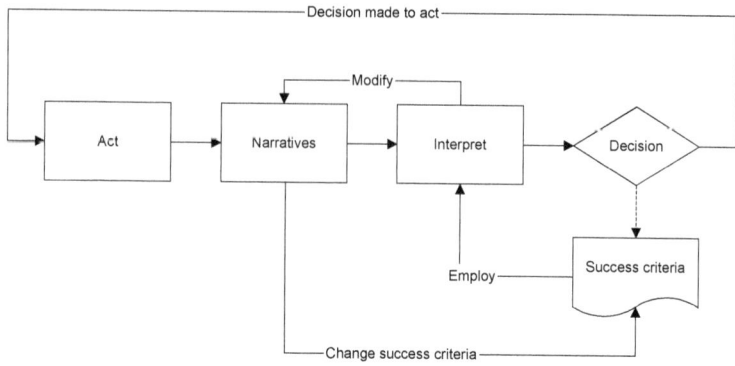

Figure 2: Proposed schematic evaluation process

Narratives used could range from talks among employees to published business cases describing the "good" use of IS. Thus, the actual implications for practice might not be so great, since narratives are used in business to convey meanings and to persuade people to act.

Due to their nature, narratives can carry much information and handled with care they can be used to reach procedural results and process improvements at the same time. Used as for evaluation, they are perhaps the best-suited tool for doing continuous improvements of both subject and evaluation process. The narratives interpreted and may lead to action (decisions) or be modified. New action creates the foundation for new narratives which include both the formal success criteria and the users perceived success stories. Narratives and stories may take role of communicating how to use IS better, e.g. to spread "best practice" use. Social and complex tasks are difficult to convey by other means than stories, which may develop and grow through face-to-face communication. Stories might inspire users of information systems, within the organisation or in other organisations, to investigate the possibilities in systems and ultimately change their mental models, which can lead to better use of information systems. Narratives is a communication medium with a high degree of media richness, which a suitable approach when there is a high degree of uncertainty and equivocality (Daft and Lengel 1986; Daft, Lengel and Trevino 1987). Other stories might reveal institutionalised work practice, inefficiencies of the system, how users manage those inefficiencies and to be used to convince consultants or managers about necessary changes in the system, where narratives can be used as tools to make the irrational become rational.

The use of narratives as an approach to measure and evaluate information systems might involve paradigm shifts in the existing control system and how to evaluate information systems. Changes of existing norms, behaviours, and procedures are difficult (Weick 1996). Resistance to change is likely to come. This is a rational behaviour for those who are affected by any change and not a dysfunctional behaviour (Markus 1983). The formalisation of narratives might also create new positions, such as chief storyteller. Storyteller might become the new power position. Narratives are powerful tales that can be manipulated by different stakeholders, such as managers, project leaders, and storytellers. The process of changing the organizational culture to accept narratives will be a challenging process for most organizations and business managers. Besides changing the culture, there is a need for developing support tools, e.g. story boards, and procedures to create, store, and spread stories (Snowden 2002; Swap et al. 2001).

A last issue discussed in this section is the validity of the proposed model. The validity of the evaluation model can be assessed by three particular criteria: the integration of the model (logical coherence), its practical and theoretical relevance, and relative explanatory power.

The evaluation model steps are casually inter-related; including not just the tools and methods, but also the impacts and consequences of the proposed use of narratives in evaluation. An important aspect of the model is the feed-back loop, modify and employ and change success criteria, i.e. the learning process. Failure to interpret narratives might lead to less learning and no improvement of system use. Potentially, this also clarifies some of the practical problems with action theory and what it is that should be learned in relation to system use.

The evaluation model is characterised by an integration of various theoretical perspectives, and addresses the interdependency between the evaluation and the actions taken based on the evaluation. There are other studies addressing the same issue. One notable study is Remenyi and Sherwood-Smith (1999) who proposed a formative evaluation process, which in idea is similar to the proposed one. The main difference that Remenyi and Sherwood-Smith (1999) evaluation approach address evaluation during the development of IS, whereas the proposed model address evaluation during use of system. Another difference is that the proposed model suggest narratives as a tool in formative evaluations.

Conclusion

The literature (e.g. Hirschheim and Smithson 1998; Walsham 1993) have proposed interpretative approaches to information systems evaluation. Hirschheim and Smithson (1998) suggest that interpretative approaches are a way of gaining a deeper understanding of the process itself. Symons (1991) supports this by suggesting that evaluations means understanding the different perspectives of individuals and Walsham (1993, p. 179) states that "interpretative evaluations designs focus on learning and understanding" however, none has yet explicitly mentioned narratives as an interpretive evaluation approach. Neither has "doing better next time" (which would be typical process improvement) been replaced by "doing better all the time". Learning continuously about the possibilities and difficulties we believe is the key to successful understanding of an information system before and during and installation, and use after an installation. Organisations use myths and narratives to make sense of equivocal situations and they are used as precedents for future actions, serving as "blue-prints" for desirable behaviour (Alvarez and Urla 2002). Narratives appear to be aptly suited as tools in furthering understanding of and support for improved system.

Still there are research implications and opportunities by acknowledging narratives as an evaluation approach of information systems. The implication is that narratives should not only be used as inputs in research, which is the traditional input in case research, it should also be a research output (Llewellyn 1998), where narratives can be used to reason and learn. Quantitative data can also form the bases of narratives. For instance, instead of stating the correlation between X and Y in statistical term it can put in words. The consequence of narratives as research outputs is that researchers have to be able to interpret and evaluate stories in the same way as other research output.

Thus, we conclude that information systems evaluation is highly contextual and measurements of impact on organisations from large and complex information system on business performance are interchangeable with measurements of general improvements. For such measurements to be relevant they have to be used over a long period of time and the measuring would have to be initiated before the implementation is started (Hoebeke, 1990), e.g. in the requirements specification phase. As Strassmann (1985) claimed, we argue that we need to measure impact of information systems with the same measurements that are used on a specific organisation before the implementation, and that any changes recorded are attributable to a combination of information system implementation, organisational changes and changes in method of measurement. Thus, measuring or quantifying isolated impact from information systems implementation is close to impossible. Instead of trying to measure the impossible, we propose the use of narratives as the means to spread knowledge, which ought to lead to better action and improvements during the implementation and usage of systems.

References

Alvarez, R. (2002) "The Myth of Integration: A Case Study of an ERP Implementation," in: Enterprise Resource Planning: Global Opportunities & Challenges, L. Hossain, J. Patrick and M. Rashid (Eds), Idea Group Publishing, Hershey, PA, pp 17-42.

Alvarez, R., and Urla, J. (2002) "Tell Me a Good Story: Using Narrative Analysis to Examine Information Requirements Interviews during an ERP Implementation," The DATA BASE for Advances in Information Systems, Vol 33, No. 1, pp 38-52.

Antón, A., and Potts, C. (1998) "A Representational Framework for Scenarios of Systems Use," Requirements Engineering, Vol 3, No :3-4, pp 219-241.

Argyris, C. (1976) Increasing Leadership Effectiveness Wiley, New York, NY.

Argyris, C. (1980) Inner Contradictions of Rigorous Research Academic press, New York, NY.

Argyris, C., and Schön, D. (1974) Theory in Practice: Increased Professional Effectiveness Jossey-Bass, San Francisco, CA.

Brown, A. (1998) "Narrative, Politics and Legitimacy in an IT Implementation," Journal of Management Studies, Vol 35, No 1, pp 35-59.

Bødker, S. (2000) "Scenarios in User-centered Design: Setting the Stage for Reflection and Action," Interaction with Computers, Vol 13, No 1, pp 61-76.

Clausen, H. (1994) "Designing Computer Systems from a Human Perspective: The Use of Narratives," Scandinavian Journal of Information Systems, Vol 6, No 2, pp 37-44.

Daft, R.L., and Lengel, R.H. (1986) "Organizational Information Requirements, Media Richness and Structural Design," Management Science, Vol 32, No 5, pp 554-571.

Daft, R.L., Lengel, R.H., and Trevino, L.K. (1987) "Message Equivocality, Media Selection, and Manager Performance: Implications for Information Systems," MIS Quarterly, Vol. 11, No 3, pp 355-366.

Deschoolmeester, D., Braet, O. and Willaert P. (2004) "On a Balanced Metodology to Evaluate a Portfolio of ICT Investments", ECITE 2004.

Dubé, L., and Robey, D. (1999) "Software Stories: Three Cultural Perspectives on the Organizational Practices of Software Development," Accounting, Management and Information Technologies, Vol 9, No 4.

Farbey, B., Land, F.F., and Targett, D. (1995) "A Taxonomy of Information Systems Applications: The Benefits' of Evaluation Ladder," European Journal of Information Systems, Vol 4, No 1, pp 41-50.

Hirschheim, R.A., and Newman, M. "Symbolism and Information Systems Development: Myth, Metaphor and Magic," Information Systems Research (2:1) 1991, pp 29-62.

Hirschheim, R.A., and Smithson, S. (1998) "Evaluation of Information Systems: A Critical Assessment," in: Beyond the IT Productivity Paradox, L. Willcocks and S. Lester (Eds), pp. 381-409.

Hoebeke, L. "Measuring in Organisations," Journal of Applied Systems Analysis, Vol. 17, pp 115-122.

Irani, Z., and Love, P.E.D. (2001) "Information Systems Evaluation: Past, Present and Future," European Journal of Information Systems, Vol. 10, No 4, pp 183-188.

Jarke, M., Bui, X., and Caroll, J. (1998) "Scenario Management: An Interdisciplinary Approach," Requirements Engineering, Vol. 3, No. 3-4, pp 154-173.

Jones, S., and Hughes, J. (2001) "Understanding IS Evaluation as a Complex Social Process: A Case Study of a UK Local Authority," European Journal of Information Systems, Vol. 10, No 1.

Klein, H.-K., and Meyer, M. (1999) "A Set of Principles for Conducting and Evaluating Interpretive Field Studies in Information Systems," MIS Quarterly, Vol. 23, No 1, pp 67-94.

Kumar, K. (1990) "Post-implementation Evaluation of Computer Based Information Systems (CBIS): Current Practices," Communications of the ACM, Vol. 33, No 2, pp 203-212.

Llewellyn, S. (1998) "Narratives in Accounting and Management Research" Accounting, Auditing and Accountability Journal, Vol. 12, No 2, pp 220-236.

Markus, M.L. (1983) "Power, Politics, and MIS Implementation," Communications of the ACM, Vol 26, No 6, pp 430-444.

Meyer, J.W., and Rowan, B. (1977) "Institutionalized Organizations: Formal Structure as Myth and Ceremony," American Journal of Sociology, Vol. 82, No 2, pp 340-363.

Murphy, K. E. and S. J. Simon (2002). "Intangible Benefits Valuation in ERP Projects." Information Systems Journal, Vol 12, No 4, pp 301-320.

Porter, M.E. (1985) Competitive Advantage: Creating and Sustaining Superior Performance Free Press, New York, NY.

Remenyi, D., and Sherwood-Smith, M. (1999) "Maximise Information Systems Value by Continuous Participative Evaluation," Logistics Information Management, Vol 12, No 1, pp 14-31.

Seddon, P.B., Graeser, V., and Willcocks, L.P. (2002) "Measuring Organizational IS Effectiveness: An Overview and Update of Senior Management Perspectives," The DATA BASE for Advances in Information Systems, Vol 33, No 2, pp 11-27.

Seddon, P. B., S. Staples, S. Patnayakuni and M. Bowtell (1999). "Dimensions of Information Systems Success." Communications of the AIS 2(15).

Serafeimidis, V., and Smithson, S. (2000) "Information Systems Evaluation in Practice: A Case Study of Organizational Change," Journal of Information Technology, Vol 15, No 2, pp 93-105.

Serafeimidis, V., and Smithson, S. (2003) "Information Systems Evaluation as an *Organizational Institution – Experience from a case study. " Information Systems Journal, Vol 13, pp 251-274.

Sinclair, D., Zairi, Mohamed (1995) "Performance Measurement as an Obstacle to TQM," The TQM Magazine, Vol 7, No 2, pp 42-45.

Snowden, D. (2002) "Complex Acts of Knowing: Paradox and Descriptive Self-Awareness," Journal of Knowledge Management, Vol 6, No 2.

Strassmann, P.A. (1985) Information Payoff: The Transformation of Work in the Electronic Age Free Press, New York, NY.

Swap, W., Leomard, D., Shields, M., and Abrams, L. (2001) "Using Mentoring and Storytelling to Transfer Knowledge in the Workplace," Journal of Management Information Systems, Vol 18, No 1), pp 95-114.

Symons, V.J. (1991) "A Review of Information Systems Evaluation: Content, Context and Process," European Journal of Information Systems, Vol 1, No 3, pp 205-212.

Walsham, G. (1993) Interpreting Information Systems in Organisations Wiley, Chichester.

Walsham, G. (1995) "The Emergence of Interpretivism in IS Research," Information Systems Research, Vol 6 No 4, pp 376-394.

Walsham, G. (1999) "Interpretive Evaluation Design for information Systems," in: Beyond the IT Productivity Paradox, S. Lester (Ed), Wiley, Chichester.

Weick, K.E. (1996) "Drop Your Tools: An Allegory for Organizational Studies," Administrative Science Quarterly, Vol 41, No 2, pp 301-331.

Venkatraman, N., and Ramanujam, V. (1986) "Measurment of Business Performance in Strategy Reserach: A Comparision of Appraoches," Academy of Management Review Vol 11, No 4, pp 801-814

e-Commerce Investments from an SME perspective: Costs, Benefits and Processes

Sandra Cohen and Kallirroi Georgila
Athens University of Economics and Business, Greece
Originally Published in EJISE (2006) Volume 9: issue 2

Editor's Comment
The strength of this paper lies in the empirical results which it supplies and which are discussed. SME are always interesting. They have much the same challenges as large organisations and much less resources at their disposal with which to overcome them. Although the literature for SME continues to grow it is still quite small relatively to the rest of scholarly endeavours. The introduction of e-Commerce into the IT Evaluation decision make the situation even more interesting. One issue of particular interest in this paper is the fact that there is a comparison between SMA and other organisation of a more substantial size. This paper draws on some interesting findings from the field and
provides an excellent example of financial analyses in a less straightforward industry.

Abstract: The scope of this paper is to investigate whether SMEs take into consideration the cost dimensions (tangible and intangible, direct and indirect) and follow the investment appraisal techniques proposed in literature as relevant and suitable in relation to e-commerce adoption. More specifically, we analyse the importance placed by the EC adopters on specific cost elements, types of budgets and investment appraisal techniques in relation to EC decision. Furthermore, we aim at understanding the reasons, both quantitative and qualitative, that drive SMEs to embark on such an investment. Our empirical evidence is based on the responses to questions found on a structured questionnaire answered by Greek firms that have already adopted EC. Our findings indicate that cost, in general, is not a major issue for Greek SMEs when deciding to implement EC, while the strategic benefits they aim at gaining from EC applications play a critical role in the adoption decision.

Keywords: e-commerce, IT investment, SMEs, IT costs, IT investment appraisal, Greece

1. Introduction

Information and communications technologies (ICT) are radically changing the competitiveness of organisations. Electronic commerce (EC), defined as the use of electronic methods, means and procedures to conduct various forms of business activity in cyberspace (Brian, 1998) has become a priority for many corporations within the context of ICT, since managers see it as a way to overcome certain limitations of the traditional distribution channels. In this paper we take into consideration all the perspectives of EC that have been defined in recent literature, i.e. the communication, the business process, the service and the online perspective of EC[1]. EC has reduced the cost of trading among companies and in the same time has helped them tighten their relationships and collaboration. Through EC, companies are now able to connect with their trading partners for "just in time production" and "just in time delivery" (Ngai and Wat, 2002). The coordination of strategic movements has been improved and the response to customers' needs has become faster, more flexible and of higher quality. Moreover the World Wide Web has given the opportunity to firms, irrespective of their size, to enter the fields of international marketing and trade their products and services on a global scale regardless of geographical, national, financial or other limitations. e-Commerce has the ability to change the way companies compete with one another, since the new technologies influence the strategic plans of organizations and they offer competitive advantages on both local and global level (Doukidis et al., 2001). According to Currie (2000), the cost/performance benefits of e-commerce can be categorized in four (4) groups. The first group relates to the reduction of

---

[1] As presented in Turban et al. (2002) EC can be viewed in various perspectives. These perspectives are the communications perspective (i.e. the delivery of goods, services, information, or payments via computers networks, or by any other electronic means), the business process perspective (i.e. the application of technology towards the automation of business transactions and work flow), the service perspective (i.e. the use of EC as a tool that addresses the desire of firms, consumers and management to cut service costs while improving the quality of goods and increasing the speed of service delivery) and finally the online perspective (i.e. the capability of buying and selling products and information on the Internet as well as providing other online services).

external and internal communication expenses, the second to the revenues generated either from current business or from new initiatives, the third to the tangible benefits, such as reduced costs and more flexible working practices, and the final group refers to intangible benefits such as enhanced competitive positioning and enhanced customer relationships.

Thus, small and medium sized companies, SMEs[2], that have limited opportunities and strengths when trying to compete against the big multinational corporations may find a way to overcome the obstacles incurred by their small size through the multiple benefits that EC offers.

Although EC is considered to be one of the main forces towards a new business environment, there is limited empirical evidence in relation to the extant evaluation process regarding its implementation. Even though many organizations have adopted EC, a lot of them are unaware of the total costs associated with this investment, as web technology is relatively new (Avram, 2001; Larsen and Bloniarz, 2000). However, according to Porter (2001), no organization should embark on the undertaking of an EC project without understanding the costs and performance of such issues. The scope of this study is to investigate whether SMEs take into consideration all the cost dimensions and follow the investment appraisal techniques proposed in literature as relevant and suitable in relation to EC adoption. More specifically, we analyze the importance placed by EC adopters on specific cost elements, types of budgets and investment appraisal techniques in relation to the EC project. Furthermore, we aim at understanding the reasons, both quantitative and qualitative, that drive SMEs to embark on such an investment.

The structure of the paper is the following. The second section is devoted to analysing ICT and EC from a SME perspective. The third section refers to specific cost issues that have been presented in literature as relevant to EC investments. The fourth section outlines the investment appraisal techniques that on theoretical grounds are applicable for ICT investments. In the fifth section the methodological aspects of our empirical survey are

---

[2] According to the definition of the European Commission (1996) a small and medium sized company is characterised by three major factors. Firstly it should employ less that 250 employees, secondly its annual turnover should not exceed the amount of €40 millions and finally it should not belong by a percentage of 25% or more to another company or companies that are not defined as SMEs.

analyzed. The sixth section is dedicated to the presentation of the empirical evidence regarding the financial aspects of EC adoption in Greek SMEs. Finally, in the last section, a discussion of the main conclusions of our research is undertaken.

2. ICT and EC in SMEs

In most developed countries SMEs constitute a highly dynamic and important sector of the economic activity that, nevertheless, has to deal with high competitive pressures and scarcity of resources. Information and communication technologies (ICT) offer SMEs significant opportunities to grow and to compete in the current business environment. There are several studies indicating that Information Systems can add value to SMEs. Heeks and Duncobe (2001) refer to the way that companies in developing countries can use IT/IS in order to build businesses. Domaracki (2001) explains how the differences in technology acquisition between large and small enterprises are smoothing out and thus the gap is being bridged. Blili and Raymond (1993) recognize the need for SMEs to use IT as a means of integration within the industry supply chain and of cost minimization. However, as presented in Levy and Powell (1998), the flexibility that characterizes SMEs in relation to their responsiveness to customers' requirements is not reflected in IS adoption or use. This is mainly due to the fact that SMEs consider IT projects to be investments that absorb a significant part of their constrained resources rather than an opportunity for growth. Moreover, SMEs fail to identify the change in organizational and management structures that may be required due to IT adoption as they do not usually incorporate an IT strategy approach that would permit a thorough examination of these aspects (Levy and Powell, 2000). Levy, Powell and Yetton (2001; 2002) have recently developed a focus-dominance model that explains how SMEs use information technologies to accomplish different goals. Their model refers to four different scenarios within a matrix that correspond to a combination of customers' dominance level within the market and the strategic focus of the company.

Internet in general is usually considered as an opportunity for smaller firms to reduce transaction costs and level the playing field (Evans and Wurster, 1997). Often cited benefits include expanding the scope of marketing, wider and richer communications, reaching new markets, reducing the cost of operations and partnering with suppliers and other collaborators. However, there are also certain limitations that make the adoption of EC by

SMEs more difficult and hazardous. The cost of in-house EC applications development can be very high and mistakes caused by the lack of experience and know-how may result in delays. Moreover, security and privacy aspects should be dealt with caution especially in the Business to Customers area. Therefore the EC industry has a very long and difficult task of convincing customers that online transactions and privacy are in fact secure. In addition customers in many cases do not trust an unknown, faceless seller, paperless transactions and electronic money. Finally, many legal issues are unresolved and in several circumstances government regulations and standards are not yet refined enough to deal with the intricacies of EC (Turban et al., 2002).

A few studies (Kleindl, 2000; Steinfield and Whitten, 1999) have identified possible shortcomings that smaller businesses can experience due to internet usage. Competitive threats may increase as the new medium allows larger firms to mimic the traditional strength of SMEs in serving niche markets, developing customer intimacy and exploiting local knowledge. For example, a regional firm, which previously had limited local competition, may be confronted with new threats from across the country or the globe. The new technology may also increase competitive rivalry and the pace of competition by reducing barriers to entry and increasing the rate of product and process innovation (Drew, 2003).

In literature, there are several empirical studies that deal with the level of EC adoption by SMEs (Damaskopoulos and Evgeniou, 2003; Santarelli and D'Altri, 2003, Doukidis et al., 2001). The above-mentioned surveys, as well as the European E-business Report (2002/2003), reveal that the full implementation of e-business solutions is still in its infancy for the majority of SMEs. A recent research performed by the Information Society (2003) in relation to internet usage and EC activities of SMEs in Greece, revealed that SMEs with more than 11 employees use Internet at a rate of 92%, 82% of them have at least one PC and 48% have a presence in the World Wide Web. The relevant figures in EU for the year 2002 were 94%, 83% and 52%, respectively. However, IT/IS usage is relatively low for Greek SMEs in total (PC usage 34% and internet usage 18%) due to the low level of electronic processes in small businesses (1 to 5 employees), which account for almost 95% of the total SMEs population[3].

3. e-Commerce cost implications

Clearly electronic commerce is part of investments in information and communications technology (ICT). Since the literature is mostly focused on the evaluation of ICT projects we will concentrate on the basic elements of this procedure having in mind that they are also applied to EC project evaluation[4]. According to Hinton and Kaye (1996), the evaluation of information technology investments relies on the satisfactory assessment of costs and benefits. However, all costs and benefits in these applications cannot easily be allocated. This is mainly due to the fact that there are two categories of costs and benefits when it comes to information technology (IT) applications, the tangible and the intangible ones. The tangible costs and benefits address the parts of an investment decision, which the manager can easily identify and attach a quantifiable value to. These elements have a historical cost in accounting terms and usually have some physical form. On the other hand, the intangible elements refer to the costs of an investment, that commonly do not have a physical form and are accounted for in terms of some expected future value rather than a past cost. It is the intangibility associated with IT investments which creates problems for the organization in initially justifying and later assessing the costs and benefits of their spending (Ward et al., 1990).

Except for the tangible and intangible cost elements there are direct and indirect elements of cost as well. Direct costs are those factors that can be easily attributed to the implementation and operation of an e-commerce application or of an IT system in general. These costs are often underestimated and go beyond the obvious hardware, software and installation costs. Direct costs may also include unexpected additional accessories, consultancy support, etc. However, the indirect costs associated with the adoption of EC projects are usually the most significant ones. Indirect costs can largely be divided into human and organizational factors with one of

---

[3] According to the data provided by the Greek Organisation of Small and Medium Sized Enterprises and Handicraft (EOMMEX, 2003) SMEs in Greece account for the 99.5% of the total population of firms as well as the 87.5% of private sector workforce employment.
[4] However, from another point of view an EC project could be considered as a business project which encompasses IT features.

the largest indirect human costs being that of management time (Irani et al., 1997). On the other hand one of the most significant indirect organizational costs relates to the transformation from old to new work practices and any influence of the system on work activities (Love et al., 2004). Because of the existence of such hidden costs most companies tend to underestimate the total cost of the IT projects with 30-50% of costs occurring out of the official IT budget (Hochstrasser, 1992). It has also been estimated that support costs represent 73% of total costs of an IT investment (Gartner Group, 1995).

Another particularity of investments in EC-IT is the dependency, legacy and heritage as described by Hinton and Kaye (1996). Certain attributes are lost when an organization moves from a human dominant system to a technology dominant system. The flexibility and organizational behaviour associated with the human systems are traded for the mechanistic attributes of the technological system. While the benefits of automation are initially appealing to organizations, the costs associated with the incapacity to adapt systems to a changing business environment are not considered. It is suggested that dependency occurs when organizations throw away a significant part of the human elements of a system and therefore become more and more reliant to the system itself with the risk of not being able to overcome a possible system failure. Without the effective control of costs an EC project is likely to become a "sinkhole". In order to effectively control the costs of an EC project an understanding of the total lifecycle cost of an information system investment is needed. According to Whelan and McGrath (2002), even though the start up cost of a website is quite small, the ongoing development and maintenance costs can be excessive. Thus, management must ensure that the full lifecycle costs, including all potential hidden costs, are identified.

4. Investment appraisal techniques and E-commerce

As we have already mentioned in the second section, EC is part of investments in information and communications technology (ICT). ICT investments have special characteristics (i.e., high risk, long term results, large proportion of intangible/hidden costs and benefits), which make the use of traditional appraisal techniques difficult, and the reliability of the outcome most uncertain (Millis and Mercken, 2003). Techniques such as payback period, accounting rate of return, and various discounted cash flows methods, such as net present value (NPV) and internal rate of return (IRR) have been heavily criticized. These methods have been accused that they have a rather narrow perspective, do not include non-financial benefits in the analysis, overemphasize short-term results, wrongly assume preservation of the status quo, treat inflation in an inconsistent manner and finally that they promote non-value-adding behaviour (Adler, 2000).

In order to overcome these problems, there have been proposals in literature for alternative appraisal techniques that better suit investments in IT projects. A first alternative suggests that managers should estimate the intangible costs and benefits of a project using different scenarios and include these estimations in the calculation of NPV. This would allow a sensitivity analysis for the realization of these hypotheses (Willcocks, 1994). A second alternative is the strategic fit approach, originally proposed by Porter (1985), which explicitly addresses the strategic dimensions of the competitive advantage perspective of an IT project. According to this approach, investments in information technology should be evaluated primarily in terms of their contribution to the competitive advantage of a firm adopting them (Millis and Mercken, 2003).

Another approach for the evaluation of IT projects is the information economics method, introduced by Parker and Benson (1987). Information economics in essence uses a process of assigning point-rating scores to assess the investment benefits and strategic relevance of IC technologies (Millis and Mercken, 2003). One of the most recent developed investment appraisal techniques is based on the concept of expert systems and fuzzy logic techniques (Irani et al., 2002). There are also alternatives that deploy both the traditional and the modern appraisal techniques. The most common one is the balanced scorecard developed by Kaplan and Norton (1992). Finally, Farbey et al. (1993) and Farbey et al. (1994) have attempted to develop a procedure that could match the proper IT evaluation procedure to a number of dimensions, such as the evaluation constraints, the role of IT, the dependence of IT projects on other projects, the uncertainty of the investment as to objectives and as to cause and effect. However, despite the advantages that the sophisticated methods have over the traditional ones, these adjusted techniques are seldom used in practice (Ballantine and Stray, 1998).

5. Research design and data collection

The sample surveyed included mainly SMEs Greek companies that had already implemented E-commerce. These companies were identified by a thorough investigation of relevant Greek sites on the Internet. In our analysis we focused on the Business-to-Consumer (B2C) nature of transactions, i.e. the retail transactions with individual shoppers. Furthermore we mainly included companies that combine an online presence with their physical retail stores ("brick-and-mortar" stores). This strategy of having both an off-line and online presence is found in literature as "click-and-mortar" model or it is sometimes called "brick-and-click" (Turban et al., 2002). As the nature of the survey was to monitor the investment appraisal process that is related to EC implementation and the financial implications of such a decision we excluded from our sample all the companies that were solely hosted in shopping portals[5]. The reason for this exclusion was that these companies had not actually undertaken an EC project, but they had rather developed an informative page for their presentation on the Internet. In these cases, the customers were not able to place orders directly to the company but only through the host's site address. The final sample included 162 SMEs. Except for the SMEs companies, we also developed a small sample of larger Greek companies (non – SMEs) in order to control whether there are any significant differences among SMEs and non – SMEs as far as financial considerations regarding EC are concerned. This sample consisted of a smaller number of firms (29 companies) as this type of companies was not the main target group of the analysis.

We did not expect to find differences among SMEs and non – SMEs in their perceptions of the benefits deriving from EC as such differences are not justified on both empirical and theoretical grounds. However, we expected to find that non-SMEs, given that they have more financial resources and are able to attract more educated personnel, apply more sophisticated management accounting practices and financial appraisal techniques in comparison to SMEs. Numerous studies have witnessed that large firms are more apt to management accounting innovation adoptions (Innes et al., 2000). Furthermore, Love and Irani (2004) have found that there are significant differences between firm size (calculated as turnover and num-

---

[5] Shopping portal is a site that has organised links to e-tailers, often with comparisons, reviews, or shopping tools for consumers. Many shopping portals are targeted towards a specific market niche (Turban et al., 2002).

ber of employees) and the evaluation process followed for IT investments. The field survey was conducted via questionnaires from June to October 2003. We contacted all the sample companies by phone before sending them the questionnaire in order to inform them about our research and ask for their contribution. Forty one (41) SMEs and 5 non-SMEs refused to participate in the survey for a variety of reasons. A five-page questionnaire mostly including questions rated in Likert scale was then sent only to the companies that agreed to participate in the survey. Thus, 145 questionnaires were sent mainly by e-mail and only in a few occasions by fax to 121 SMEs and 24 non-SMEs. After a follow up phase of telephone calls, 50 firms returned the questionnaire completed. The overall response rate was 34.5% (31.4% for the SMEs and 50.0% for the non-SMEs). Two questionnaires were completed only partially and therefore were excluded from the analysis. Thus, the final sample contains 48 companies, 36 Greek SMEs and 12 Greek non – SMEs.

6. Survey results and descriptive statistics

6.1. Sample statistics

The companies that participated in the survey belong to the following sectors:

Table 1: Final sample composition

Sector	Number of firms		Percent %
	SMEs	Non-SMEs	
Information Technology	14	1	31.3
Wholesale –Retail	13	2	31.3
Telecommunications	2	3	10.4
Financial services	1	3	8.3
Tourism	1	3	8.3
Other	5	0	10.4
Total	36	12	100.0

As indicated in Table 1 above, the different sectors are not evenly distributed in the final sample. However, the initial sample had a similar pattern. The majority of the sample Greek companies have introduced EC during the last 4 years as shown analytically in the following table (Table 2).

Table 2: Year of EC introduction

Year of e-commerce introduction	Number of firms	Percent %
Before 1999	4	9.3
1999	9	20.9
2000	11	25.6
2001	10	23.3
2002	9	20.9
Total	43	100.0

$N = 43$

This finding indicates that the introduction of EC has been rather delayed in relation to the pace of its development in other European countries. Nevertheless, it follows the trend in relation to Internet penetration in Greece (Doukidis et al., 2001).

6.2. EC contribution to revenues and costs

The analysis of the data revealed that EC sales account approximately for the 9.5% of the total revenues of SMEs sample companies (Table 3).

Table 3: Percentage of EC sales to total revenues

N = 17	Median	Mean	Standard deviation
% of total revenues that is due to sales through Internet	3.00%	9.53%	18.27%

Our evidence does not deviate significantly from the findings presented in the European E-business Report (2002/03). This research that included 9,264 SMEs from the 15 countries members of the EU indicates that only 13% of the sample companies used EC for selling purposes. Moreover, forty five percent (45%) of these companies reported that the share of goods and services sold online was less than 5% of their total revenues while another 25% experienced EC sales revenues that lay between 5 to 10%. In our analysis, 58.8% of SMEs achieved EC revenues less than 5% of their total revenues and in 23.6% of the cases EC revenues fell between 5%-10% of their total yearly turnover. Almost half of SMEs (47.1%) spend amounts that fall between 2% to 4% of their year expense budget for EC purposes (Table 4).

Table 4: Percentage of total yearly budgeted expenses dedicated to EC

% of total budgeted operating expenses that are dedicated to EC on a yearly basis	Number of firms	Percent %
2-4%	8	47.1
4-6%	1	5.9
6-8%	3	17.6
8-10%	3	17.6
>10%	2	11.8
Total	17	100.0

This finding is consistent with the level of revenues that is generated from e-commerce. This consistency is also statistically significant. The correlation between the % of total revenues that is due to sales through Internet and the % of total budgeted expenses that are dedicated to e-commerce on a yearly basis is statistically significant at 1% significance level (spearman correlation = 0.741, p-value = 0.001). Moreover, this finding is close to that reported by Damaskopoulos and Evgeniou (2003) in a recent research that was based on a sample of more that 900 SMEs in 4 countries of Eastern Europe and Cyprus. Their empirical evidence showed that the majority of SMEs in their sample dedicated less than 5% of the yearly operational budget for EC support. However, the more developed countries, Slovenia and Cyprus, had the lowest expenditure rates.

The majority of SMEs sample companies (64.7%) have a separate department that deals with e-commerce. The average number of employees working in these departments is 3.6 employees. The human resources that are dedicated to EC (i.e. number of employees devoted to the EC department) are also statistically related to the % of total revenues that is due to sales through Internet.

More specifically a statistically significant correlation at 5% significance level exists between these two variables (spearman correlation = 0.619, p-value = 0.014). From the analysis presented above, it is evident that Greek SMEs try to balance the resources they devote to EC in relation to the revenues they obtain from this way of making business.

6.3. Importance of EC's investment appraisal questionable areas

Before analysing the importance of specific cost elements and budgets in relation to the EC adoption decision, we asked the companies to present their opinion of the significance of a number of parameters. These factors have been encountered in literature as "grey zones" that trouble companies when analysing and appraising the EC prospect. Through these questions we identified indirectly the importance of cost issues in relation to the investment decision. The parameters that should be considered carefully due to their importance during the investment appraisal process according to our sample views are the following (Table 5):

From the analysis of Table 5, it is clearly inferred that Greek companies do not perceive issues that are related to cost, in general, as issues that should be dealt with exceptional consciousness during the investment appraisal process, as they grade them as of medium importance.

Table 5: Important factors during the EC appraisal process

Items	N	Mean	Std.Dev
The benefits from EC are visible only in the long run	48	3.65	1.176
EC benefits are mainly of qualitative nature	48	3.40	1.047
Need for continuous upgrades of EC systems	48	3.08	1.145
Traditional investment appraisal techniques are not applicable to EC	48	3.04	1.148
A part of the total cost of EC is not easily quantifiable	48	2.94	1.060
The lack of historical data makes EC appraisal difficult	48	2.92	1.127
EC creates unbudgeted expenses for system support during its operation	46	2.74	1.124
It is difficult to calculate the cost of capital for EC assessment	48	2.54	1.071
It is difficult to monitor EC implementation progress	47	2.36	1.258

The scale is 1 = very small significance to 5 = great significance.

More specifically, the theoretically justified inadequacy of traditional investment appraisal techniques (mean value 3.04) and the non-easily quantifiable EC costs (mean value 2.92) do not trouble significantly Greek companies.

Also, the unbudgeted expenses that appear for EC support during its operation (mean value 2.74) and the difficulties regarding the cost of capital calculation (mean value 2.54) are ranked even lower in significance. As all companies that participate in our survey use EC already, they have probably answered this question on the basis of their experience. So, it seems that they did not encounter significant problems with the issues mentioned above in relation to their EC project. However, the significance of the proposition that the total cost of EC is not easily quantifiable is statistically related, at 5% statistical level, to the year of EC adoption. In other words, earlier adopters consider this parameter more significant in relation to more recent ones (spearman correlation =-0.304, p-value=0.047). Probably as time passes companies become more familiar with all cost parameters that are related to EC and they are able to quantify greater parts of its total cost, a situation that could have been vague some years ago.

6.4. EC success factors

The following Table 6 presents the importance given to a number of factors that, according to the respondents, play an important role in relation to EC adoption and implementation in a successful manner.

Table 6: Evaluation of success factors for the EC appraisal process

Issue	N	Mean	Std.Dev
Proper selection of the planning and development team	48	4.27	.792
EC application development by experienced personnel	47	4.26	.736
Alignment with corporate strategy	48	4.19	.842
Top management support	48	4.13	.937
Rational allocation of resources	48	3.92	.846
Systematic personnel training	48	3.90	.928
EC follow up at frequent intervals	48	3.85	.825
Clear mechanisms of evaluation and reward	47	3.51	.906
Accurate cost estimation	48	2.85	.989

The scale is 1 = very small significance to 5 = great significance.

As indicated in Table 6, Greek firms implementing EC consider rational allocation of resources as an important success factor (mean value 3.92) but allocate less than medium importance to the accurate estimation of cost (mean value 2.85). These findings are in alignment with the fact that EC cost per se does not trouble significantly Greek companies that apply EC as long as its application provides a balanced dedication of resources.

6.5. Analysis of EC costs

The analysis of the responses revealed the degree of significance that is given to numerous cost parameters that are related to EC. The answers given are consistent with the overall attitude of Greek companies towards EC. They do not consider, as shown already by the presiding answers, that EC, as an investment, is extremely resource demanding. A possible explanation for that may be that EC applications in Greece, as they account only for a small proportion of total revenues and yearly budget costs, are not difficult applications and thus the cost of their initial implementation as well as their maintenance is not exorbitant. Greek companies devote resources primarily to software (mean value 3.75) and planning and development (mean value 3.67). On the contrary, they consider the costs that are related to personnel training (mean value 2.83) and consultancy (mean value 2.83) of being less than medium significant.

The cost items presented in Table 7 can be categorized into three groups on the basis of factor analysis. These three groups account for the 68.97% of the total variance of the answers to the relevant question (Table 8).

Table 7: Significance of cost items

Cost items	N	Mean	Std.Dev.
Initial software cost	48	3.75	1.042
Planning and development costs	48	3.67	.953
Possible failure cost	48	3.54	1.237
Maintenance and upgrading cost	48	3.40	.939
Initial hardware cost	48	3.23	1.057
Cost of top management involvement	46	3.04	1.095
Cost related to depend-ency on new technologies	47	2.85	1.122
Consultancy cost	47	2.83	1.148
Personnel training cost	46	2.83	.973

The scale is 1 = very small significance to 5 = great significance.

Table 8: Factor analysis of cost parameters

Factors*	Factor loading	% of variance explained by each factor	Cronbach's alpha
Factor 1: EC Preparation and maintenance cost		30.35%	0.7789
Consultancy cost	0.811		
Maintenance and upgrading cost	0.803		
Personnel training cost	0.755		
Planning and development costs	0.720		
Factor 2: Direct implementation cost		20.83%	0.7896
Initial software cost	0.909		
Initial hardware cost	0.832		
Factor 3: Indirect organizational costs		17.78%	0.6006
Cost of top management involvement	0.866		
Cost related to dependency from new technologies	0.625		
Possible failure cost	0.457		
Total variance explained		68.97%	

*The factors were identified by using the principal component analysis extraction method and the varimax with Kaiser Normalization rotation method. The KMO measure of sampling adequacy is 0.713 and the Barlett's test of sphericity is 124.930 (sig. 0.000). Also, the conventional recommendation of five observations per parameter is met. The factors were also tested for reliability using Cronbach's coefficient alpha (α). An α value of 0.60 or above indicates a reliable measurement instrument (Bagozzi, 1994). The factor analysis revealed that the costs that are relevant to EC could be categorized into three groups. The first group that was given the name "Preparation and maintenance cost" contains all costs that are relevant to the preparation of EC introduction as well as its maintenance. The second group, which was called "Direct implementation cost", is composed of all the direct initial EC adoption costs, i.e. direct software and hardware acquisition and installation costs. Finally, the third factor that was named "Indirect organizational costs" contains costs that are related to influences caused to the organization by the EC. The first and the second factor above correspond to the direct costs in relation to EC. The third factor is related to the indirect cost. From another point of view, the first two factors contain the cost parameters that are usually identified as tangible costs while the third shares features in the intangible cost category. As discussed in section 2, the dedication of resources during the life cycle of an EC project differs. The perceptions of Greek companies implementing EC in relation to this issue (Table 9) are very close to those already depicted in recent empirical surveys. More specifically EC adopters perceive EC implementation phase as the most demanding one (65.0%) followed by the EC operation and maintenance phase (57.5%), while the takeout phase is considered to impose a minor financial burden on the company (10%).

Table 9: Cost requirements through EC life cycle phases

Phase	% of respondents*
EC implementation	65.0%
EC operation and maintenance	57.5%
EC development and maturation	45.0%
Idea generation and investment appraisal	37.5%
Acquisition of the necessary equipment	32.5%
EC retraction	10.0%

*Respondents could give multiple answers to the question. N = 40

6.6. Investment appraisal techniques used

We investigated the techniques used by the sample companies during the EC investment appraisal process. As EC investment is an ICT investment we expected the implementation of a suitable method to evaluate such a long-term project. However, we expected differences between SMEs and non-SMEs as to the sophistication of the techniques adopted. More specifically, we hypothesized that SMEs would apply less sophisticated investment appraisal techniques in comparison to the non-SMEs mainly due to limitations that SMEs usually experience in relation to the knowledge prerequisites and the financial means that are related to these methods.

Table 10: Investment appraisal techniques used

Investment appraisal technique used	Total sample % (Rank)	SMEs % (Rank)	Non-SMEs % (Rank)	Difference between SMEs and Non-SMEs* t value (prob. value)	Difference between SMEs and Non-SMEs * Mann – Whitney U test, z score (prob.value)
Cost - benefit analysis	79.2% (1)	68.4% (1)	31.6% (4)	3.669 (0.001)	-2.030 (0.042)
IRR	33.3% (2)	19.4% (3)	75.0% (1)	4.025 (0.000)	-3.499 (0.000)
Pay back period	31.3% (3)	30.6% (2)	33.3% (2)	0.176 (0.861)	-0.178 (0.859)
NPV	18.8% (4)	13.9% (4)	33.3% (2)	1.265 (0.225)	-1.479 (0.139)

*As the number of observation within each sub-sample (SMEs and non-SMEs) is rather small we used both parametric (t test of equality of means) and non parametric (Mann – Whitney U test) tests in order to assess the existence of statistically significant differences between the two groups. The results of the tests are consistent.

The most common investment appraisal technique used in order to assess EC projects for the total sample companies (Table 10) is the cost-benefit analysis followed by Internal Rate of Return method (IRR), the Payback Period method and the Net Present Value method (NPV).

However, as expected, the selection of investment appraisal method is influenced by the firm's size. SMEs use more often cost-benefit analysis in comparison to non-SMEs (statistical significant difference at 1%). On the other hand, non-SMEs tend to use more frequently IRR (statistical significant difference at 1%). Thus, SMEs companies prefer less sophisticated and easier to apply investment appraisal techniques such as cost-benefit analysis and payback. Non-SMEs, as they employ personnel adequately experienced and educated in financial appraisal methods, apply more frequently discounted cash flow methods such as IRR and NPV.

7. Budget development and follow up

Table 11: Budget time frame

Budget time frame	SMEs (% of SMEs)	Non-SMEs (% of non-SMEs)	Total (% of total)
1 semester	1 (4.2%)	0 (0.0%)	1 (2.9%)
1 year	12 (4.2%)	3 (27.3%)	15 (42.9%)
2 years	5 (50%)	4 (36.4%)	9 (25.7%)
3 years	5 (20.8%)	2 (18.2%)	7 (20.0%)
3 to 5 years	1 (4.2%)	2 (18.2%)	3 (8.6%)
Total	24 (100.0%)	11 (100.0%)	35 (100.0%)

Table 12: Frequency of budget follow up

Frequency of budget follow up	SMEs (% of SMEs)	Non SMEs (% of non SMEs)	Total (% of total)
Every month	6 (25.0%)	2 (18.2%)	8 (22.9%)
Every trimester	11 (45.8%)	4 (36.4%)	15 (42.9%)
Every semester	4 (16.7%)	3 (27.3%)	7 (20.0%)
Once a year	3 (12.5%)	2 (18.2%)	5 (14.3%)
Total	24 (100.0%)	11 (100.0%)	35 (100.0%)

It should be mentioned that 74.5% of the respondents had developed a budget prior to EC adoption (66.7% of SMEs and 100.0% of non-SMEs). The development of an EC budget is significantly statistically related to the type of the firm. Non-SMEs tend to develop budgets more systematically than SMEs (t= 4.183, p-value = 0.000). The range of these budgets covers a period from 6 months to 5 years. The most common time frame for these budgets is one year (42.9%) and the period that is commonly used for its follow up is one trimester (42.9%). Both the budget time frame and the frequency of budget follow-up do not differ, at a statistically significant level, between SMEs and Non-SMEs. Table 11 and Table 12 present more details regarding the budget time frame and its follow up frequency.

The follow up of the budgets in the majority of the sample companies (65.7% of the cases) reveals the existence of variances. The occurrence of these variances is more frequent for SMEs in comparison to Non-SMEs (t = 2.661, p-value = 0.012). Non-SMEs, due to their familiarity with budgets in a variety of occasions regarding their business activities, are probably more experienced in developing accurate forecasts. However, only 31.4% of the respondents reported that these variances were due to cost issues and more specifically to cost issues that were not included in the initial budget. Change to the primary plans regarding the EC implementation is considered to be a more important driver for these discrepancies (46.4%).

7.1. Qualitative reasons for EC adoption

Finally, we asked respondents to select from a given list the motives as well as the expected benefits that had driven them to EC adoption. As shown in Table 13, Greek companies do not perceive cost reduction as a main driving force for EC introduction (37.5%).

Table 13: Motives for EC adoption

Motives	% of respondents
Preservation of competitive position	75.0%
Entering into new markets	62.5%
Technological modernization	58.3%
Differentiation	37.5%
Cost reduction	37.5%

N=47

Even though cost reduction is a popular justification in relation to IT investments in general (Hinton and Kaye, 1996) this is not the case as far as

EC is concerned according to our sample companies. Other reasons, that are mainly strategically oriented, have driven Greek companies to undertake this investment as presented in Table 13.

Moreover, cost reduction, in relation to production, selling, administrative and order handling costs, was ranked again as having medium importance in relation to other more quantitative and customer oriented benefits (Table 14). Similar conclusions have also been reported in Paris et al. (2004) in relation to a survey of "brick and mortar" organizations.

Table 14: Perceived benefits for EC adoption

Perceived benefits	% of respondents
Facilitation of customer informing	83.3%
Means of entering new markets	81.3%
Approaching new customers	75.0%
Acquisition of competitive advantage	66.7%
Increase of sales	58.3%
Reduction of operating costs	54.2%
Exploitation of new distribution channels	52.1%
Flexibility in customer service	52.1%
Quality in customer service	50.0%
Reduction of selling and administrative costs	47.9%
Reduction of order handling time	45.8%

N=48

As an epilogue, we can claim that both motives and benefits presented by Greek companies in relation to EC adoption are comparable to those reported in other recent studies (Damaskopoulos and Evgeniou, 2003; Santarelli and D'Altri, 2002, Doukidis et al., 2001).

8. Summary and discussion

In this paper we studied the significance of cost issues as a dimension of the overall assessment of an EC project by Greek SMEs. More specifically, we investigated the importance placed by EC adopters on specific cost elements (tangible and intangible, direct and indirect) in relation to EC and the cost requirements during the investment's life cycle. Also, we analyzed the time frame and the follow up of the cost budgets used by EC adopters. Furthermore, we studied the investment appraisal techniques used by SMEs for evaluating EC. In order to identify whether SMEs differentiate from non –SMEs, i.e. larger Greek companies, we also used a small control sample in order to test for significant variations to numerous issues presented above.

The majority of Greek companies that have introduced EC have done so during the last 4 years. This finding indicates that the introduction of EC has been rather delayed in relation to the pace of its development in other European countries. Greek SMEs that apply EC gain approximately 10% of their revenues from sales through internet. They also devote an analogous portion of their yearly budgeted operating expenses to EC. This relation, that is statistically significant, raises a number of issues. A first interpretation is that Greek SMEs companies appear to be realistic in their expectations in relation to EC and tend to balance the resources they devote to EC to the revenues they obtain from this way of making business. On the other hand, this relation may signal that Greek SMEs have a significant potential to increase their EC revenues by dedicating more resources to EC.

Greek companies do not perceive issues that are related to cost, in general, as issues that should be dealt with exceptional consciousness during the investment appraisal process, as they grade them with medium importance. However, this attitude is not homogeneous through time. Probably, as time passes, the cost parameters that are related to EC become more transparent and the vagueness of several cost items related to EC is resolved. Moreover, Greek companies do not perceive EC as an investment that is extremely resource demanding. A possible explanation for this may be that EC applications in Greece, due their small scale, as only a small proportion of yearly budget costs is devoted to them, are not difficult applications and thus the cost of their initial implementation as well as the cost of their maintenance is not excessive.

Greek EC adopters are aware of the fact that EC has different resource requirements during the different phases of its life cycle. They also anticipate that EC is related to both direct and indirect costs as well as tangible and intangible costs but they usually rank direct tangible costs as being more significant. This is not in alignment with IT literature where it is clearly stated that the intangible costs are far greater than the visible ones (Hinton and Kaye, 1996). As far as investment appraisal techniques are concerned, SMEs prefer less sophisticated and easier to apply techniques such as cost-benefit analysis and payback. Non-SMEs, as they employ personnel adequately experienced and educated in financial appraisal methods, apply more frequently discounted cash flow methods such as IRR and NPV. This finding is partially consistent with international practices, where discounted cash flows techniques are perceived more difficult and thus are used to a lesser extent for ICT investments (Ballantine and Stray, 1998). The majority of Greek companies develop a budget prior to EC adoption. The range of these budgets covers a period from 6 months to 5 years. The most common time frame for these budgets is one year and the period that is commonly used for its follow up is one trimester.

Cost reduction has not been considered as the main driving force in relation to the introduction of EC. On the contrary, other more qualitative and customer oriented benefits have driven Greek firms to adopt EC. Thus, as already indicated in other studies (Remenyi et al., 2001), EC is perceived rather as a strategic issue and within this context operational aspects such as costs are somewhat downplayed. Finally, from the analysis above we can conclude that Greek SMEs are aware of the whole range of EC perspectives as they use it as a tool for communicating purposes, for business process improvement, for service amelioration and for online transactions. The conclusion that can be drawn, as a synopsis of the survey results, is that Greek SMEs can adopt EC without incurring unbearable costs. Moreover, these costs are rather easily quantifiable, manageable and controllable and above all revenues counterbalance them. However, even though in quantitative terms EC is not a major tool for cost reduction, it provides significant recourses and qualitative benefits that can help SMEs to become more competitive in the market overcoming the limitations of their size.

Our findings are based on the analysis of an adequate sample of SMEs and a small sample of larger companies implementing EC. The analysis of the two sub-samples (SMEs and Non-SMEs) has not revealed any statistically significant differences that could induce noise in the empirical evidence, apart from the expected variation in the use of investment appraisal techniques and the frequency of budget development. Moreover, our analysis in relation to the actual financial resources devoted to EC and the revenues steaming from it is exclusively concentrated on SMEs in order our findings to be comparable with other SMEs studies. Thus, the fact that the sample is not homogeneous does not undermine the relevance of our conclusions. However, a limitation in our research is the small number of observations in absolute terms. Also, the composition of the sample due to the uneven representation of different sectors may induce some sort of bias to the conclusions

References

"European e-Business Report 2002/03", March 2003, [Online], Available: http://www.ebusiness-watch.org/resources/synthesis.htm [30 May 2005].

Adler, R., (2000) "Strategic Investment Decision Appraisal Techniques: The Old and The New", Business Horizons, Voll 43, No. 6, pp15-22.

Avram, G., (2001) "Evaluation of investment in E-commerce in the Romanian business environment", Electronic Journal of Information Systems Evaluation, Vol 4, No.1.

Bagozzi, R. P. (1994) Measurement in marketing research: Basic principles of questionnaire design. In. R. P. Bagozzi (Ed.), Principles of Marketing Research. Oxford: Blackwell.

Ballantine, J., & Stray S., (1998) "Financial appraisal and the ICT investment decision making process", Journal of Information Technology, Vol 13, pp3-14.

Blili, S., & Raymond, L., (1993) "Information technology: threats and opportunities for small and medium-sized enterprises", International Journal of Information Management, Vol 13, pp 439-448.

Brian, W., (1998) "Your network's not ready for e-commerce", Network Computing, Vol 9, pp22-25.

Currie, W., (2000) The global information society, Chichester: Wiley.

Damaskopoulos, P., & Evgeniou, T., (2003) "Adoption of New Economy Practices by SMEs in Eastern Europe", European Management Journal, Vol 21, pp133-145.

Dans, E. (2001), "IT investments in Small and Medium Enterprises: Paradoxically productive?", Electronic Journal of Information Systems Evaluation, Vol 4, No 1.

Domaracki, G.S., (2001) "The Dynamics of B2B E-Commerce", AFP Exchange, Vol 21 (4), pp 50-57.

Doukidis, G., Poulymenakou, A., Georgopoulos N., & Motsios Th. (2001) E-Commerce in Large Greek Enterprises: Issues and Prospects, EASE (Confederation of CEOs of Greek Enterprises), (In Greek).

Drew, S. (2003) "Strategic uses of e-commerce by SMEs in the East of England", European Management Journal, Vol 21, pp 79-88

EOMMEX, (2003) "The SMEs sector in Greece" (in greek).

European Commission, (1996) "Definition of Small and Medium Sized Enterprises" [Online], Available: http://europa.eu.int/comm/enterprise/consultations/sme_definition/ [30 May 2005].

European Communities, (2002) SMEs in Europe: Competitiveness, innovation and the knowledge-driven society, [Online], http://epp.eurostat.ec.europa.eu/cache/ITY_OFFPUB/KS-CJ-02-001/EN/KS-CJ-02-001-EN.PDF, Accessed on August 12th 2006.

Evans, P.B., Wurster, B.S. (1997) "Strategy and the new economics of information", Harvard Business Review, Vol 75(5), pp70-83

Farbey, B., Targett, D., & Land, F., (1994) "Matching an IT project with an appropriate method of evaluation: a research not on Evaluating investment in IT", Journal of Information Technology, Vol 9, pp239-243.

Farbey, B., Targett, D., & Land, F., (1993) How to evaluate your IT investment, Butterworth Heinemann, Oxford.

Gartner Group (1995) A guide for estimating client/server costs, Gartner Group, High Wycombe.

Heeks, R., & Duncombe, R. (2001) "Information, Technology and Small Enterprise: A Handbook for Enterprise Support Agencies in Developing countries", Institute for Development Policy and Management, University of Manchester.

Hinton, C.M., & Kaye, G.R., (1996) "The Hidden Investments in Information Technology: The Role of Organisational Context and System Dependency", International Journal of Information Management, Vol 16, No. 6, pp413-427.

Hochstrasser, B., (1992) "Justifying IT investments". Conference proceedings: Advanced information systems; The new technologies in today's business environment, pp17-28.

Information Society, (2004) "Survey on new technologies adoption in Greek SMEs" (in greek).

Innes, J., Mitchell, F., & Sinclair, D., (2000) "Activity based costing in the UK's largest companies: a comparison of 1994 and 1999 survey results", Management Accounting Research, Vol 11, pp349-362.

Irani, Z., Ezingeard, J-N., & Grieve, R.J., (1997) "Integrating the costs of a manufacturing IT/IS infrastructure into the investment decision-making process", Technovation, Vol 17, No. 11-12, pp695-706.

Irani, Z., Sharif, A., Love, P.E.D., & Kahraman, C., (2002) "Applying concepts of fuzzy cognitive mapping to model: The IT/IS investment evaluation process", International Journal of Production Economics, Vol 75, No. 1-2, pp199-211.

Kalakota, R., & Whinston, A.B., (1997) Electronic Commerce: A Manager's Guide, Massachusetts: Addison - Whesley

Kaplan, D., & Norton, D., (1992) "The Balanced scorecard – Measures that drive performance", Harvard Business Review, January – February, pp71-79.

Kleindl, B. (2000) "Competitive dynamics and new business models for SMEs in the virtual market place", Journal of Developmental Entrepreneurship, Vol 5(1), pp 73-85.

Larsen, K., & Bloniarz, P., (2000) "A cost and performance model for web service investment", Communications of the ACM, Vol 43, No. 2, pp109-116.

Levy, M., & Powell, P., (1998) "SME flexibility and the role of information systems", Small Business Economics, Vol 11, pp 183-196

Levy, M., & Powell, P., (2000) "Information systems strategy for small and medium sized enterprises: an organisational perspective", Journal of Strategic Information Systems, Vol 9, pp 63-84

Levy, M., Powell, P., & Yetton, P. (2001) "SMEs: Aligning IS and the Strategic Context", Journal of Information Technology, Vol 16, pp 133-144.

Levy, M., Powell, P., & Yetton, P. (2002) "Critical Issued for Growing IS Capabilities in SMEs", Small Business Economics, Vol 16, pp 341-354.

Love, P., & Irani, Z., (2004) "An exploratory study of information technology evaluation and benefits management practices for SMEs in the construction industry", Information and Management, Vol 42, No. 1, pp227-242

Love, P.E.D., Irani, Z., Standing, C., Lin, C., & Burn, J.M., (2004) "The enigma of evaluation: benefits, costs and risks of IT in Australian small-medium-sized enterprises", Information & Management, Vol 42, No. 7, pp947-964.

Milis, K., & Mercken, R., (2003) "The use of the balanced scorecard for the evaluation of information and communication technology projects", International Journal of Project Management, Vol 21, No. 2, pp83-91.

Ngai, E., & Wat, F., (2002) "A literature review and classification of electronic commerce research", Information and Management, Vol 39, No. 5, pp415-429.

Parker, M., & Benson, R., (1988) Information Economics: Linking business performance with Information Technology, Prentice Hall.

Piris, L., Fitzgerald, G., & Serrano, A., (2004) "Strategic motivators and expected benefits from e-commerce in traditional organizations", International Journal of Information Management, Vol 24, pp489-506.

Porter, M., (2001) Strategy and the Internet, Harvard Business Review, March, pp63-78.

Remenyi, D., Money, A., & Price, D., (2001) "Concepts of drivers of e-business success", Electronic Journal of Information Systems Evaluation, Vol 4, No. 1.

Santarelli, E., & D'Altri, S., (2003) "The Diffusion of E-commerce among SMEs: Theoretical Implications and Empirical Evidence", Small Business Economics, Vol 21, No. 3, pp273-283.

Turban, E., King, D., Lee, J., Warkentin, M., & Chung, H.M., (2002) Electronic Commerce 2002: A managerial perspective, Prentice Hall.

Ward, J., Griffiths P., & Whitmore, P., (1990) Strategic planning for information systems, Wiley, Chichester.

Whelan, E. & McGrath, F., (2002) "A study of the total life cycle costs of an E-commerce investment: A research in progress", Evaluation and Program Planning, Vol 25, No. 2, pp191-196.

Willcocks, L., (1994) Information Management: the evaluation of information systems investments, Chapman & Hall.

A Holistic Framework on Information Systems Evaluation with a Case Analysis

Petri Hallikainen[1] and Lena Chen[2]
[1]Information Systems Science, Helsinki School of Economics, Finland
[2]General Education Center, National University of Arts, Taiwan
Originally Published in EJISE (2006) Volume 9: issue 2

Editor's Comment
Holism is a relatively rare concept in IT Evaluation. Historically speaking the accounting approaches to IT Evaluation discussed in the introduction were high level but high level should not be confused for holistic. For holistic analysis a case analysis is useful and Hallikainen and Chen have taken this approach to their research. Only one case study has been conducted so the question of any degree of generalisability is not raised. Drawing together of the information obtained by the case study is always a challenging issue and it is interesting to see how this has been done on this occasion.

Abstract: This paper presents a framework for understanding IS evaluation in its broader context. The role of IS evaluation is emphasised on integrating the IS development process into business development process. The framework is applied to analyze a single IS project in details. The results show that sometimes formal IS evaluation might not be important or necessary, but rather it may be more important, with an informal and flexible evaluation process, to quickly gain experience of a new kind of business and system to maintain a leading position in the competitive market.

Keywords: information systems projects, IS evaluation, organisational context, holistic framework on IS evaluation

1. Introduction

It has been widely noticed in the literature that information system (IS) evaluation is a very difficult task involving a variety of dimensions (Smithson and Hirschheim, 1998; Irani, 2002; Peffers and Saarinen, 2002) and various stakeholders (McAulay et al., 2002). IS investments often include intangible benefits (Powell, 1992) and the benefits are often realised during a long period of time (Saarinen and Wijnhoven, 1994). Ad hoc practices for IS evaluation are frequently reported (Irani and Love, 2001) and only simple methods, like payback period, are used in evaluation (Lederer and Mendelow, 1993). This is in sharp contrast to management theory suggestions that IS investments should be evaluated using a covering set of criteria. For example, Peffers and Saarinen (2002) stated that evaluation of IT in financial terms may be biased toward the most easily measured benefits and prone to manipulation to justify predetermined investment decisions, resulting in systematic over or under-investment in IT. Some contingency models for selecting evaluation methods for IS investments have been presented in the literature. At organisational level, contingency factors may include, for example, the industry situation (stable or changing), and the leadership role of the organisation (pioneer or follow) (Farbey et al., 1992). At IS project level, contingency factors may include, for example, project types, project sises, the type of expected benefits (qualitative vs. quantifiable), the stages of the system's life cycle, and development and procurement strategy (see e.g. Farbey et al., 1992; Hochstrasser, 1990).

As a result of their study on IS evaluation methods, Peffers and Saarinen (2002) divided evaluation criteria into five broad categories as follows: Strategic value; Profitability; Risk; Successful Development and Procurement; and Successful Use and Operations. The above categories might be seen as universal for evaluation in any particular case. Moreover, Irani and Love (2002) presented a comprehensive frame of reference for ex-ante IS investment evaluation. However, the need for a better understanding of in-context IS evaluation still exists. This paper aims to provide an instrument for understanding IS evaluation in a broader context. The instrument is expected to be of value to both researchers and practitioners. In the next section, a holistic framework on IS evaluation is presented. Then the empirical research methodology is described and the presented framework is applied in a case analysis. Finally, the paper concludes with discussions and conclusions.

2. A holistic framework for analysing IS evaluation in context

The outset situation of the IS investment project consists of the organisational norms and values, project specific contextual factors and the resources given to the project. The actual outcomes of the IS investment project are produced in conjunction with the business development process, the IS development and procurement processes. The outcomes of the IS project are defined by the success of the system with respect to the investment perspective, the success of the IS project implementation and the success of the desired IS functionality. The basic idea in our analytical framework, presented in Figure 1, is the inclusion and integration of the IS evaluation process into business development and IS development processes. The evaluation categories defined by Peffers and Saarinen (2002) are suggested to be applied in all IS projects, and in projects with great uncertainty they should be applied frequently, to iteratively assess the system investment throughout its life-cycle. Furthermore, the IS evaluation process should also adapt to the possible changes in the assumptions that the IS investment is based on, thus in our conceptual framework there is a two-way relationship between the IS evaluation process and, business development and IS development processes. The components of the framework are discussed in more details.

2.1. Outset situation

2.1.1. Organisational norms and values

The investment characteristics and the organisational environment affect the way in which the evaluation is conducted (Huerta and Sánchez, 1999). Organisations operate and survive through organisationally accepted rules that are justified by goals or a hierarchical goal system. Within organisations, there are individual goals, objectives, desires, wishes, intentions, etc, as well as organisational goals, objectives, missions, etc. (Kivijärvi, 2004). As pointed out by Hallikainen et al. (2002), any strategic investment process employs individual and organisational values and preferences, goals and objectives as an input. At best, evaluation would help the organisation to understand its processes, problems and opportunities, thus facilitating organisational learning (Barrow and Mayhew, 2000).

2.1.2. Project contingencies

An information system can, on the one hand, be a small application supporting only one single activity, but on the other hand, it can be a wider system supporting the whole company, or it can even be an inter-organisational system. There is one additional type of information system that deserves special attention, namely infrastructure investments. Infrastructure investments are of high importance because they create the platform on which future applications can be built (see e.g. Dos Santos, 1991). Moreover, why the information system is actually built, depends on several factors. In some situations a company may be forced to build a new information system, e.g. because of legislation changes. Additionally, the senior management may perceive that the system needs to be built, for example, to support a business strategy. Finally, the arguments for building the system can be from the expected and clear quantitative or qualitative benefits from the investment perspective.

The nature of the investment varies according to the novelty of the system. An investment can deal with improving an existing system, replacing an old system or developing an entirely new system. The nature of the investment differs according to how common this type of system is in the field of industry where the company operates (see e.g. Saarinen and Vepsalainen, 1994). For example, investment in a routine system is different from an investment in an innovative system.

2.1.3. IS project resources

Both the material and the immaterial resources are crucial while developing information systems. The integrating role of evaluation includes detecting possible problems and as a result of evaluation it may be noticed, for example, that the project needs more system development resources.

2.2. Business development process

As information technology can make alternative operational designs possible, it in many cases plays a central role when developing the company's business strategy. Furthermore, IT enables new kinds of flexible inter-organisational arrangements (Venkatraman, 1994). Moreover, information technology can support the development of new business, or new products and services. Thus, IS projects are often connected to larger strategic business development programs and the role of IS evaluation would be to ensure that the IS project would deliver the required technological capabilities for achieving the strategic business objectives. The degree that an

IS project is involved in business development can range from a system that supports the current business strategy to a system that creates competitive advantages and new business opportunities to the company. An information system investment is in many cases an important part of a business process re-engineering project. The actual aim of the system investment would be cutting costs, improving products or services, or serving a certain customer group better.

2.3. IS development process

In the ever-changing business environment it is very important to be aware of the possible changes that may, in some situations, affect the underlying assumptions that the investment is based on. Thus, it would be essential to conduct evaluation regularly during the development process. According to Burns and Dennis (1985) there are basically three development strategies: to use a system life cycle -based methodology, an iterative methodology (e.g. prototyping) or a mixed methodology. The choice of the development method obviously affects the way evaluation is conducted; for example, prototyping can be considered an evaluation methodology in itself.

There are several factors that affect the risk of the development process. First, the risks would be decreased if parts of existing systems or existing knowledge can be exploited in system development (see Davis, 1982). Secondly, there are some factors related to project management (see McFarlan and McKenney, 1983): the knowledge and skills of the system developers and the representatives of the users affect the risks of the IS development project; the co-operation within the project group and between the project group and the users must be active in order to minimise the project risks; and the risks of the project could be decreased by using formal project management and control methods.

In summary, Barki et al. (1993) presented the following factors affecting the risk of a system development project: 1. Technological newness; 2. Application size; 3. Expertise of development team and users; 4. Application complexity; 5. Organisational environment (e.g. conflicts, role definitions).

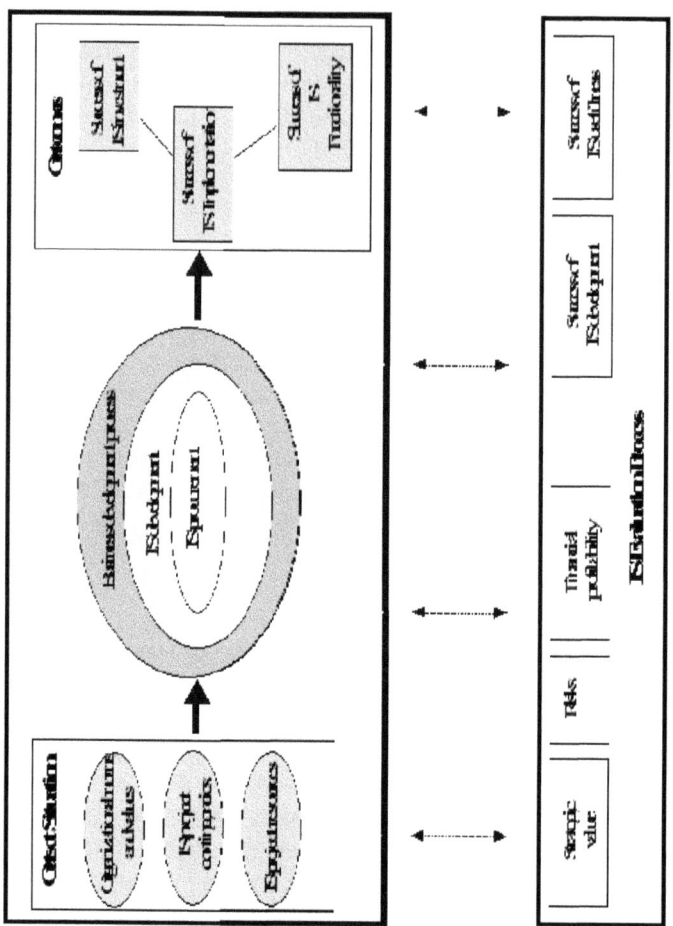

Figure 1 A holistic framework on IS evaluation

2.4. IS procurement process

Basically, an information system may be developed in-house, it may be developed by a software vendor, or the company may purchase a software package. Heckman (1999) described two recent trends in information resource acquisition: firstly, the process has changed from an internal to market-oriented; second, there is a more distinct focus on business processes. When using an outside vendor to develop the system, evaluation procedures should be explicitly designed for contracting purposes, since all individuals acting as clients for IS projects may not be knowledgeable about the technology related issues (Kirsch et al., 2002). While IS often plays a central role in developing new business processes, the choice of the IS procurement strategy is critical for company operations. For different kinds of systems different kinds of resources are needed and consequently different procurement strategies are applicable. According to the procurement principles for choosing the efficient procurement strategy, presented by Saarinen and Vepsalainen (1994), routine systems should be implemented by acquiring software packages from implementers, while standard applications require software contracting by analysts and possibly other outside resources for implementation, and speculative investments are best left for internal development by innovators.

2.5. IS evaluation process

The evaluation process should identify and control the critical areas of an IS project. Before selecting the evaluation criteria and methods and deciding who would be involved in the evaluation, it is important to identify all the relevant interest groups for the IS project (Serafeimidis and Smithson, 2000). A covering set of evaluation criteria should be used to make sure that all dimensions of the IS endeavour are taken into account and assessed. The IS evaluation process must be integrated into business development process, the IS development process, and the IS procurement process.

Wen and Sylla (1999) suggested a three-step process for IS evaluation: 1. Intangible benefits evaluation, 2. IS investment risk analysis, and 3. Tangible benefits evaluation. The steps should be taken in this order, i.e. intangible benefits and risks should be evaluated prior to evaluating the tangible benefits. In our framework, the order of the evaluation categories "strategic value", "risks" and "financial profitability" reflects this suggestion. The "success of IS development" category is placed prior to the "success of IS usefulness" since the usefulness can only be observed after the IS has been used for a while. Ideally, IS evaluation would cover all the above categories, but, however, it is expected that the focus of evaluation is different depending on who conducts the evaluation and where the initiative for the evaluation comes from. Farbey et al. (1992) stated that the focus of evaluation changes according to the organisational interests, which may be on a number of levels, e.g. costs and benefits, organisation's competitive position or industrial relations. We argue, however, that whether the organisation's interests are taken into account appropriately depends on the knowledge and skills of the evaluator. Thus, the senior management should carefully consider who should be involved in the evaluation.

The result of the evaluation should be delivered to each person related to the project so that the information received from the evaluation can be employed in the decision making phase. Most likely, the decision itself would be continuing with the investment (maybe after some minor changes), changing the specifications, range or implementation method of the system, or 'freezing' the project. In addition, the changes might include e.g. schedule changes; reorganisation of the project (e.g. project management can be changed); or vendor changes. The reasons for these changes may be obvious mistakes, unexpected problems, a new experience about the project that changes the idea of the right course of action, or changes in the company's environment, that are beyond the company's control.

2.6. Outcomes

The outcomes of an IS project are identified as the success of 1) IS implementation, 2) IS investment, and 3) IS functionality. IS Evaluation should not work only as a justification mechanism but as a tool for experience learning. During the IS development process, feedback from the evaluation process should lead to corrective actions if necessary. These actions might include, for example, a change in the information system development or procurement strategy, or a change in the resources that are given to the project.

Evaluating the success of an IS implementation should consider at least two dimensions: the process and the product success (Saarinen, 1993). Evaluating the conduct of the IS development process would facilitate the learning for future projects. *The product success includes both the IS functionality and the realisation of the expected benefits from the IS investment.*

To learn conducting evaluation and managing information system projects more effectively, the perceived success of the evaluation process itself can be measured in terms of: evaluation efficiency, precision, and effectiveness (Hallikainen et al., 1998). Evaluation efficiency can be divided into efficiency of evaluation process and cost of evaluation. Evaluation precision can be further divided into satisfaction with evaluation criteria and methods used; and satisfaction with contents, usability and reliability of information produced by evaluation. Finally, evaluation effectiveness can be divided into usefulness of the results of evaluation when making decisions concerning this particular project; and evaluation supporting in aligning information technology and business functions.

3. Research methodology

We conducted a case study in a major Finnish insurance company to investigate how IS evaluation was conducted in an environment where information technology was extensively used in daily operations. The company covers the entire spectrum of insurance services with about 3 700 employees. Based on the above-presented framework (Figure1), we designed a research instrument, a questionnaire, to be used as a basis for interviews. A questionnaire was used, because this study was a pilot study for a survey to be conducted later and one objective was to test the research instrument. The original research instrument is in Finnish language, but the main issues addressed are listed in Appendix 1. Although the interview instrument was rather structured, we let the interviewee talk freely also about issues not mentioned in the instrument to get as rich a picture of the case as possible. We first interviewed the corporate IS manager to get an overview of the use of information technology in the company and to select an appropriate project for the detailed analysis. We selected a pilot project through which the company wanted to gain experience about a new kind of insurance policy and system. We believe this project represents rather well a typical IS project in contemporary organisations where new business processes are frequently developed, information systems being a crucial part. Moreover, the case has revelatory power, because it is about entering a totally new business area, thus making it feasible to use a single case study research strategy (Yin, 1994). We interviewed the project manager because he was considered to have the widest knowledge of the project. The interviews were recorded on tape, and the interviewee has checked and commented on our written case report.

4. Findings of the case study

4.1. Project characteristics
The system takes care of unit-linked insurance policies, including both life assurance of endowment type and pension insurance. The yield on the unit-linked policies is determined merely in accordance with the return

gained by the investment funds chosen by the client. The client is free to choose both domestic and foreign equity and bond funds. The system is characterised as a wide system supporting one business unit. There were about 15 persons who participated in the system development project. The estimated workload was about 30 person months and the estimated calendar time was about one year. It was difficult to define the benefits gained from the investment in monetary terms.

The implementation of the investment was based on the senior management's vision of its necessity. The system was seen as an important source of competitive advantages based on a determined business strategy and product differentiation. It was expected that the system would create possibilities for new business. When the system was developed in 1993, this kind of insurance was not legal in Finland, but it became legal at the beginning of 1994. According to the project manager, the background of the investment was that it was known this kind of insurance policies represented in the USA about 30%, in Sweden 50% and in England 80% of all savings insurances, and the company believed that the development would be alike also in Finland. The company attempted to make sure that it could have this product in the market from the beginning. Since the project was about going to a new business area, even the product itself was developed during the system development process (work processes were reconsidered). The basic idea of the project, actually, was that the company would gain a few-year experience of using this kind of a system. It was known when developing the system that it would not last long since it was implemented in PC-environment. Later the volumes would increase and more powerful computing would be needed. According to the project manager, this experience has been very valuable.

4.2. IS development/procurement process

There was no prior experience of exactly this kind of systems in Finland. That is why the company investigated a possibility to co-operate with a foreign company. However, this co-operation failed because of some political reasons. Also procurement of a software package was investigated but it was considered too expensive. It was decided that the system would be developed using external resources, i.e. a consulting company. This system was planned to be based on the so called "universal life" principle, which in practice means that the customer pays first an amount of money to an account and the insurance company then debits the account with transaction and other payments and credits it with compensations; the customer just follows the balance of the account. Because of the tight schedule, it was concluded that the most suitable way would be hiring the consulting company to develop the system, using as a basis another system that they had developed earlier, applying the similar "universal life" principle, in the company.

So, existing knowledge and experience, and also existing parts of another system could be exploited in system development. This was expected to lower the risks of delayed schedule. An iterative method was used in system development (not actual prototyping though) because the desired system features were not entirely clear at the beginning. As to the project risks, all the people participating in the project were experts but most of the issues were completely new, which according to the project manager was actually a very rare situation. However, co-operation worked well and people were very active in the project. Formal methods were applied in the project management. The issues concerning the project were discussed about once a week in a steering group. The project manager had the general responsibility of the project. In addition there were meetings for discussing the business dimensions and issues related to, for example, marketing and personnel training. Some members of the board of the company also participated in these meetings. The technology used in the project was very new, but according to the project manager it was not considered a big problem. The project was considered medium sized and technically complex, but that was not considered to create uncertainty because the system was not supposed to handle large amounts of information and the system code was not very complex. Moreover, the system did not cause greater changes in the company's functions, but rather the changes concerned the product range.

4.3. Evaluation process

The concepts presented in the theoretical framework in section 2 are developed into a more operational level in Figure 2 to describe the evaluation process of the case project. The evaluation process and the results for the case company are discussed below. The project was formally evaluated only in the investment proposal phase. The costs of both in-house development and outsourcing alternatives were assessed. A project overview is usually conducted after implementation in the company, but it was not conducted for this project. However, the costs were investigated after the project had been implemented. Moreover, the type of vendor agreement

Leading Issues in IS Evaluation Research

used was assessed. The agreement with the vendor was considered appropriate and the project manager believed that this project encouraged the use of outside vendors. The project manager stressed that the aim of this project was to engage in an entirely new business area. That is why evaluation had to concentrate more on the substance and not so much on the system investment itself. According to the project manager it was most important, in this case, to evaluate whether the business would be successful or not. The project manager and the representatives of the business management conducted the evaluation.

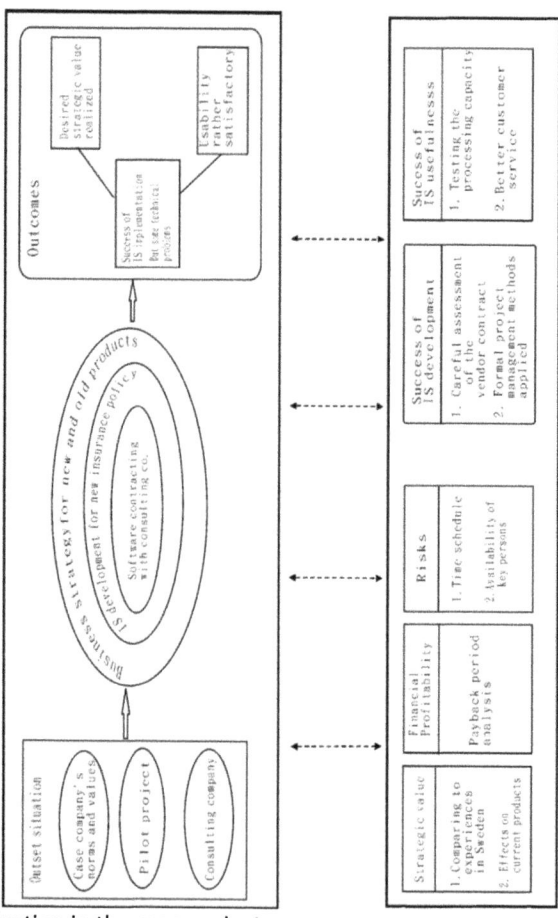

Figure 2 IS evaluation in the case project.

Strategic value was considered as a very important criterion in evaluation. Comparing to the experiences in Sweden assessed the volume of the business. It was important to the company to be in the leading position in the competitive market in Finland. The evaluation concentrated on the following issues: 1. Whether this kind of products could be successful (market shares were compared in different countries) 2. Whether this could be a way to expand to the banking area 3. Whether this investment could bring new sales volume. During the evaluation process it was also investigated whether this kind of products would replace current products or affect negatively the sales volumes of the current products. Payback period was used while evaluating the financial productivity. The break-even point of costs and incomes was also calculated. The aim of this investment was not to create any big business but expressly to gain experience of this kind of business. Risk was evaluated on several dimensions. There was the risk that the sales of the traditional insurances would decrease because of these new products. Moreover, it was important that the system would be implemented according to the schedule. Further, there were a number of key persons who only had the knowledge and skills required in the project. The schedule affected the decision of choosing the procurement method a lot. Time schedule was a problem because it was not known exactly when the new law would come into effect. Processing capacity was tested because pension insurance was one part of the system and it requires a lot of calculation. Otherwise, efficiency of use was not considered one of the most critical considerations. There were a lot of new qualitative objectives like transparency (information to the customer about how their money changes into benefits) and clarity; in other words, sufficient customer information, which was taken into account when evaluating the system. Although some technical problems could not be anticipated in the early stages of the project, the project manager was quite satisfied with the evaluation process as a whole. The costs of evaluation were not high. However, the project manager was only moderately satisfied with the contents of information produced in evaluation and the usability of the results of evaluation when making decisions concerning this project.

4.4. Success of the information system project
Generally speaking, the project has been successful. The estimate of the vendor's work amount was exceeded but no big surprises occurred. The strategic benefits expected from the system investment have realised quite well. The project manager considered financial profitability of the

project sufficient enough. The procurement process was effective because the same vendor had worked with the company earlier. Only the problems related to the new technology should have been anticipated better.

5. Discussion and conclusions

In this study we have presented a framework for understanding IS evaluation in its broader context. Based on the operationalisation of the framework, we analysed one IS project in details. The first impression of the analysis is that evaluation is highly contextually specific. Although the literature of IS evaluation suggests the use of formal evaluation methods, sometimes it is important to quickly gain experience of a new type of information system or product with a rather informal evaluation process. Formal evaluation does not seem to be important or necessary in every case. Moreover, in the case presented in this study the evaluation process was more concerned about evaluating the business substance, rather than evaluating the information system investment alone. In the case investigated in this study, the evaluation did not cause any major changes in the IS project. There were no major unexpected changes in the business environment that would have caused a larger scale re-consideration of the IS investment. The interviewees were rather satisfied with the evaluation process, but on the other hand, based on our study, we are not able to detect the actual effects of the above IS investment on the business functions of the company. Only the improvements in the business processes would actually prove that the evaluation process has been successful in integrating IS development into business development process. Finally, we were not able to find any established practices for learning about IS evaluation itself. One of the challenges for the case company, and other companies, would be making the tacit evaluation knowledge more explicit so that it could be exploited in future projects. The investigation of how companies adjust their evaluation procedures to the rapidly changing business environment would be one of the interesting areas for future research. Taking the changes in the environment into account would require a continuous evaluation process over the information system life cycle. Another challenging area for future research is certainly the development of evaluation methodologies for new Internet technology based IS. In contemporary IS projects where development time is short, and modifications easy to make, collecting customer feedback efficiently would play the crucial role. Finally, the question how much IS evaluation should be formalised remains a contradictory issue and an interesting topic for future research.

It seems that the formalisation of conducting evaluation might not be applicable in the rapidly changing business environment of today, but evaluation knowledge should rather be developed and managed as a continuous process.

References

Barki, H, Rivard, S and Talbot, J 'Toward an Assessment of Software Development Risk' *Journal of Management Information Systems*, Vol 10 No 2 (Fall 1993) pp 203-225.

Barrow, P D M and Mayhew, P J 'Investigating principles of stakeholder evaluation in a modern IS development approach' *The Journal of Systems and Software*, Vol 52 No 2-3 (2000) pp 95-103.

Burns, R N and Dennis, A R 'Selecting the appropriate application development methodology' *DATA BASE*, Vol 17 No 1 (1985) pp 19-24.

Davis, G B 'Strategies for information requirements determination' *IBM Systems Journal*, Vol 21 No 1 (1982) pp 4-31.

Dos Santos, B L 'Justifying Investments in New Technologies' *Journal of Management Information Systems*, Vol 7 No 4 (1991) pp 71-90.

Farbey, B, Land, F and Target, D 'Evaluating investments in IT' *Journal of Information Technology*, Vol 7 No 2 (1992) pp 109-122.

Hallikainen, P, Kivijärvi, H and Nurmimäki, K Evaluating Strategic IT Investments: An Assessment of Investment Alternatives for a Web Content Management System, Proceedings of the HICSS-35, Big Island, Hawaii (2002).

Hallikainen, P, Heikkilä, J, Peffers, K, Saarinen, T and Wijnhoven, F 'Evaluating Information Technology Projects in Finland: Procedures, Follow-through, Decision-Making and Perceived Evaluation Quality' *Journal of Global Information Management*, Vol 6 No 4 (1998) pp 23-33.

Heckman, R 'Managing the IT Procurement Process' *Information Systems Management*, Vol 16 No 1 (1999) pp 61-71.

Hochstrasser, B 'Evaluating IT Investments: Matching Techniques and Projects' *Journal of Information Technology*, Vol 5 No 4 (1990) pp 215-221.

Huerta, E and Sánchez, P J 'Evaluation of information technology: strategies in Spanish firms' *European Journal of Information Systems*, Vol 8 No 4 (1999) pp 273-283.

Irani, Z 'Information systems evaluation: navigating through the problem domain' *Information & Management*, Vol 40 No 1 (2002) pp 11-24.

Irani, Z and Love, P E D 'Developing a frame of reference for ex ante IT/IS investment evaluation' *European Journal of Information Systems*, Vol 11 No 1 (2002) pp 74-82.

Irani, Z and Love, P E D 'The Propagation of Technology Management Taxonomies for Evaluating Investments in Information Systems' *Journal of Management Information Systems*, Vol 17 No 3 (2001) pp 161-177.

Kirsch, L J, Sambamurthy, V, Ko, D G and Purvis, R L 'Controlling Information Systems Development Projects: The View from the Client' *Management Science*, Vol 48 No 4 (2002) pp 484-498.

Kivijärvi, H *Knowledge Conversion in Organizational Context: A Framework and Experiments*, Proceedings of the 37th Hawaii International Conference on System Sciences (2004).

Lederer, A L and Mendelow, A L 'Information systems planning and the challenge of shifting priorities' *Information & Management*, Vol 24 No 6 (1993) pp 319-328.

McAulay, L, Doherty, N and Keval, N 'The stakeholder dimension in information systems evaluation' *Journal of Information Technology*, Vol 17 No 4 (2002) pp 241-255. McFarlan, W F and McKenney, J L Corporate information systems management: The issues facing senior executives, Richard D Irwin, INC. (1983).

Peffers, K and Saarinen, T 'Measuring the Business Value of IT Investments: Inferences from A Study of Senior Bank Executives' *Journal of Organizational Computing and Electronic Commerce*, Vol 12 No 1 (2002) pp 17-38.

Powell, P 'Information Technology Evaluation: Is It Different?' *Journal of the Operational Research Society*, Vol 43 No 1 (1992) pp 29-42.

Saarinen, T Success of Information Systems. Evaluation of Development Projects and the Choice of Procurement and Implementation Strategies, PhD Dissertation Helsinki School of Economics and Business Administration A-88 (1993).

Saarinen, T and Vepsalainen, A P J 'Procurement Strategies for Information Systems' *Journal of Management Information Systems*, Vol 11 No 2 (1994) pp 187-208.

Saarinen, T and Wijnhoven, F *Organizational Learning and Evaluation of Information Systems*, Working Papers W-111 Helsinki School of Economics and Business Administration (1994).

Serafeimidis, V and Smithson, S 'Information systems evaluation in practice: a case study of organizational change' *Journal of Information Technology*, Vol 15 No 2 (2000) pp 93-105.

Smithson, S and Hirschheim, R 'Analyzing information systems evaluation: another look at an old problem' *European Journal of Information Systems*, Vol 7 No 3 (1998) pp 158-174.

Wen, H J and Sylla, C *A Road Map for the Evaluation of Information Technology Investment*, in Mahmood and Szewczak (Eds.) Measuring Information Technology Investment Payoff: Contemporary Approaches, Idea Group Publishing (1999).

Wen, H J and Sylla, C *A Road Map for the Evaluation of Information Technology Investment*, in Mahmood and Szewczak (Eds.) Measuring Information Technology Investment Payoff: Contemporary Approaches, Idea Group Publishing (1999).

Venkatraman, N 'IT-Enabled Business Transformation: From Automation to Business Scope Redefinition' *Sloan Management Review*, Vol 35 No 2 (1994) pp 73-87.

Yin, R K *Case Study Research: Design and Methods*, Sage Publications, Newbury Park, (1994).

Appendix 1: The main issues in the interview instrument

1. General description of the information system under study
2. Specific characteristics and objectives of the system investment
3. Description of the IS development and procurement process
4. Description of the IS evaluation process
    a. Stages of evaluation
    b. Who conducted evaluation?
    c. What were the evaluation criteria and methods applied?
    d. What were the decisions made based on evaluation?
5. Was the evaluation process perceived as successful in terms of:
    a. Evaluation efficiency?
    b. Evaluation precision?
    c. Evaluation effectiveness?
6. Is the IS project considered successful?

An Interactive and Iterative Evaluation Approach for Creating Collaborative Learning Environments

Anita Mirijamdotter[1], Mary M. Somerville[2] and Marita Holst[1]
[1] Luleå University of Technology, Social Informatics, Sweden
[2] Dr. Martin Luther King Jr. Library, San José State University, USA
Originally Published in EJISE (2006) Volume 9: issue 2

Editor's Comment

This is an unusual paper both in terms of the subject it addresses and the way that the research was conducted. Collaborative learning is at first sight not a topic that one would count on seeing in a set of IT Evalauition papers. However as IT is a major facilitator of collaborative activities then it quickly become apparent that it is perfectly reasonable to include such a paper in this set. The paper describes a research initiative involving sixty-two students in four disciplines on three campuses – two in the USA and one in Sweden. What is more interesting is that the research involves an Interactive and iterative basis which is unusual.

An interactive and iterative evaluation approach for creating collaborative learning environments (2006). Authors A Mirijamdotter, M M Somerville and M Holst. Essentially, evaluation is about learning. This paper very well illustrates this issue.

Abstract: Inspired by a three-year Creative University 'arena' initiative at Luleå University of Technology in Sweden, an international team of faculty researchers conducted an exploratory study in 2005, which aimed to investigate the efficacy of an interactive design and evaluation process for technology-enabled collaborative learning environments. This applied research approach was designed as a collaborative evaluation process for co-creation of technology-enabled, learning-focused physical and virtual 'learning commons.' Faculty researchers from Sweden and the United States used Soft Systems Methodology tools, including the Process for Organisational Meanings (POM) model, to guide sixty-two students' participatory co-design and evaluation activities. In this paper, the POM evaluation model is explained and related to the Japanese concept Ba. Application of the models is illustrated within the context of student learning through boundary crossing information exchange and knowledge creation. As evidenced in their iterative and interactive evaluative recommendations, students' learning outcomes included development of improved capabilities for identifying socio-technical elements of distributed learning environments, suggesting that student beneficiaries can successfully reflect upon their experiences and provide valuable evaluation insights. In addition, when this evaluation is iterative, students' insights into project management, software needs, and services design can improve their technology-enabled learning experiences. Concluding comments explore the efficacy of the POM model implementation for guiding other learning-focused, user-centric initiatives, which aim to promote interdisciplinary, or boundary crossing, exchanges concurrent with advancing team-based knowledge creation proficiencies among project participants.

Keywords: interactive formative evaluation, learning commons, soft systems methodology, process for organisational meanings (POM) model, Ba, higher education pedagogy

1. Introduction

Between January and June 2005, an international research team investigated the efficacy of an interactive design and evaluation process for technology-enabled collaborative learning. The research subjects in this study involve sixty-two students in four disciplines - computer science, library and information science, computer and systems science, and social informatics - on three campuses - California Polytechnic State University (Cal Poly) and San José State University (SJSU) in the United States and Luleå University of Technology (Ltu) in Sweden. Faculty supervisors and student participants in two graduate courses – information science and knowledge management – and two undergraduate courses – social informatics and human computer interaction (HCI) – explored a shared topic of inquiry: a 'learning commons'. The research team also applied a shared research methodology, which assumes that student beneficiaries are able designers and evaluators of socio-technical learning spaces and places. In our paper, we present the theoretical framework informing this user-centred process for co-creation of collaborative physical and virtual learning environments through interactive and iterative evaluation processes. Selected research results provide additional detail on the evaluation process and learning outcomes.

The 'commons' construct emerges from a three-year Creative University 'arena' initiative at Ltu, Sweden (Andersson 2003; Andersson et al. 2002; Edzén 2005; Edzén et al. 2004; Holst 2004; Holst and Mirijamdotter 2004; 2005; 2006; Sandström 2004). It also acknowledges the contemporary transformation of information commons (Bailey 2005; Bailey and Tierney 2002; Beagle 1999; 2002; Crockett et al. 2002) into learning commons, where the focus is on learning rather than technology (Beagle 2004) and relates to the shift from a teaching culture to a culture of learning (Bennett 2003); a change sweeping American higher education as necessitated by the distinctively different expectations and preferences of the NetGeneration student population (Brown 2005; Lippincott 2005). Similarly, the Swedish Creative University initiative also originated in response to changing assumptions and requirements among the populations they sought to serve. Expressed need on both continents to revisit traditional assumptions – toward the end of reinventing education – prompted this international research alliance.

This research collaboration is unique in its involvement of student beneficiaries in design and evaluation activities for collaborative learning environments. To date, the learning and design planning principles (Johnson and Lomas 2005) for "learning ecosystems" (Alexander 2004) reflective of expanded teaching and learning ambitions has explored such disparate elements as the relationship between learning technologies and innovative space design (Joint Information Systems Committee, 2006; Brown and Lippincott 2003). Included in the exploration are also strategies for community-based planning processes, collaborative service and system delivery models, and collaborative project planning and implementation considerations (Lippincott 2004a; 2004b; Wedge and Kearns 2005). But none explicitly involve students substantively in the design and evaluation activities. In response, the interdisciplinary research team sought to evolve a formative evaluation approach which both advanced learning commons design and student learning outcomes. Employing interactive and iterative evaluation methodology, we introduced a variety of technology supported tools for initiating and advancing physical, virtual and mental facets of collaborative learning environments, including two Learning Management Systems

(LMSs), two e-meeting software, 3-way video conferencing, Instant Messenger (IM), wikis, and email. We were also attentive to the social factors affecting tool utility, including cultural expectations, time zone differences, and role variation among both faculty and student learning groups. Throughout, we employed the lens of interactive design and evaluation (Newman and Lamming 1995; Preece et al. 2002), which has similar objectives as formative evaluation, for creating and sustaining dynamic technology-enabled, dialogue-driven communities of inquiry.

Our interactive and iterative evaluation methodology applied knowledge creation and systems thinking theories, especially the work of Nonaka (Nonaka 1994; Nonaka and Toyama 2003; von Krogh et al. 2000) and Checkland (Checkland 1981; 2000; Checkland and Holwell 1998; Checkland and Scholes 1990). We used the principles of knowledge exchange embedded in the concept of Ba, as advanced by Nonaka and others (Nonaka and Konno 1998; Nonaka et al. 2000), in coaching our students in their collaborative development process to make tacit information explicit. According to Nonaka et al, making tacit explicit is a prerequisite to enable information sharing and knowledge creation and also to establish shared physical, virtual and mental contexts. To collaboratively evaluate this development, i.e., the practical feasibility of constituting and linking learning communities to create new disciplinary knowledge, share it across disciplinary communities, and co-create dynamic technology-enabled learning environments, we employed systems thinking methodology. This methodology involves discourse, dialogue and communication and thus enabled faculty and students to create shared meanings. Inter-subjective sense making discourse, hence, served to define purposeful actions to be taken in the light of negotiated intentions and accommodations. In this paper, we outline the approach, which provided the analysis model for evaluating the efficacy of the interactive design and evaluation process. Thereafter we introduce the design of the learning commons project followed by illustration of students' process and lessons learnt. Lastly, we discuss findings from this collaborative learning environment study.

2. Interactive evaluation for collaborative learning

Interactive and iterative evaluation contrasts with more traditional methodologies in which researchers act as experts in the evaluated domain and defines what is to be evaluated and how. It is often assumed that the evaluation is conducted 'objectively', i.e., independent of social and political context, and the intention is to measure some phenomenon to find out its status. Moreover, evaluation results are oftentimes assumed to be an accurate representation of the actual situation (Guba and Lincoln 1989). While evaluation may have many purposes, e.g., control, change management, policy making and learning (Hansen 2005; Hedman and Borell 2005; Mackenzie and Blamey 2005; Oliver et al. 2005), in interactive design and evaluation, the purpose is improving through continuous learning. Therefore, according to Newman and Lamming (1995), it corresponds to a formative evaluation approach. Where the intention of the evaluation is to create learning and thereby improvements, formative evaluation based on a stakeholder model involving interactive and qualitative processes is necessary (Hansen 2005). With this approach, user-generated interpretations are viewed as 'meaningful constructions' - meaningful to the people involved in the situation because the interpretations make the situation of which people are a part more intelligible to them. Furthermore, such an approach assumes that evaluation is a social-political process in which social, cultural, and political factors are viewed as significant aspects of the process – i.e., 'meaning creators' – not 'annoying inconveniences' that threatens research validity. Evaluation, in this perspective, is a process to create shared reality and meaning (Guba and Lincoln 1989) which leads to an awareness of social and political aspects influencing both evaluation and learning processes.

In the information science (IS) field, there is increasing awareness of the importance of an ongoing evaluation process as a basis for action (Hedman and Borell 2005). Over the last years various action-oriented evaluation models have been developed (e.g., Guba and Lincoln 1989; Patton 1990). Common for these models, according to Rolfsen and Torvatn (2005), is that evaluators and stakeholders should work together in real-time and co-create knowledge useful for both the evaluation and the stakeholders, in this case, participants in the evaluation process. To manage ongoing evaluation processes and action-oriented evaluation, a model of processes is required. Hedman and Borell (2005) suggest integrating organisational sense-making and double loop learning as developed by Argyris and Schön (Argyris 1976; 1991; Argyris and Schön 1974). However, given our focus on collaborative learning environments, we adopted the Process for Organisational Meanings (POM) model (Checkland and Holwell 1993; 1998) to manage the formative evaluation, i.e. interactively and iteratively. The POM model depicts ongoing processes, which occur in interaction between the components Agents, Organisation and Technology, which is why we find it suitable for capturing processes aimed at creating collaborative, learning environments. The people who interact to create the wholly, or partially, shared meanings and thereby make sense of their world, are called Agents. The interactions take place via various forms of Organisations which can be embodied in a division or project team, but may also include tasks, patterns of communication and reporting. Finally, the processes of the POM-model acknowledge Technology, through which information support is provided. See Figure 1

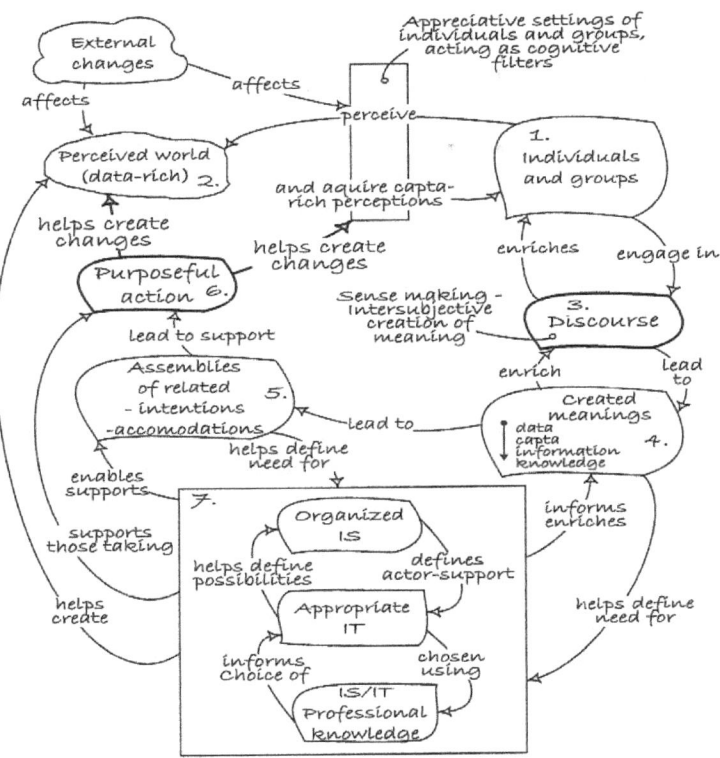

Figure 1: Process for Organisational Meanings (POM) Model. After Checkland and Holwell (1998: 106)

The POM-model offers a process-based organisational model for application to information systems design. The model emerges out of Vickers's concept of an appreciative system (Checkland 1994a; 1994b; Checkland and Casar 1986; Vickers 1983a; 1983b) as well as Soft Systems Methodology (Checkland 1981; 2000; Checkland and Scholes 1990). The POM-model addresses the relationship-maintaining aspects of organisations and also visualises them as ongoing processes of creating meaning through organisational discourse. It has in earlier studies been used for information systems development (Checkland and Holwell 1998; Rose 2002), in relation to project management (Costello et al. 2002), and as a sense making model for knowledge creation in multi-disciplinary settings (Holst and Mirijamdotter 2004; 2006; Mirijamdotter et al. 2005) and for understanding emerging work practices (Köhler et al. 2005; Mirijamdotter and Somerville 2005). In this context, we use the model, its elements and their relations, to assess and evaluate the learning processes involved in effective design and application of collaborative learning environments. We want to understand what hinders and what enables collaborative virtual processes where the focus is purposeful communication and dialogue aimed at creating shared reality and meaning. Furthermore, this evaluation approach offers a dynamic process model for continuous on-going group learning and strong participatory involvement while concurrently advancing negotiated actions.

Figure 1 depicts the model's seven elements that address the relationship-maintaining aspects of – in this case – virtual learning communities, and the underlying social, cultural, and political context. Elements 1-2 represent identification of relevant environmental elements, an exercise that both depends upon and extends project participants' data collection and analysis expertise. The notion that information exchange drives ongoing processes of creating meaning through dialogue and discourse is expressed in elements 3-4-5. The intention is to affect collaborators' appreciative settings (top of Figure 1). It follows then that dialogue and negotiation processes inform purposeful actions (element 6), based on accommodated views. Shared understanding then informs the formally organised distributed learning systems (element 7), by means of which needed social and technical support is identified, iteratively, through these recurring processes. In using a systems thinking approach for interactive, formative evaluation and collaborative learning, as depicted in the POM model, we honour the mental constructs that people generate to understand – or to obtain an improved understanding of a situation. We recognise that these mental constructs are largely formed by individual worldviews, perceptions, and values that, in turn, are based on individual background and previous experience. This corresponds to the concept of social-cultural learning, which is the essence of collaborative learning (Selzer and Woodbridge 2004).

To deepen reflective insight through dialogue-based collaborative interaction, we draw from Nonaka's SECI model of the knowledge creation process (Nonaka et al. 2000; Nonaka and Takeuchi 1995; Nonaka and Toyama 2003). The model delineates four phases, Socialisation, Externalisation, Combination, Internalisation, that characterise effective information exchange for knowledge creation. Ideally, dialogue is held over a prolonged period of time because occasional interaction is insufficient to produce knowledge creation. The human activity of knowledge creation, which crosses existing boundaries (Holst 2004; Holst and Mirijamdotter 2005; Nonaka 1994; von Krogh et al. 2000), occurs through the interaction between individuals, and between individuals and their environment. Over time, through face-to-face – or 'face-to-face like' – experiences, as individuals share feelings and emotions as well as information including mental models, commitment and trust emerges adequate to support knowledge creation. The SECI model is embedded in the concept of Ba (Nonaka and Konno 1998; Nonaka et al. 2000). Ba is the context, place and space, shared by those who interact successfully – physically, virtually, and mentally – for the purpose of knowledge creation. It expands the dialogue and interaction illustrated in the 3-4-5 elements of the POM model. In our interactive and iterative evaluation approach, Ba epitomises the desired outcome of the learning commons – i.e., boundary crossing information exchange for knowledge creation, enabled appropriately by information and communication technology (ICT).

3. The collaborative learning environment project

Universities in Sweden, as in many other countries, are experiencing major changes due to, for instance, cut backs and budget reductions caused by fluctuations in government funding, variability in students' decisions about when or whether to choose university studies, and last but not least advances in ICT. As a consequence of these environmental changes, Luleå University of Technology (Ltu) made the strategic decision to transform into "The Creative University." University leaders encouraged innovative thinking by constituting cross-functional or multidisciplinary faculty and student groups comprised of members with differentiated knowledge. Recognising the power of crossing knowledge boundaries, the university next created meeting places, called Arenas, for the purpose of encouraging intentional integration and creation of knowledge through interdisciplinary research and education. This is, in short, the background for the present interactive evaluation project in which findings informed collaborative investigations among Ltu, California Polytechnic University (Cal Poly), and San José State University (SJSU) participants focusing on the shared concept of a learning commons.

Learning commons initiatives benefit from a decade of information commons development in North America. Typically located in libraries, information commons normally provide computing equipment and information services to students and faculty. They reflect varying degrees of shared service and support responsibilities between staff members in university libraries and information technology services (Bailey 2005; Bailey and Tierney 2002). The commons construct stems from the British academic tradition of gathering in public rooms, typically after a meal, where academians with various disciplinary backgrounds met to discuss contemporary issues with their students (Bennett 2003). From these early origins, the concept has now matured to embrace virtual as well as physical learning. While there is widespread agreement that learning commons places and spaces should enable collaborative learning (Brown and Duguid 1991; Brown 2005; Johnson and Lomas 2005; Wedge and Kearns 2005), there is a paucity of literature on how best to design for this. Furthermore, the evaluation literature is limited to measuring user satisfaction with services and facilities with only occasional attention to assessing learning outcomes for collaborative learning commons projects (Gillette and Somerville 2006; Somerville and Gillette 2006/7).

Thus, this project significantly advances the emerging learning commons literature. This was accomplished by providing a common 'learning object' across two undergraduate courses and two graduate courses, as well as a shared metaphor facilitative of information exchange among these student-learning communities. In addition, the four researchers and sixty-two students shared a common purpose – to evaluate the efficacy of an interactive evaluation process model for collaborative design and collaborative learning in a virtual learning environment. The scope of the four courses were intentionally complementary, to encourage the need for information exchange in order to obtain a 'big picture' of the holistic Learning Commons initiative.

- The fourth-year Ltu students were pursuing degrees in computer and systems science, and social informatics. They were well versed on Ltu's innovative construction of interdisciplinary learning environments or 'arenas.' They also had extensive experience in team-based project management intended to enable knowledge creation, in line with Nonaka's SECI and Ba constructs. In this course, they intended to further their proficiency in research methodology, data collection and analysis, and report writing. Within this framework, Ltu students developed and implemented a strategic design process for a campus learning commons that would be managed by students for learning purposes that varied greatly and changed frequently, (reported in Lundkvist et al. 2005). The learning commons would also benefit from partnerships with collaborating campus partners - i.e., Ltu faculty, librarians, and technologists.

- The SJSU graduate students were completing their degree requirements in library and information science. In this course, they investigated the impact of ICT on interdisciplinary exchange and knowledge creation. This focus intended to prepare them for information provision, as well as knowledge enablement, in their future careers as information and knowledge professionals in academic, public, and corporate environments. To ready themselves, students completed team-based projects on the design and development of the services and systems necessary for collaborative learning in the Cal Poly Learning Commons.

- The undergraduate and graduate Cal Poly students were enrolled in computer science courses. Their human-computer interaction and knowledge management assignments involved design and development of software applications that could be implemented in the Cal Poly Learning Commons. With the intention to enable information exchange and knowledge creation among student beneficiaries, they gathered information from student peers and used these needs assessment findings to inform their team-based projects.

In addition to classroom activities, students from the four courses on the three campuses regularly exchanged information for the purpose of stimulating synergistic, interdisciplinary insights. Students' cooperative exploration and collaborative engagement around the common learning object required their usage of a wide variety of application tools, supplemented by other commercial and open source communication technologies. Students pursued projects aligned with their disciplinary focus – for instance, Ltu students embraced the university's 'arena' pedagogy, students in library and information science explored implications for information and knowledge management systems, and computer science students designed and developed Internet2 broad bandwidth applications. Group information exchange was facilitated through four video conferencing sessions of between from one to three hours in length. In addition, four Ltu students and three SJSU students conducted more frequent information exchanges. Throughout the research project, these students – and also faculty – communicated through additional technology such as e-mail, learning management systems, e-meeting software, wikis, and a web conferencing system.

Design of the student projects originated in the five energisers described by Nonaka et al (2000). The project start-up activity provided 'creative chaos' through a short presentation on the concept of a learning commons, followed by distribution of background documents. From here the student groups worked autonomously to select their topic and design their processes. In the most highly functioning group, the Ltu team, the students assessed team members' knowledge assets. In addition to variety in work styles, the disciplinary differences complicated communication challenges – while ensuring the presence of the requisite variety necessary to creative thinking. To varying degrees, the fifth element of energising Ba, trust, developed. Faculty support consisted of responsive modification of learning environment elements, including technologies, as well as coaching students on enabling processes, structures and means for communicating successfully. In this way, amidst the variety of investigatory approaches to a common topic, all students' learning experiences shared a common pedagogical strategy.

The interactive and iterative evaluation process for student groups and faculty researchers was designed according to the POM model. The students had meetings, both physically and virtually, with supervisors at regular intervals when they presented their progress. Additionally, they wrote interim reports and shared them with other teams. Streaming video archives of the videoconference sessions also encouraged reviewing proceedings. The process and progress in each team project was assessed and evaluated collaboratively by students and faculty, as were cross team successes and failures, leading to accommodated decisions on future actions and activities, including the technologies component. A formal group interview with the Ltu students provided additional information on learning experiences achieved through the course and assignment. The interaction between the four Ltu students and three SJSU students, which we discuss below in some detail, provides a textured look into the interactive evaluation process and learning outcomes.

4. Student process and findings

The following highlights express the Ltu students' processes in attempting to establish communication and collaboration with the SJSU students, and their recommendations on creating a distributed learning commons. Subsequently we report lessons learned from our interactive and formative evaluation study on technology-enabled distributed collaborative learning: on the design of a collaborative learning environment and on its processes for collaboration. We emphasise the interactive social networking processes embedded in the POM-model, with the aim of creating a shared (accommodated) vision for virtual collaborative learning participants. We are especially interested in the information systems, which support both the interaction and the activities that result from the accommodations. In so doing, we explore the efficacy of POM to both design and learning through iterative formative evaluation.

4.1. Social implementation factors

The Ltu students began their project through a videoconference with faculty from Ltu and Cal Poly in which they discussed the concept of a learning commons and the Ltu students' plan for their part of the project. Three students from SJSU had volunteered to interact with the Ltu students to obtain first-hand experience working in a distributed international learning commons. However, because of practical problems, the SJSU students did not participate in this first videoconference. In retrospect, students recognised that their inability to interactively communicate early on in the proposed collaboration proved irreparable. Though students experimented with various communication technology media, such as e-mail, a learning management system, Instant Messenger (IM), and a wiki, their attempts to overcome time differences and cultural differences remained unsuccessful. They never progressed beyond the first 'intention' phase of forming a viable international working group. Cultural complications played an especially significant factor, as expressed in assumptions about independent versus team action and autonomous versus collaborative work decisions, causing insurmountable difficulties in reaching an accommodated understanding of common purpose and goals. From reflection on this data, participants concluded that great difficulties arose which interfered with evolving common appreciative settings (see top of Figure 1) and thereby prohibited reaching inter-subjective creation of meaning. Communication improved somewhat when the students used a chat function, which also showed when students were on-line. By chatting they got a better understanding of each other's social and working/studying conditions. However, the SJSU students were available on-line at different times during the day due to other existing work and study obligations. In contrast, the Swedish students' workday was focused exclusively on this project – though 'nine hours ahead' of the California students because of time zone differences. As their frustration over communication difficulties increased, students increasingly recognised the critical importance of understanding the cultural and situational context of potential collaborators. Interpersonal communication differences were further complicated by time zone differences. Frequently, a day was 'lost' – between questions and answers – when e-mailing. Attempts to establish synchronous interaction meant scheduling virtual conversations 'in the middle of the night' on one side or the other of the Atlantic. Therefore, in retrospect, students realised the value of deciding well in advance on a time for chatting and/or for being on-line and accessible.

4.2. Technology for collaboration

As the project evolved, students realised that when separated by distance and reliant on ICT, it is of utmost importance to come to agreement early on about how to communicate. The students explored various software with only intermittent success during their collaborative attempts. To enable created meanings (element 4 of Figure 1), they found that technology which supports both voice and picture is the best way for establishing and furthering information exchange and collaboration. Particularly for initial contact, the Ltu students preferred video conferencing as it provided both audio and visual information and thereby avoided the best opportunity to establish rapport with potential partners using IT (element 7) – rather than relying exclusively on text-based media. Chat was another highly rated technology but, since the US students were monolingual, this medium required usage of written English, which is the Ltu students' second language. In addition, the information gleaned by body language – not only through gestures but also by tone of voice – was unavailable in a chat. Chat moderation presented another complication, students came to realise, as did the requirement for 'speed on the keys'. During the course of the project, participants demonstrated increasing sophistication in articulating both their communication and learning needs and also their judgments about potentially useful hardware and software. In addition, they learned that baseline proficiency in 'tech know how' was essential and a common 'tech platform' was desirable.

4.3. Collaborative learning process

In reflecting on the collaborative learning process, students recommended clear objectives for distributed collaboration. This is in contrast to the assumption in the POM model (see element 5, Figure 1) which suggests that shared purposes will 'naturally' evolve through stakeholder negotiations about common intentions and accommodations. However, in this case, students experienced great difficulty in establishing communication, which complicated sense making activities. The Ltu students were especially sensitive to the lack of shared purpose. Its absence disabled efforts to initially understand US students' possible contributions to their work in Sweden.

In addition, both US and Swedish students recommended establishing protocols for bridging cultural differences, which influenced team operations and impeded cross-team interactions. This proved to be less necessary within a homogeneous team. For instance, when carrying out their own part of the project, the Swedish students praised the 'independence' approach which allowed them to form their own work, testing their abilities to manage information and create knowledge from original data on a topic of their own choosing. They developed considerable ownership of the project and declared that this pedagogy has been the most valuable during their four year of studies (Lundkvist et al. 2005). It gave them strong motivation and meaningful knowledge transferable to future research work. Their common culture and shared work styles and work values permitted them to work effectively together, without need of extensive faculty supervision.

However, both Swedish and American students recognised that the formative phase of group work requires specific direction in a distributed environment where the members do not know each other. In contrast, they were able to collaborate easily in a physically gathered group where proximity made others' knowledge assets more easily recognisable. Also, in a distributed team, personal and cultural experiences and expectations have to be shared explicitly through 'leading questions', which reveal unspoken assumptions and expectations. Otherwise it is easy to assume that potential collaborators are 'just like us'. Ultimately, although the Ltu students did not manage to come to an agreement on a common purpose for collaboration with the three SJSU students, they benefited from the course-to-course video conferencing system-mediated information exchange that provided new ways of understanding approaches for the Swedish learning commons project.

While many of the environmental characteristics, as expressed in the above, are within the 'hands' of the faculty, it is the student participants who 'drive' these changes within an interactive and formative evaluation context. For instance, students recognised that more robust technology was required, as context and meaning evolved, and as their reflective dialogue on design/redesign advanced. They then explored additional technologies, like chat, wikis and blogs, to find suitable means for social information exchange. This experimentation advanced their insights into technology purposes. For illustration, they found that chat was quite good to learn to know each other. On the other hand, it was not enabling when discussing the project and seeking agreement on purposes, forums for dialogue and interaction, and division of work tasks. Students also concluded that a more robust medium was needed to formulate a knowledge-sharing context.

5. Discussion of findings

From the iterative and interactive evaluation findings, the faculty research team learned that common purpose, structure, and forums for dialogue and interaction are necessary to teamwork, as are enabling technologies appropriate to negotiating and accommodating quickly and efficiently. Video conferencing was a preferred medium for more sophisticated information sharing across teams. It permitted participants to make their disciplinary tacit knowledge explicit, thus creating sufficient shared understanding to facilitate cross team communication – i.e., to move beyond the 'single lens' of 'discipline bounded' training. Additionally, when we began to schedule time for reflection during video conferencing sessions, interdisciplinary insights began to unfold. We conclude, while 'creative chaos' (Nonaka et al. 2000) is useful within limits, it should be managed to avoid disablement arising from insurmountable differences in experience and expectations of project work, cultural background and time zones, living and working conditions, and technological access, awareness and proficiencies. Discourse and dialogue emerged as a means of advancing collective understanding through information exchange, knowledge sharing and meaning creation illustrated in the POM (Checkland and Holwell 1998) and Ba models. This took the form of defining purposeful actions to be taken in the light of negotiated intentions and accommodations. Building on these models can potentially mediate the challenges present in international collaborations and improve cultural conversance through negotiation of regional, national, or ethno-cultural differences. Preliminary findings also suggest that the socialisation aspect (Nonaka et al. 2000) of Ba could, over time and with proper management, have moderated the continuum of orientations from individualistic to teaming behaviours, and advanced appreciative recognition of other team members' knowledge assets. When the groups depend on enabling and supporting technologies, as in a distributed virtual learning community, these challenges are heightened and therefore need to be consciously addressed. The results, presented and discussed in this paper, suggest significant promise for this user-centered design and evaluation approach when energising interactions of Ba and dialogue-driven insights of POM are embedded into the collaborative learning environment. Additionally, besides addressing facets involved in distributed collaboration for knowledge exchange and knowledge creation, this action-oriented approach implies value for higher education pedagogy; in the interactive and iterative process students demonstrated improved capabilities for their own learning – i.e., for learning how to learn. Such skills are recognised as very important and valuable when educating students for business and industry.

6. Acknowledgements

We are most grateful for the students' willingness to participate in this research project. The Pitepojkarna team from Luleå University of Technology – Markus, Robert, Seppo, and Peter - were especially enthusiastic and forthcoming. On the other side of the Atlantic, we are most indebted to Dr. Franz Kurfess and his HCI and KM students, who participated at Cal Poly and the Information Science students at SJSU. In addition, Dr. Erika Rogers, Dr. Hiram L. Davis, and Ms. Helen Y. Chu from Cal Poly contributed to the 'creative chaos' portion of the course curricula. Lastly, we acknowledge our source of funding: "Interactive Design and Evaluation of a Learning Environment for Distributed Collaboration over Internet2: An Applied Research and Training Project" was funded as a subaward of the U.S. Office of Naval Research grant #N00014-04-1-0436

References

Alexander, B. (2004) New Learning Ecosystems. *2004 Annual Meeting NLII National Learning Infrastructure Initiative,* Washington, DC.

Andersson, M. (2003) Drivhusmodellen i teori och praktik - ett verksamhetsintegrerat forsknings- och utvecklingsarbete för integration av utbildning, forskning och samverkan vid Luleå tekniska universitet, Licentiate Thesis, Department of Applied Physics and Mechanical Engineering, Luleå University of Technology, Luleå, Sweden.

Andersson, M., Jonsson, M. and Söderlund, A. (2002) The Greenhouse Learning Concept: a new pedagogical approach. *30th SEFI Annual Conference,* Florence, Italy. Edizioni Polistampa.

Argyris, C. (1976) Increasing Leadership Effectiveness, New York: Wiley.

Argyris, C. (1991) Teaching Smart People How to Learn. *Harvard Business Review,* vol. 69, pp. 99-109.

Argyris, C. and Schön, D. (1974) *Theory in Practice: Increased Professional Effectiveness,* San Francisco, CA: Jossey Bass.

Bailey, R. (2005) Information commons services for learners and researchers: Evolution in patron needs, digital resources and scholarly publishing. *INFORUM 2005: 11th Conference on Professional Information Resources,* Prague. Available: http://www.inforum.cz/inforum2005/pdf/Bailey_Russell.pdf.

Bailey, R. and Tierney, B. (2002) Information commons redux: Concept, evolution, and transcending the tragedy of the commons. *Journal of Academic Librarianship,* vol. 28, no. 5, pp. 277-286.

Beagle, D. (1999) Conceptualizing an information commons. *Journal of Academic Librarianship,* vol. 25, no. 2, pp. 82-89.

Beagle, D. (2002) Extending the information commons: From instructional testbed to Internet2. *Journal of Academic Librarianship,* vol. 28, no. 5, pp. 287-296.

Beagle, D. (2004) From Information Commons to Learning Commons. *Leavey Library 2004 Conference: Information Commons: Learning Space Beyond the Classroom,* Los Angeles, CA. Available: http://www.usc.edu/isd/libraries/locations/leavey/news/conference/presentations/presentations_9-16/Beagle_Information_Commons_to_Learning.pdf. [25 Jan. 2005].

Bennett, S. (2003) *Libraries designed for learning,* Washington DC: Council on Library and Information Resources. Available: http://www.clir.org/pubs/reports/pub122/ pub122web.pdf.

Brown, J. S. and Duguid, P. (1991) Organizational Learning and Communities-of-Practice: Toward a Unified View of Working, Learning, and Innovation. *Organization Science,* vol. 2, no. 1, pp. 40-57.

Brown, M. (2005) Learning Space Design Theory and Practice. *Educause Review,* vol. 40, no. 4, pp. 1. Available: http://www.educause.edu/ir/library/pdf/erm0544.pdf.

Brown, M. B. and Lippincott, J. K. (2003) Learning spaces: More than meets the eye. *Educause Quarterly,* vol. 26, no. 1, pp. 14-16. Available: https://www.educause.edu/ ir/library/pdf/eqm0312.pdf.

Checkland, P. (1981) *Systems Thinking, Systems Practice,* Chichester: John Wiley & Sons.

Checkland, P. (1994) Conventional Wisdom and Conventional Ignorance: The Revolution Organization Theory Missed. *Organization,* vol. 1, no. 1, pp. 29-34.

Checkland, P. (1994) Systems Theory and Management Thinking. *American Behavioral Scientist,* vol. 38, no. 1, pp. 75-91.

Checkland, P. (2000) Soft Systems Methodology: A Thirty Year Retrospective. *Systems Research and Behavioral Science,* vol. 17, no. S1, pp. 11-58.

Checkland, P. and Holwell, S. (1993) Information Management and Organizational Processes: An Approach through Soft Systems Methodology. *Journal of Information Systems,* vol. 3, pp. 3-16.

Checkland, P. and Holwell, S. (1998) Information, Systems and Information Systems - making sense of the field, Chichester: John Wiley & Sons.

Checkland, P. and Scholes, J. (1990) *Soft Systems Methodology in Action,* Chichester: John Wiley & Sons.

Checkland, P. B. and Casar, A. (1986) Vickers' Concept of an Appreciative System: A Systemic Account. *Journal of Applied Systems Analysis,* vol. 13, pp. 3-17.

Costello, K. L., Bentley, L. and Pollack, J. (2002) Connecting Soft Systems Thinking With Project Management Practice: an organizational change case study. In Ragsdell, G., West, D. & Wilby, J. (Eds.) *Systems Theory and Practice in the Knowledge Age.* New York, NY: Kluwer Academic/Plenum Publishers.

Crockett, C., McDaniel, S. and Remy, M. (2002) Integrating services in the information commons: Toward a holistic library and computing environment. *Library Administration and Management,* vol. 16, no. 4, pp. 181-186.

Edzén, S. (2005) *Datorstöd för identifiering av individernas kunskap och kompetens inom organisationer,* Licentiate Thesis, Department of Business Administration and Social Sciences, Luleå University of Technology, Luleå, Sweden.

Edzén, S., Holst, M. and Sandström, A. (2004) *Answers to Questions About the Creative University,* Technical report, Luleå University of Technology, Luleå, Sweden.

Gillette, D. D. and Somerville, M. M. (2006) Toward lifelong 'knowledge making': Faculty development for student learning in the Cal Poly Learning Commons. In *Lifelong Learning - Partners, Pathways, and Pedagogies: Proceedings of the 4th International Lifelong Learning Conference,* Rockhampton, Queensland, Australia, Central Queensland University, pp. 117-123.

Guba, Y. and Lincoln, E. (1989) *Fourth generation evaluation,* Newbury Park: Sage Publications.

Hansen, H. F. (2005) Choosing Evaluation Models. *Evaluation,* vol. 11, no. 4, pp. 447-462.

Hedman, J. and Borell, A. (2005) Broadening Information Systems Evaluation Through Narratives. *The Electronic Journal of Information Systems Evaluation,* vol. 8, no. 2, pp. 115-122. Available: www.ejise.com.

Holst, M. (2004) *Knowledge Work across Boundaries - Inquiring into the processes of creating a shared context,* Licentiate Thesis, Department of Business Administration and Social Sciences, Luleå University of Technology, Luleå, Sweden.

Holst, M. and Mirijamdotter, A. (2004) Logically Created Organizations for Multi-disciplinary Settings: Understanding Their Systemic Structure. *International Conference of Systems Thinking in Management (ICSTM04),* Philadelphia, PN, May 19-21, 2004. University of Pennsylvania (CD-ROM). Available: http://www.acasa.upenn.edu/icstm04/.

Holst, M. and Mirijamdotter, A. (2005) An application of Ba: Deconstructing formative processes in multdisciplinary work groups. *The International Journal of Knowledge, Culture and Change Management,* vol. 4, pp. 1051-59. Available:
http://ijm4.cgpublisher.com/product/pub.34/prod.107.

Holst, M. and Mirijamdotter, A. (2006) Sense Making Through the POM-Model: Experiences from Set-up of Multidisciplinary Teams. *Systems Research and Behavioral Science,* vol. (submitted for publication).

Johnson, C. and Lomas, C. (2005) Design of the learning space: Learning & design principles. *Educause Review,* vol. 40, no. 4, pp. 16-28. Available: http://www.educause.edu/ir/library/pdf/erm0540.pdf.

Joint Information Systems Committee (2006). Designing spaces for effective learning: A guide to 21st century learning space design. Available: http://www.jisc.ac.uk/uploaded_documents/JISClearningspaces.pdf

Köhler, V., Mirijamdotter, A. and Söderhamn, O. (2005) People, Technology and Work Practices: understanding the processes of sensemaking when using IT in a nursing context. *The 16th Australasian Conference on Information Systems: People, Technology and Work Practices,* Sydney, Australia, 29 Nov - 2 Dec.

Lippincott, J. K. (2004) Co-location, Cooperation & Collaboration within the Information Commons. *Leavey Library 2004 Conference,* Los Angeles, CA. USC Leavey Library: Information Commons. Available: http://www.usc.edu/libraries/locations/leavey/news/conference/presentations/presentations_9-16/Lippincott.ppt.

Lippincott, J. K. (2004) New Library Facilities: Opportunities for Collaboration. *Resource Sharing & Information Networks,* vol. 17, no. 1/2, pp. 147.

Lippincott, J. K. (2005) Net Generation students and libraries. In Oblinger, D. G. & Oblinger, J. L. (Eds.) *Educating the Net Generation.* Boulder, Co: Educause.

Lundkvist, P., Sundlöf, R., Tanskanen, S. and Tiburzi, M. (2005) *Strategic Design of a Learning Commons at Luleå University of Technology,* Technical report, Luleå University of Technology, Luleå, Sweden. Available: http://epubl.ltu.se/1402-1536/2005/19/. [2006-07-31].

Mackenzie, M. and Blamey, A. (2005) The Practice and the Theory. Lessons from the Application of a Theories of Change Approach. *Evaluation,* vol. 11, no. 2, pp. 151-168.

Mirijamdotter, A. and Somerville, M. M. (2005) Dynamic Action Inquiry: A Systems Approach for Knowledge Based Organizational Learning. *The 11th International Conference on Human-Computer Interaction,* Las Vegas, Nevada, July 22-27. Lawrence Erlbaum Associates, Inc. (CD-ROM).

Mirijamdotter, A., Somerville, M. M. and Holst, M. (2005) An interactive evaluation approach for the creation of collaborative learning commons. In Remenyi, D. (Ed.) *The 12th European Conference on Information Technology Evaluation (ECITE 2005),* Turku, Finland, pp. 337-347. Available: http://www.academic-conferences.org/ecite2005/ecite05-home.htm.

Newman, W. and Lamming, M. (1995) *Interactive System Design,* Cambridge: Addison-Wesley Publishers Ltd.

Nonaka, I. (1994) A Dynamic Theory of Organizational Knowledge Creation. *Organization Science,* vol. 5, no. 1, pp. 14-37.

Nonaka, I. and Konno, K. (1998) The Concept of "Ba": Building a Foundation for Knowledge Creation. *California Management Review,* vol. 40, no. 3, pp. 40-54.

Nonaka, I., Konno, N. and Toyama, R. (2000) SECI, Ba and leadership: A unified model of dynamic knowledge creation. *Long Range Planning,* vol. 33, pp. 5-34.

Nonaka, I. and Takeuchi, H. (1995) *The Knowledge-Creating Company - How Japanese Companies Create the Dynamics of Innovation,* New York: Oxford University Press.

Nonaka, I. and Toyama, R. (2003) The knowledge-creating theory revisited: knowledge creation as a synthesizing process. *Knowledge Management Research & Practice,* vol. 1, pp. 2-10.

Nonaka, I., Toyama, R. and Nagata, A. (2000) A Firm as a Knnowledge-creating Entity: A New Perspective on the Theory of the Firm. *Industrial and Corporate Change,* vol. 9, no. 1, pp. 1-20.

Oliver, S., Harden, A., Rees, R., Shepherd, J., Brunton, G., Garcia, J. and Oakley, A. (2005) An Emerging Framework for Including Different Types of Evidence in Systematic Reviews for Public Policy. *Evaluation,* vol. 11, no. 4, pp. 428-446.

Patton, M. Q. (1990) *Qualitative Evaluation and Research Methods,* 2nd ed. Newbury Park: Sage Publications.

Preece, J., Rogers, Y. and Sharp, H. (2002) *Interaction Design: Beyond human-computer interaction,* New York: John Wiley & Sons, Inc.

Rolfsen, M. and Torvatn, H. (2005) How to 'Get Through'. *Evaluation,* vol. 11, no. 3, pp. 297-309.

Rose, J. (2002) Interaction, transformation and information systems development - an extended application of Soft Systems Methodology. *Information Technology & People,* vol. 15, no. 3, pp. 242-268.

Sandström, A. (2004) *Innovative Policy Networks - The relation between structure and performance,* Licentiate Thesis, Department of Business Administration and Social Sciences, Luleå University of Technology, Luleå, Sweden.

Selzer, D. and Woodbridge, S. (2004) Collaborative Learning: Building Bridges to Lifelong Learning. In Danaher, P. A., Macpherson, C., Nouwens, F. & Orr, D. (Eds.) *Proceedings of the 3rd International Lifelong*

Learning Conference, Rockhampton, Queensland, Australia, Central Queensland University, pp. 314-319.

Somerville, M. M. and Gillette, D. (2006/7) The California Polytechnic State University Learning Commons: A case study. In Tierney, B. & Bailey, R. (Eds.) *Information Commons Case Studies: Academic, Community College and Public Libraries.* Chicago, Illinois: ALA Editions. (in press).

Wedge, C. C. and Kearns, T. D. (2005) Creation of the learning space: Catalysts for envisioning and navigating the design process. Educause Review, vol. 40, no. 4, pp. 32-38. Available: http://www.educause.edu/ir/library/pdf/erm0541.pdf.

Vickers, G. (1983) The Art of Judgment. A Study of Policy Making, London: Harper & Row Ltd.

Vickers, G. (1983) *Human Systems Are Different,* London: Harper & Row Ltd.

von Krogh, G., Ichijo, K. and Nonaka, I. (2000) Enabling Knowledge Creation. How to Unlock the Mystery of Tacit Knowledge and Release the Power of Innovation, New York: Oxford University Press, Inc.

Does ROI Matter? Insights into the True Business Value of IT

A J G Silvius
Utrecht University of Professional Education, Netherlands
Originally Published in EJISE (2006) Volume 9: issue 2

Editor's Comment
This paper provides a very interesting synopsis of academic thinking about ICT evaluation and research. This in itself is of considerable value. The perennial question of does ROI matter and if so to what extent? As this paper illustrates ROI and IRR are still very much in use. But as we all known there is much more to IT evaluation than simple arithmetic and this paper provides an excellent review of much of the literature in this field. However author A J G Silvius like the word 'true' which is a word about which there is much controversy. This paper is one that everyone in the field of IT evaluation should read.

Abstract: Ever since the introduction of an 'IT productivity paradox' by Robert Solow, the business value of information technology (IT) has been the topic of many debates by practitioners as well as by academics. In these discussions a distinction can be made between the variance approach, investigating what the relationship between IT investments and organisational performance is, and the process approach, investigating on how this relationship works. Following the process approach, this paper describes a useful framework for assessing the organisational impact of IT. Secondly the paper considers the relation between IT impact and organisational performance and reviews the IT investment evaluation methods. The paper concludes with a proposal for a multivariable value assessment sheet, based on insights derived from the balanced scorecard theory.

Keywords: IT business value, return on investment, real option valuation, balanced scorecard

1. Introduction

The business value of information technology (IT) is a topic that is cause for a lot of discussion. Scepticism roars again in the boardrooms of many companies, as the e-business hype explodes in the face of many 'believers' of the new-economy gospel. Without strong technological developments to thrive upon and an uncertain economic perspective the pressure on IT budgets is high. For investments in IT the requirement of sufficient returns and a clear 'business case' is even more severe than before. Several surveys indicate that the issue of measuring benefits of IT investments is a concern in many organisations (Whitling et al, 1996). Measuring IT benefits and value is frequently reported as one of the most important issues for senior IT management. (Brancheau and Wetherbe, 1987; Niederman, Brancheau and Wetherbe, 1991; Watson, Kelly, Galliers and Brancheau, 1997). Based on research into 'the changing role of finance executives regarding Information and Communication Technology' (Paul and Tate, 2002) it can be concluded that CFOs use typical financial methods to evaluate IT investments. Over 86%, of the 288 CFOs that responded claim to use traditional capital budgeting methods like Return on Investment, Pay-back period, Discounted Cash Flow and Internal Rate of Return. This can be seen in Figure 1. The strong use of financial appraisal techniques is also found in surveys of Ballantine et al. in the United Kingdom (Ballantine et al, 1997) and Wong and Behling in Australia (Wong and Behling, 1997).

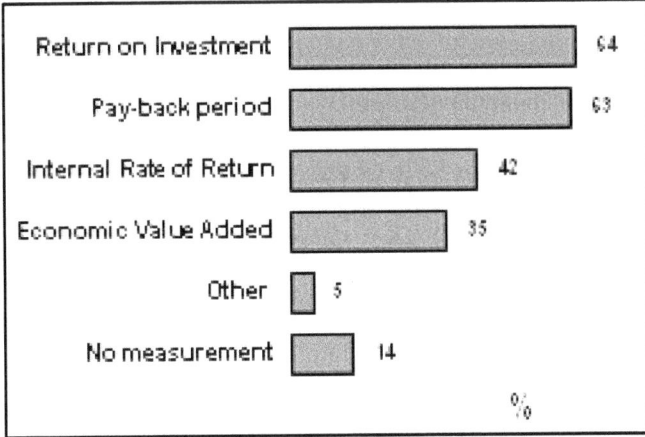

Figure 1: Use of investment evaluation methods by CFOs.

However, CIOs tend to estimate the use of these financial methods a lot lower. Of the 456 CIOs and senior IT managers that responded in the research into 'the issues and challenges facing senior IT executives' (IDG Research and Getronics, 2002) only 18% indicated using Return on Investment. As can be seen in Figure 2, for the CIOs the mere effects of the investment, like decreased costs and increased productivity, topped the list. The different results of the research illustrate the problems in capturing the full business value of IT investments in an understandable measure. This paper aims to give some insight into the concepts, possibilities and limitations in this quest for value.

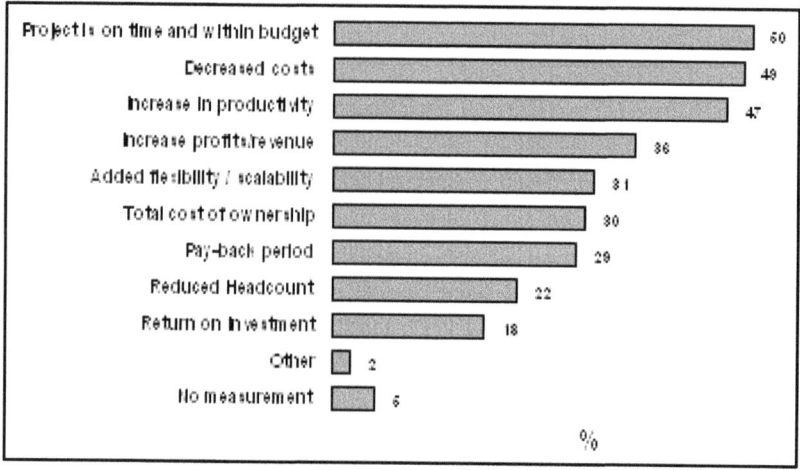

Figure 2: Use of investment evaluation methods by CIOs.

2. The quest for business value

In research into the value of IT two approaches can be distinguished: the variance approach and the process approach (Davaraj and Kohli, 2002).

2.1. The variance approach

The variance approach measures the relationship between IT investments and organisational performance in terms of higher revenues, lower costs, improved market share, etc. This approach focuses on the 'what' question. *What* is the relationship between IT investments and organisational performance? Over the years, a vast amount of work has been done regarding this relationship. Several studies showed that the relationship between IT investments and organisational performance could not be proven (Loveman, 1988; Salmela, 1997). This result became known as the 'IT productivity paradox' (Brynjolfsson, 1993). Probably the best-known statement about this paradox was done by Robert Solow when he stated: 'You can see the computer age everywhere but in the productivity statistics'. Notorious as this 'IT productivity paradox' may be, it does not turn up in all studies about IT returns. Table 1 provides an overview of selected firm-level studies.

Table 1: Selected firm-level studies of IT returns (Dedrick et al., 2003)

Study	Data Sample	Findings
IT and Firm Performance		
Strassmann (1990)	38 U.S. companies	No correlation between IT spending and firm performance.
Loveman (1994)	60 Business units in 20 US firms	IT investments add nothing to output.
Barua et al. (1995)	Same as Loveman (1994)	IT improves intermediate output if not final output.
Brynnjolfsson and Hitt (1993)	Large U.S. manufacturers	Gross-marginal product of IT is over 50% per year in manufacturing.
Brynnjolfsson and Hitt (1995)	Large U.S. manufacturers	Firm effects account for half of productivity benefits of earlier study.
Lichtenberg (1995)	U.S. firms, 1989-1991	IT has excess returns; one IS employee can be substituted for six non-IS employees without affecting output.
Brynnjolfsson and Hitt (1996)	367 Large U.S. firms	Gross return on IT investments of 81%. Net return ranges from 48% to 67% depending on depreciation rate.
Brynnjolfsson and Hitt (1996)	370 U.S. firms	IT investments increase firm productivity and consumer welfare, but not profitability.
Dewan and Min (1997)	300 Large U.S. firms	IT is a net substitute for both capital and labour, and shows excess returns relative to labour input.
Black and Lynch (1997)	1621 U.S. manufacturing establishments	Productivity not affected by presence of particular management practice but by implementation, especially degree of employee involvement.
Brynjolfsson et al. (1998)	Sample of Fortune 1000 U.S.	The stock market value of $ 1 of IT capital is the same as $ 5 - $ 20 of other capital

Study	Data Sample	Findings
	firms, 1987 – 1994	stock.
Gilchrist et al. (2001)	Sample of Fortune 1000 U.S. firms	IT productivity is greater in IT producer firms than in user firms and in durable manufacturing.
Gilchrist et al. (2001)	French firms	Gross returns to IT investments are positive and greater than returns to non-IT investments.

The advantage of this approach is that it reveals statistically 'proven' effects of IT. These effects are of particular relevance for the development of economic policy. The disadvantage of the approach is that the effects are valid in general, but might not appear for a particular investment in a particular company. This notion is illustrated in table 2, which shows another overview of firm-level studies.

Table 2: Selected firm-level studies of IT returns if combined with organisational transition (Dedrick et al., 2003).

Study	Data Sample	Findings
Organisational Complements and IT Returns		
Bresnahan et al. (2002)	400 Large U.S. firms, 1987 – 1994	The effects of IT on labor demand are greater when IT is combined with particular organisational investments.
Brynjolfsson er al. (1998)	Sample of U.S. firms, 1996	Decentralised organisational practices, in combination with IT investments, have a disproportional positive effect on firm market value.
Ramirez et al. (2001)	200+ U.S. firms	Firm use of employee involvement and total quality management enhances IT returns.
Francalanci and Galal (1998)	52 U.S. life insurance companies, 1986 - 1995	Productivity gains result from worker composition (more informational workers) and IT investments.
Deveraj and Kohli (2002)	8 hospitals, over 3 years	IT investment combined with business process reengineering positively and significantly influences performance.
Tallon et al. (2000)	300+ U.S. firms, 1998	Perceived business value of IT is greater when IT is more highly aligned with business strategy.

hese studies however analysed the returns of IT investments in combination with organisational and process changes. The results of these studies show that the return on IT is influenced by the organisational transition that accompanies it. The same IT investment therefore can have a positive return in organisation A and a negative or neutral return in organisation B. This raises the question how IT is used in an organisation, a question that is better addressed with the process approach. For corporate decision makers therefore the variance approach is of limited use.

2.2. The process approach

On a company level more insight into the 'how' question is required. *How do IT investments improve organisational performance?* This question is addressed in the process approach (Mooney et al, 1995). Soh and Markus synthesised the different models of the process approach into a comprehensive framework for the IT value creation process (Figure 3, Soh and Markus, 1995). This paper is constructed along this framework. First we will explore the relation between IT expenditures and IT assets: the IT efficiency question. In the next paragraph the organisational impacts of IT will be discussed in search of IT effectiveness. The following paragraph considers the relation between IT impact and organisational performance: the question of business and IT alignment.

The paper will be concluded with an overview of investment valuation techniques and a proposal for a more balanced understanding of the value of IT.

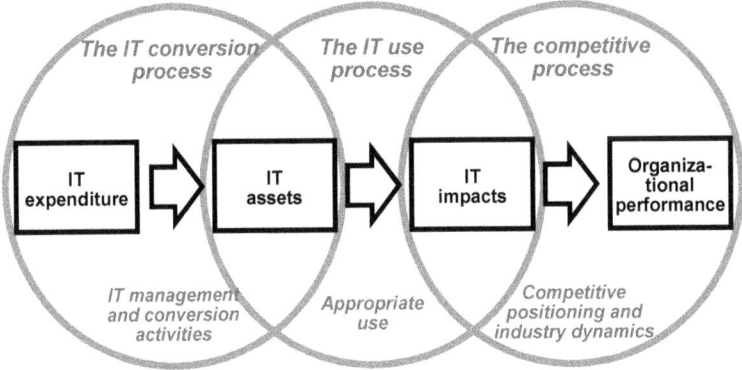

Figure 3: The process approach for understanding IT value. (Soh and Markus, 1995)

3. IT efficiency

One of the core concepts of the process approach is the time dimension of IT value (Bannister, 2001). Most technologies have a life cycle, i.e. value dissipates over time, utilising available technologies as optimally as possible and switching to new technologies at the right moment are the keys to a minimal cost of managing and maintaining the IT in an organisation. A well-established concept is this area is that of the Total Cost of Ownership (TCO). TCO covers all costs related to the asset. All cost meaning both registered and unregistered 'hidden' costs, for example peer support in solving a problem. Regarding the optimal use of technologies, and the effects on the TCO, a lot of research has been done by the Gartner Group. The relationship between TCO and the life cycle of a technology is a less researched field (Davaraj and Kohli, 2002). Figure 4 shows the expected relationship between the TCO and the life cycle of a technology.

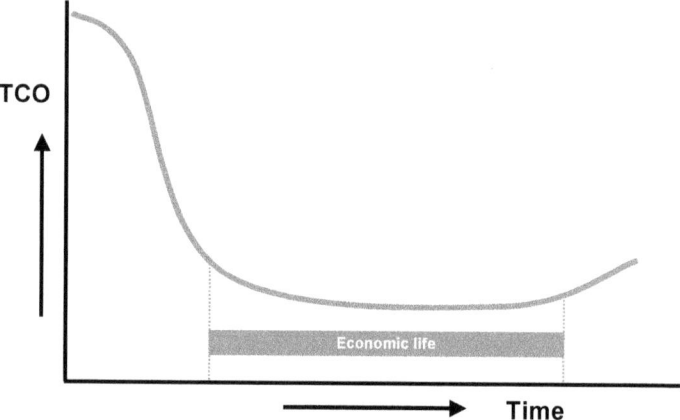

Figure 4: The expected relationship between TCO and the life cycle of a technology.

In its younger years, the knowledge and utilisation of a technology are less developed, resulting in a relatively high TCO. If the technology evolves into an industry standard, the TCO will decline as the technology matures. At the end of its life cycle the use of the technology will decline and the TCO will rise again as a result of scarcity of resources. Its economic life has passed and the technology is outperformed, probably both technically and economically, by a newer technology. An example of this lifecycle is the rise of MS-DOS and its replacement by MS-Windows as the standard operating system for personal computers. Within a technology a similar life cycle pattern can be expected for successive versions or releases. For a discussion about the value of IT, it should be understood that TCO does not express a value. TCO expresses a cost! This cost reflects the IT Efficiency challenge; one of the most important challenges for CIOs and IT Executives:

How to minimise the cost of utilising, managing and maintaining the current IT, whilst delivering the agreed 'quality of service'? Notwithstanding the fact that TCO has no value on its own, a decline in TCO has! IT investments that result in a higher IT efficiency, for example the implementation of a IT management suite, contribute to a lower TCO of the managed IT systems or components. The decline of TCO that can be achieved is a return on the investment involved.

4. IT effectiveness

Another challenge for CIOs is the question: How to maximise the 'business value' of IT investments? This challenge addresses not the efficiency of IT, but its effectiveness. How does IT contribute to the business strategy and goals?

4.1. Understanding the impact of IT

The impact of IT on business is rapidly shifting from an efficiency enhancing production factor towards a source of business innovation. This development is illustrated in Figure 5.

The changing role of IT has to be reflected in the way IT investments are evaluated. The traditional 'IT-economics' focus on cost savings should evolve to also include productivity and business value drivers. This notion has inspired several authors (e.g. Hammer and Mangurian, 1987, Riggins, 1999, Smit and Silvius, 2001) to provide frameworks for identifying value of IT solutions. From these frameworks a common understanding arises that IT can make a business more *efficient*, more effective, more flexible and/or more innovative. These four 'sources of value' identify the way IT creates value for an organisation. The four terms mentioned summarise the development of the value of IT over the past decades. Starting from a calculation tool to improve efficiency in administrative processes, the opportunity to provide decision makers with more detailed information much quicker than before arose, hereby improving the effectiveness of the organisation.

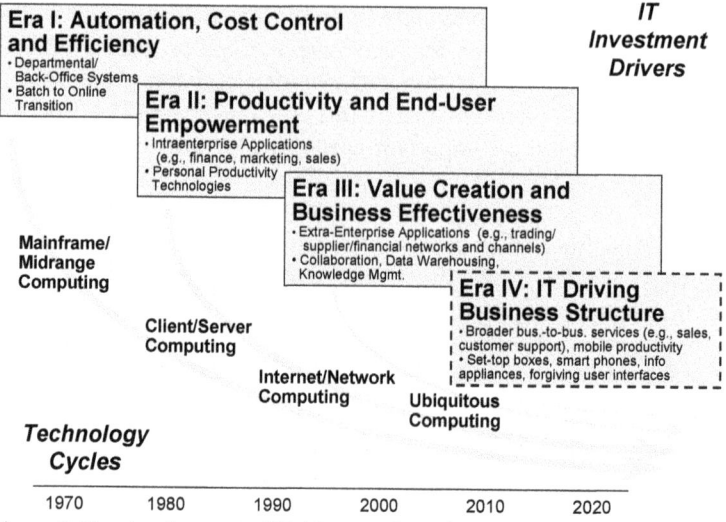
Figure 5: The development of IT. (Gartner Group)

In recent years it has become clear that a revolutionising technology like the Internet can open up new markets, new products or provide new means of developing customer loyalty, thereby innovating the business of a company. So, from an enabler of business IT developed into an innovator of business. The latest notion is that the lower cost of communication, which IT provides, enables organisations to swap resources more easily, e.g. moving business activities offshore, thereby enhancing the managerial flexibility.

4.2. Understanding more of the impact of IT

Thus, for a better understanding of the impact of IT on an organisation we should consider its effect in terms of efficiency, effectiveness, innovation and flexibility. Logically, these 'sources of value' can be applied to the external positioning of the organisation or to the internal business processes.

Understanding the external positioning marketing, provides us with the four 'P's: Price, Product, Placement and Promotion. Combining the sources of value with these fields of competition provides a practical 'grid' to identify the possible effects of an IT investment. For example, an IT system that allows a company to differentiate its prices is identified on the grid as having an impact in the field effectiveness combined with price. To understand how IT adds value to the internal business processes, these processes are categorised in main business functions as illustrated in Figure 6. The 'Generic Business Model', as developed by James Martin and Associates, distinguishes as main business functions: adding value, innovating, controlling resources en directing

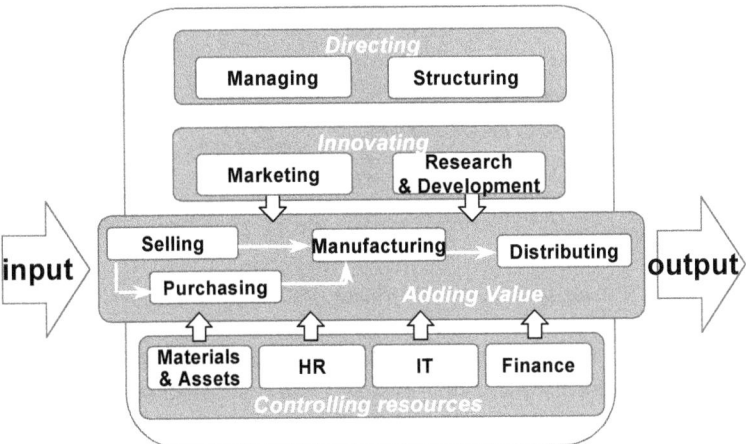

Figure 6: The generic business model.

An example of an IT investment with impact in the directing function is the implementation of a management information system that allows for better decision-making. When the variables of the 'external impact', the four 'P's, and the variables of the 'internal impact', the business functions, are plotted across the sources of value, a graphical grid can be constructed to identify the impact of IT investments on an organisation. This 'IT value grid', as shown in Figure 7 with a number of sample impacts, provides a useful aid to understand, communicate and discuss the impact of an IT investment.

Without this understanding, any discussion about the value of IT will be without foundation. A preliminary understanding however is that the relation between IT and business value is not always straightforward. Business applications will usually have an identifiable impact on business processes, but for components of the IT infrastructure their effect is mostly indirect as enabler of applications.

	4 sources of value Efficiency	Effectiveness	Innovation	Flexibility
Price		Enable for price differentiation		
Product		Enable for customization	Enable build to order	
Promotion	Enable one-to-one marketing		Create new promotion channels	
Placement		Enable when/where you want delivery		
4 dimensions of competition				
Value Adding	Increase use of production resources	Allow for outsourcing	Create new channels	Allow for deferral of investments
Innovating		Allow for interactive marketing	Allow for collaboration	
Directing		Speed-up decision making		Be informed anytime, anywhere
Controlling resources	Automate supportive tasks			Increase scalability of resources

4 groups of business processes

Figure 7: The IT value grid. (Smit and Silvius, 2001 and Targowski, 2004)

These 'levels' of impact brought us to distinguish three categories of IT 'value drivers', which are shown in Figure 8. The first category, 'IT Business Value Drivers' consists of business applications with a direct impact on the business. The second category is the 'Derived IT value drivers' and consists of the IT infrastructure and the data architecture of the organisation. The third category, 'IT value enablers', consists of the variables regarding the organisation of IT in the company.

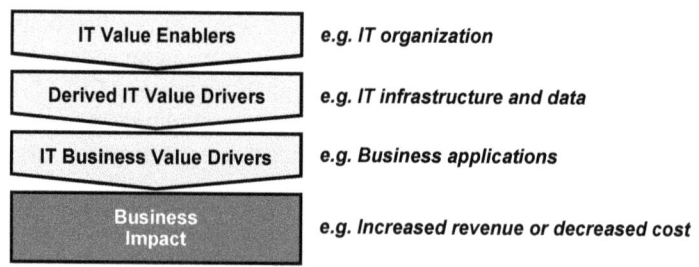

Figure 8: The complex relation between IT and business value.

Business and IT alignment

After creating a thorough understanding of how an IT investment influences the business, the next step is to come to understand the returns of this impact. Since IT itself has no returns, the returns are always in 'the business', it is helpful to have a close look at the business. First of all the strategy and goals of the business have to be considered. After all, it is this strategy IT should align with.

4.3. Aligning with business strategy

In modern business strategy literature, three dominant strategies are identified: Product Leadership, Customer Intimacy and Price Leadership (Treacey and Wiersema, 1997), which is illustrated in Figure 9.

Figure 9: Typology of business strategy

In a Price Leadership strategy the organisation only survives if it realises high volumes with low costs. IT investments that create business efficiency, for example an ERP system that optimises the utilisation of resources, are particularly relevant in this type of strategy. In Product Leadership strategy the Unique Selling Proposition of the company is that of high quality of products and services. For these companies the ability of IT systems to enable this quality would therefore probably be of greater value than the efficiency of the company. For example, a smart warehouse management system that enhances order fulfilment by optimising stock levels could fit this strategy. Finally, in a Customer Intimacy strategy the organisation will benefit most from IT systems that strengthen their ability to tailor their offer to the customer's needs. An example of such a system could be a CRM application for a fashion retailer that allows him to capture the measurements, preferences and buying history of his individual customers. The manner in which business strategy gives input to the evaluation of IT investments can be summarised as follows.

Table 3: Relationship between business strategy and dominance of the sources of value.

Dominant Business Strategy		Corresponding dominant source of value
Price Leadership	<>	Business Efficiency
Product Leadership	<>	Business Effectiveness
Customer Intimacy	<>	Business Innovation

A possible weakening of the argument made above is that all 'sources of value', efficiency, effectiveness, innovation and flexibility, are always relevant, regardless the strategy. This is true of course, but the analysis of the business strategy provides an indication of the relative weight of the criteria used in the evaluation of IT investments. However we should add that another angle is missing: the business process.

4.4. Aligning with business processes

Not all business processes 'make the difference' in the strategy of a company. In the typology of business processes provided by the Generic Business Model (Figure 6) typically the 'adding value' and 'innovating' processes create the Unique Selling Propositions of the organisation. Logically, the impact of business strategy on the valuation of IT investments will be most relevant for investments in IT systems with an impact on these 'adding value' and 'innovating' business processes. Supporting processes like facility management or personnel administration are also important but do not typically have a direct effect on the external positioning of the organisation. For IT investment supporting these business processes, 'business efficiency' will therefore be the most important source of value. Adding the volatility of the business function can further expand the alignment between the sources of value and the business process. Logically, the more volatile the business process, the more valuable becomes the flexibility that IT can add to that business process. An overview of the relationship between business strategy, business processes and the sources of value of IT is shown in Figure 10.

Several studies also show the nature of the 'adding value' business processes as a factor of influence in the value of IT investments. Studies that show returns on IT investments (Harris and Katz, 1991) typically concentrated on information intensive industries like financial services, whereas studies that concentrated on manufacturing or information non-intensive industries (Loveman, 1988; Olson and Weill, 1989) found no returns from IT.

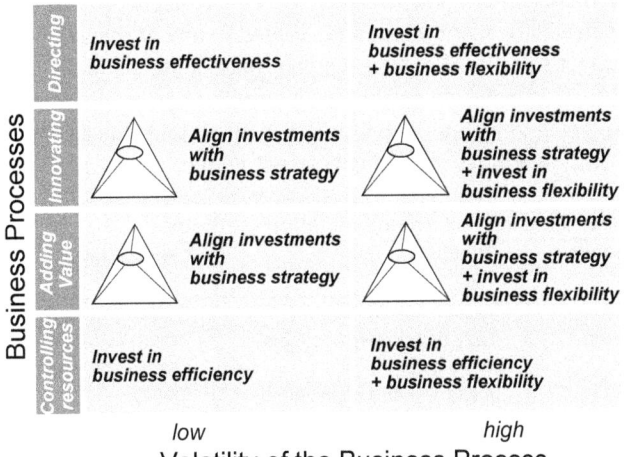

Figure 10: The relation between business processes, business strategy and the sources of value of IT investments.

5. Valuing investments

After creating an understanding of the impact of IT on business and the relevance of this impact in relation to the business strategy, the issue of valuation is next on the list. This is a typical economic issue for which it is irrelevant whether the investment is in IT or in any other resource. As long as the effects of the investment are understood, calculating the value of it is merely a financial technicality. This sounds almost too good to be true. Indeed, it is not quite that simple. Valuation methods all have assumptions and limitations.

5.1. Traditional valuation methods

Table 4 provides an overview of these valuation methods and their most important qualities and limitations.

The shortcomings of these methods are especially clear when IT investments are made to participate in today's E-Business economy. In this arena it is hard to make informed decisions when many variables are in flux. Traditional calculation methods are all limited in their ability to cope with risk and managerial flexibility. For example if a project proves to be a success, it can be sped up. If however the market deteriorates, the investment outlays of the project can be lowered or postponed. Despite the logic of this, in reality management adapts plans based on actual conditions all the time; this flexibility is not adequately valued in any of the valuation methods mentioned earlier. The result is an inadequate decision process for new projects. In some cases this even results in competitive investment proposals being rejected. Therefore it is clear that companies need to come up with new ways of judging IT investments.

Table 4: Overview of investment valuation methods

Valuation method	Qualities	Limitations
Return on investment	Easy to calculate Easy to interpret (a simple percentage) In line with the financial administration	Outcome sensitive to amortisation method Ignores the time-value of money Ignores risk
Pay-back period	Quite easy Intuitively coping with risk	Ignores part of the revenues Simplistic, does not determine value
Internal Rate of Return	Includes the time-value of money Easy to interpret (a simple percentage) Based on cash-flows	Complex Not in line with the financial administration Ignores risk Multiple outcomes, or none, possible
Discounted Cash Flow / Net Present Value	Includes the time-value of money Based on cash-flows Copes with risk	Complex Complex to interpret Not in line with the financial administration Not conclusive in case of projects with different durations
Economic Value Added	Includes the opportunity value of money In line with 'shareholder value'	Value calculation based upon one of the other methods Not in line with the financial administration

5.2. Valuing flexibility

A new insight is provided by the Real Options Valuation (ROV) theory. With ROV an additional value is calculated on top of the Net Present Value (NPV) of a project. This 'flexibility value' valuates the optionality of the investment. Optionality reflects the ability to alter the investment outlay and the timing of outlays based on changes in the competitive environment. ROV treats the possibilities of adapting the investment plan as (real) options. The opportunity to invest can be seen as a call option, involving the right to acquire an asset for a specified price (investment outlay) in a future moment. A call option gives the holder the right, for a specified price within a given amount of time, to exercise the option to acquire the underlying asset. The techniques derived from option pricing, quantify the management's ability to adapt its future plans to capitalise on favourable investment opportunities or to respond to undesirable developments in a dynamic environment by cutting losses. The ROV model is shown in Figure 11.

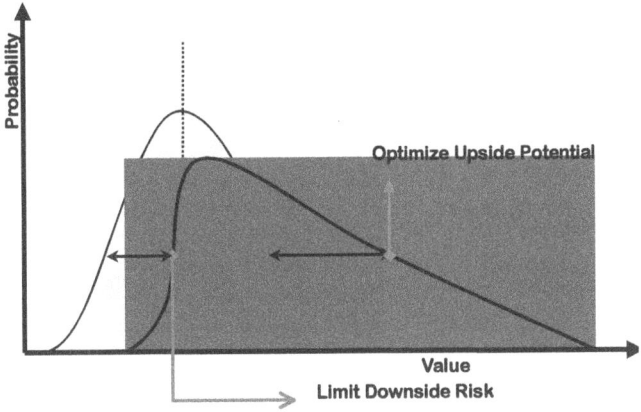

Downside risk is limited by enabling investors/ management to abandon the investment or to wait with future investments. Upside value is optimized by enabling investors/ management to expand investment, to progress with projects or to seek other opportunities for the initial investment.

Figure 11 The effect of real options on value. (Smit and Silvius, 2001)

Downside risk is limited by enabling investors/ management to abandon the investment or to wait with future investments. Upside value is optimised by enabling investors/ management to expand investment, to progress with projects or to seek other opportunities for the initial investment.
The Value of the real-option depends on three major elements:

- Maturity of the option;
- Business or project risk;
- Interest rates.

A valuable insight that can be gained from option theory is the effect of changes of the variables of the investment on the value of the investment. Table 5 shows these effects. An interesting fact is that, for example, an increase in the volatility of the returns decreases the NPV, but increases the ROV! Corporate strategists embrace the ROV approach, acknowledging the importance of active managerial flexibility in adapting to a changing market environment.

Table 5: The effect of changes in the variables of the underlying investment.

		Effect on NPV	Effect on ROV	Effect on the sum of NPV and ROV
Present Value of the cash-flows	↗ :	↗	↗	↗
Height of the investment	↗ :	↘	↘	↘
Volatility of the returns	↗ :	↘	↗	?
Level of the interest	↗ :	↘	↗	?
Maturity of the option	↗ :	↘	↗	?

5.3. Taking the competition into account

Another addition to the traditional valuation methods is the notion that the returns of an investment are not only influenced by the organisations own decisions, but also by the decisions of the competition. For example the first telecom operator that implements an innovative new service will enjoy, temporary, first mover advantages that the other players will miss when they implement the same service. Combining the real options approach with game theory, taking into account competitive counteractions, closes the gap between traditional corporate finance theory and strategic planning. Management investment decisions are made with the explicit recognition that they may invite competitive reaction, which in turn impacts the value of the firm's investment opportunity. The strategic value of early commitment in such cases must be set off against the option value of waiting and may potentially justify early investment. These decisions are often seen as strategic games against both nature and competition. Of course, in many cases the players may not exactly be 'symmetrical', with one of them enjoying a more dominant market power position. The value of organisational capabilities and of a firm's bundle of corporate real options, like uncertainty itself, is idiosyncratic to each firm. Similarly, the exercise price of a corporate real option may be idiosyncratic, depending on what other resources and assets the firm already has. Exercising the option to launch a new Windows-based software package, for instance, will be less expensive for Microsoft than for another player, by virtue of its earlier strategic investments and complementary assets that enable dominance in the desktop market. The firm pre-empted competition and captured a dominant share of the market by setting the product standard early on. Analysis of competitive behaviour and the effects on the valuation of real options is executed using elements of the Game Theory.

A 'Grab the dollar' game, for example, is a strategic context that is often associated with IT investments. Firms obtain a negative payoff when they end up investing simultaneously. 'Grab the dollar' illustrates the situation where the current market prospects are only favourable if one of the players invests, but simultaneous investment results in a battle with an expected negative payoff. Only the first player captures the dollar (e.g., patent), but when they all enter the market, they all end up loosing the battle. A dominant firm has an advantage to win this simultaneous game.

5.4. A complete valuation framework

Based on the insights provided by the real options and game theories the traditional NPV calculation can be and should be expanded to include the effects of managerial flexibility and competitive behaviour. This 'Expanded NPV' can be calculated as: Expanded NPV = NPV + Flexibility value + Strategic value

Figure 12 summarises this more complete valuation framework. This framework provides a better understanding of the value of IT investments.

What does this mean for the calculation of the value? In theory the knowledge is available to calculate a 'complete' value according to the framework. This calculation however will be complex and hard to understand in boardrooms. It is a drawback not to be taken lightly. The tendency to fall back on simple and comprehensible calculation methods leads to systematic underestimation of the value of IT investments especially when their effects are more than just efficiency improvement. This pitfall should be well understood. Financial theory just cannot provide us with a simple and undisputed figure or percentage that expresses the complete value of an investment.

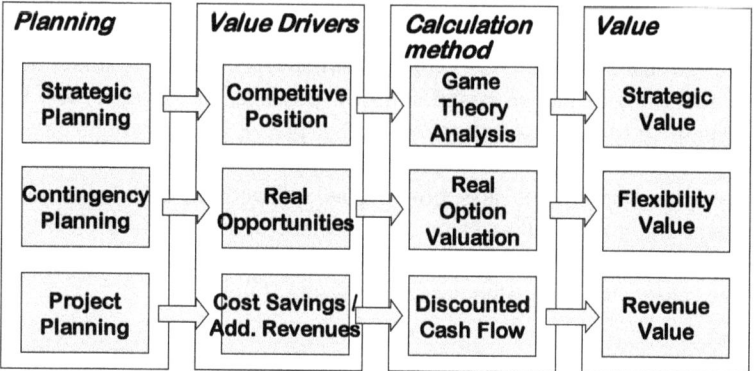

Figure 12: A complete valuation framework

It is therefore the opinion of the economist Professor Michael Brennan that :

'It is better to have the approximately optimal solution to the right problem than the exact solution to the wrong problem!!!!

(Actual quote on the 2000 Real Options Group conference, May 2000).
This opinion may not be very satisfying but it is not without grounds. A last insight to be added is the characteristic of the investment under scrutiny. For an IT system with a mainly internal 'business efficiency' impact, the additional 'flexibility value' and 'strategic value' will not be that significant. However, if an IT system has impact on the external positioning of the organisation, the additional value elements will be significant for a good valuation of the investment. Logically a relationship between the impact of the investment and the relevance of the different value elements can be suspected, as is shown in Figure 13.

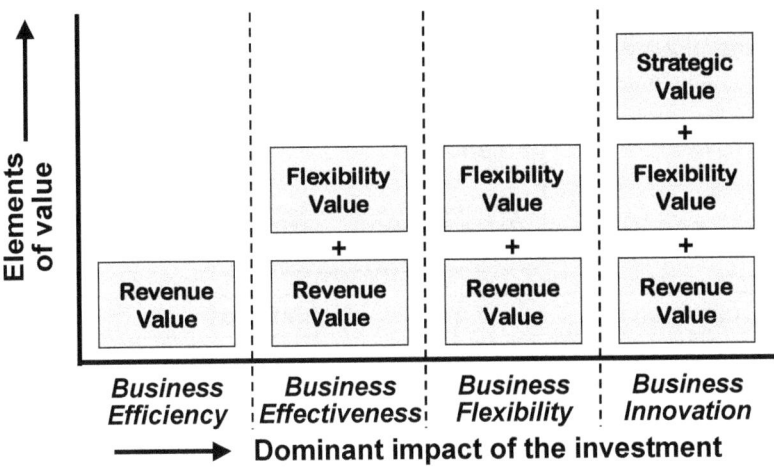

Figure 13: The relationship between the impact of an investment and the relevance of different value elements

6. Conclusion

The value of IT is a much discussed and often misunderstood subject. This paper aims to add new insight to the discussion by providing a practical grid in understanding the impact of IT investments on the organisation and by showing the conceptual relationships between IT value and business strategy and functions. In its use of the latest developments in financial theory this paper hopefully develops a more complete framework for the valuation of IT projects. This framework warns about rushing into possibly wrong decisions about IT investments based on incomplete calculations of value. Different evaluation and valuation methodologies reveal different aspects of value. However, we are still far away from a simple and easy-to-understand calculation method unveiling the complete and true value of any investment. A boardroom focus on simple Return on Investment metrics therefore should be qualified as either mismanagement or macho-talk. Company executives should focus their attention on creating a thorough understanding of how an investment in IT impacts the business of the organisation, instead of focus on oversimplified value calculations based on questionable assumptions.

Since a simple Return of Investment calculation cannot capture all elements of value, a more balanced approach is appropriate. Figure 14 shows a possible example of an 'IT investment Balanced Scorecard'

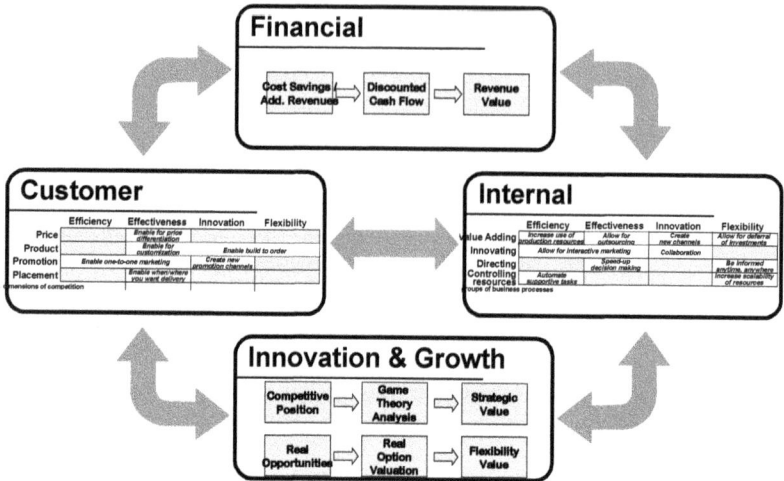

Figure 14: An IT investment Balanced Scorecard.

In this scorecard the financial perspective can be filled with the traditional Return on Investment calculation. This scorecard is enriched with the customer perspective showing the impact of the investment on the marketing proposition of the organisation. The internal perspective shows the impact of the investment on the business processes. The innovation and growth perspective finally shows the future options and possible competitive effects of the investment.

References

Ballantine, J.A., Galliers, R.D. & Stray, S.J. (1996). "Information systems/technology evaluation practices: evidence from UK organizations", *Journal of Information Technology* 11, pp. 129-141.

Ballantine, J.A., Stray, S.J. (1997). "A comparative analysis of the evaluation of information systems and other capital investments: empirical evidence". Proceedings of ECIS '97, pp. 809 – 822.

Brancheau, J.C., & Wetherbe, J.C. (1987). "Key Issues in Information Systems Management", *MIS Quarterly*, 11(1), pp. 23 - 45.

Bannister, F. (2001). "Dismantling the silos: extracting new value from IT investments in public administration", *Information Systems Journal*, 11 pp. 65 - 84.

Brynjolfsson, E. (1993). "The productivity paradox of information technology. *Communications of the ACM*, 36(12), pp. 67-77.

Davaraj, S. & Kohli, R. (2002). "The IT Payoff, Measuring the business value of information technology investments", Prentice Hall.

Dedrick, J., Gurbaxani, V. & Kraemer, K.J. (2003). "Information Technology and Economic Performance: A critical Review of the Empirical Evidence.", University of California, Irvine.

Fitzgerald, G. (1998). "Evaluating information systems projects: a multidimensional approach", *Journal of Information Technology*, 13, pp. 15-27.

Glazer, R. (1997). "Measuring the value of information: The information-intensive organisation", *IBM Systems Journal*, 32 (1), pp. 99-110.

Hammer, M. & Mangurian, G.E. (1987). "The changing value of communications technology", *Sloan Management Review* pp. 65-71.

Harris, S.E., Katz, J.L. (1991). "Firm size and the information technology investment intensity of lifer insurers", *MIS Quarterly*, 15, pp. 333-352.

IDG Research & Getronics (2002). "The CIO Agenda: Taking Care Of Business", CxO Media.

Loveman, G. (1988). "An assessment of the productivity impact of information technologies", Working Paper, Management in the 90s. Sloan School of Management, MIT.

Molenaar, T. (2002). "History learns us the value of IT investments " (in Dutch), *IT service magazine*, 5 pp. 18 - 21.

Mooney, J., Gurbaxani, V. & Kraemer, K. (1995). "A process oriented framework for assessing the business value of information technology ", *Proceedings of the Sixteenth Annual International Conference on Information Systems*, Degross, J., Ariav, G., Beath, C., Hoyer, R. & Kemerer, C., pp. 17-27, The Association of Information Systems, Amsterdam.

Niederman, F., Branchaeu, J.C. & Weaterbe, J.C. (1991). "Information systems management issues for the 1990s", *MIS Quaterly*, 15, pp. 475-499.

Olson, M.H. & Weill P. (1989). "Managing investment in information technology: mini case examples and implications". *MIS Quarterly*, 13(1), pp. 3-17.

Paul, L.G. & Tate, P. (2002). "CFO Mind Shift: Technology Creates Value", CFO Publishing Corporation, Boston, MA.

Riggins, F.J. (1999). "A Framework for Identifying Web-Based Electronic Commerce Opportunities", *Journal of Organizational Computing and Electronic Commerce* 9(4), pp. 297-310.

Salmela, H. (1997). "From information systems quality to sustainable business quality". *Information and Software Technology.* Vol 39, no. 12, pp. 819 – 827.

Smit, J. T. J. & Ankum. L.A. (1993). "A Real Options and Game-Theoretic Approach to Corporate Investment Strategy Under Competition", *Financial Management* 22, pp. 241-250.

Smit, J. T. J. & Silvius, A.J.G. (2001). "Dynamic Investment Planning; Valuing Intuition in the New Economy", *Proceedings of FESMA/DASMA conference*, Heidelberg.

Smit, J. T. J. & Trigeorgis, L. (1999). "Flexibility, Strategic Options and Dynamic Competition in Technology Industries", in "Real Options" A. Micalizzi and L. Trigeorgis eds., Egea Sda Bocconi, Milan.

Soh, C. & Markus, M. (1995). "How IT Creates Business Value: A Process Theory Synthesis", *Proceedings of the Sixteenth International Conference on Information Systems,* pp. 29-41.

Targowski, A (2004). "Making Business Sence of IT", 3rd Annual WMU-Hcob IT Forum, Western Michigan University.

Treacey, M. & Wiersema, F. (1997). "The Discipline of Market Leaders: Choose your customers, Narrow your focus, Dominate your market", Perseus Publishing.

Trigeorgis, L. (1993). "Real Options and Interactions with Financial Flexibility," *Financial Management* 22, pp. 202-224.

Whiting, R., Davies, J, & Knul, M. (1996). "Investment appraisal for IT systems" in Investing In Information Systems: Evaluation and Management. Edited by Leslie Willcocks. Chapman and Hall.

Willcocks, L., Lester, S. (1993). "How do organisations evaluate and control information systems investments? Recent UK survey evidence." *Journal of Information Systems*, 2, pp. 5-39.

Wong, J.W. & Behling, R. (1997). "Using conventional methods to perform cost-benefit analysis (CBA) on proposed information systems (IS) projects: an Australian study". *Journal of Computer Information Systems*, Summer 1997, pp.30-36.

Interpretative IS Evaluation: Results and Uses

Jenny Lagsten[1] and Göran Goldkuhl[2]
[1]Örebro University, Örebro, Sweden
[2]Linköping University, Linköping, Sweden
Originally Published in EJISE (2008) Volume 11: issue 2

Editor's Comment
This paper is useful to researchers but it may also have an application in more advanced courses in IS evaluation. The authors leave the more traditional views of IS assessment behind and explore the use of interpretative IS evaluation. Authors Langsten and Goldkuhl do this both theoretically and empirically. It is difficult to do this satisfactory but the authors mange this perfectly well in this paper. The manner in which they analyse their data and interpret it is impressive. They also take the reader through their steps of model building.

The interpretative approach is important for IT Evaluation research to grasp understanding of the situation at hand and this paper is an excellent example of its successful application.

Abstract: One major reason for doing evaluations of information systems is to take actions based on the results of the evaluation. In order to make better use of interpretive evaluation processes in practice we need to understand what kinds of results such evaluations produce and the way that the results are used to be transformed into change and betterment in the organisation. We have developed, applied and studied a methodology in support for doing interpretive evaluation. In the paper we report the case of a performed action research study that has comprised an IS evaluation. Through this action research we have transformed the theoretical principles of the interpretive approach into a useful evaluation methodology in practice. The main emphasis in this study is on the results and the uses of the evaluation process. We make a brief theoretical overview of interpretive principles for IS evaluation and of the research on evaluation use, from the field of evaluation theory, and represent a framework for analysing influences from evaluation efforts. We use this framework to analyse and identify the results and uses of the performed evaluation in order to shed light on what kinds of results that interpretive evaluation may offer. We experienced the Influence framework useful for locating and understanding the variety of results from interpretive evaluation processes. We conclude with a model depicting results and uses from interpretive IS evaluation processes. The main point we elaborate on in this paper is how evaluations influence the actions taken in the organisation in order to establish betterment. How people in the organisation use evaluation in order to establish betterment and change. Further we bounce back the insights on evaluation results and uses into the discussion on how to design interpretive evaluation processes and how to design evaluation methodology in support for those processes.

Keywords: IS evaluation, evaluation process, evaluation results, evaluation use, interpretative evaluation methodology

1. Introduction

One major reason for doing evaluations of information systems is to take actions based on the results of the evaluation. Results from evaluations form a base of knowledge that is supposed to be used to plan and perform knowledgeable actions by individuals in the organisation.

Evaluations of information systems can be performed through different approaches and methodologies and consequently evaluations aims to fulfil different kinds of purposes and produces different kinds of results (Lagsten and Karlsson 2006). The interpretive evaluation approach has been reported as a capable evaluation approach with important implications for practice (Symons and Walsham 1988; Symons 1991; Avgerou 1995; Farbey *et al.* 1999a; Hirschheim and Smithson 1999; Walsham 1999). There is a growing body of work on interpretive IS evaluation, but as Introna and Whittaker (2002) put it "most of the interpretive work on IS evaluation is interpretive in its evaluation of empirical studies, but more limited when it comes to describing IS evaluation *as* interpretation". This paper concerns the use of interpretive evaluation methodology in support for doing evaluation as interpretation.

Walsham (1999) and Hirschheim and Smithson (1999) address the problem that there does not seem to be much evidence of extensive use of interpretive evaluation approaches in practice although the approach seems well founded academically and theoretically to offer potential advantages (such as stakeholder commitment, learning opportunities). Walsham suggests that the non-use might be explained by a lack of knowledge in the IS field of the interpretive approach or that such evaluations brings into light problems that is normally hidden leading to anxiety and fear. The non-use might also be due to organisational-political motives. Hirschheim and Smithson suggests that the wide use of formal-rational evaluation methods could be explained by the ritualistic value the organisation achieve by adopting scientific (positivistic) methods and that those methods offers a rhetoric that reconciles the lack of rationality in decision making and the responsibility of the decision maker.

We suggest that one reason for the low-use is due to poor understanding of the results and uses of interpretive evaluations. The interpretive evaluation *process* is of course important to study and conceptualise, but we want to move beyond a limited process focus and direct attention to its results and uses. In a pragmatic vein, we want to study the interpretive evaluation process in the light of its uses and results. In order to do this we will provide an illustrative analysis of results and uses of a performed evaluation. In this analysis we apply a framework, from the area of evaluation research, which categorise different mechanisms through which evaluations may achieve influence. We approach the studied evaluation from its use and consequences in the organisation, from the perspective of usefulness, which is an intentionally pragmatic stance towards knowledge and understanding. "In a nutshell, the overriding issue for pragmatists is whether or not something, be it philosophical assumptions, methodology, or information, is useful in the sense that the something in question is instrumental in producing desired or anticipated results" (Goles and Hirschheim 2000). We think the analysis will help practitioners and researchers to better understand the interpretive evaluation process and contribute to better use and usefulness of interpretive evaluations in practice.

In this paper we do several things. First we make a brief overview of principles of interpretive IS evaluation in section 2 and then of the research on evaluation use where we represent a framework for analysing influences from evaluations (section 3). We shortly report the case of an action research study that has comprised an evaluation based on interpretive methodology (section 4). We use the influence framework to locate and elaborate on the results and uses of the performed evaluation in section 5.

In section 6 we present a model of interpretive evaluation results and uses. We close the paper with making conclusions on how we can use conceptions of evaluation consequences in order to establish better interpretive IS evaluations in practice.

2. Interpretive IS evaluation

In the litterateur on IS evaluation there has been several calls for interpretive methodology and researchers has suggested principles to guide interpretive evaluation processes.

Avgerou (1995) suggests a dialectic approach to undertake evaluation processes that are recognised as interpretive and political and put forward following guiding principles:

- The task of the "evaluator" is to organise and support a dialectic evaluation process, to asses methodically aspects of the system under evaluation as seen appropriate by stakeholders, and to inform about issues which, although significant according to the IS literature, might have been ignored by the participants.
- The evaluation process is participative, allowing all stakeholders to express their views and supporting them to defend their position.
- The criteria of evaluation are determined by the context and include all the concerns of the stakeholders.
- The objective is to reach consensus decisions about future systems developments, either by accepting and possibly modifying plans and proposals for new systems, or by learning the lessons of past experience.

According to Avgerou the proposed approach takes into account actions of different agents and establishes a collective responsibility for information systems changes and questions the validity of the projects initial objectives.

Jones and Hughes (2001) propose an interpretive approach that emphasises the situatedness of social action and knowledge. They argue that the social interaction and actor perception plays an important interpretive role that should be obtained and valued in the evaluation process. They characterise the interpretive evaluation process to be concerned with the context in which IS evaluation takes place, that it engages with stakeholders in process to understand assumptions and views. Furthermore the interpretive evaluation seeks multiple-stakeholder subjective views and that the process is recognised as social and political.

Additionally Jones and Hughes propose guidelines for practitioner action that maps onto the characteristics of the process:
- Articulate the importance of the stakeholder view by appointing a facilitator to elicit the views and concerns of stakeholders so that these can be disseminated. Use methods in practice similar to the GT method which provides a set of procedures for the articulation analysis and dissemination of a grounded view of stakeholders.
- Expose and document these grounded processes.
- Through seminars and group discussion expose the underlying assumptions and values.

The framework of Content, Context and Process (CC&P) (figure 1), introduced by Symons 1991, has been proposed as an analytical tool for interpretive IS evaluation. The CC&P framework elucidates the elements of IS evaluation and support the researcher with a theoretical framework for analysing evaluation in a specific context (Serafeimidis and Smithson 1996, Symons 1991, Walsham 1999). The framework can act as a foundation for discussion of the various aspects of IS evaluation in its organisational and business context (Serafeimidis and Smithson 1996). It has, for example, been used to analyse case studies in order to explain why an implementation of a new evaluation approach failed (Serafeimidis and Smithson 2000).

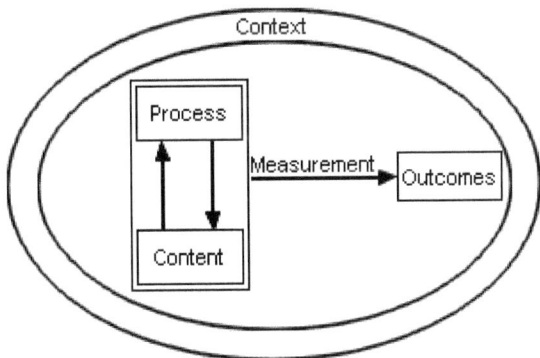

Figure 1: The elements of evaluation (the CC&P framework) (Serafeimidis and Smithson 1996).

It has been argued that the CC&P framework has implications for practice but, from our point of view, the framework is suited for analysing and understanding practical situations but is of less use when it comes to guiding evaluators and practitioners in the practical art of doing evaluation. Further, the framework gives no guidance on the important matter of how the evaluation process works in order to realise betterment (the outcome box in the framework is not connected to the context in some way). As we see it, the betterment realisation process that is supposed to follow from the evaluation comprises (at least) two stages; results and effects. Firstly, there are the immediate results that are produced within the different evaluation activities; these are the direct outputs from the evaluation, the results. Secondly, there are the effects that these results have on peoples thinking and doing and further onto the wider organisation environment; these effects could be recognised as the outcomes of the evaluation. It is the effects, or the outcomes, that are the reasons for why people engage in evaluation efforts.

3. Learnings from evaluation research

In order to better understand the way evaluations are used, and how evaluations influence on people and organisations, we have turned to the literature in the field of evaluation research. Evaluation research has developed as a field from the need of evaluating public programs of social change (within schools, health-care, and welfare enterprises) in order to show if services and improvement efforts were succeeding (Stufflebeam 2001). According to Henry and Mark (2003) is social betterment the ultimate purpose of evaluations and refer to improvement of social conditions. We agree that the concern for social betterment lies behind the widespread purposes of evaluation: to inform decision making and to improve the subject or program under study. Farbey et.al. (1999b) points out that IS evaluation has a lot to learn from the field of evaluation research and state "If IS are complex and pervasive socio-technical systems whose life extends over several months or years then IS investments can be seen as social action, based on complex technology and taking place in substantial period in time. They are thus like programmes of social action which are the subjects of evaluation research".

Alkin and Christie (2004) organize the field of evaluation research within three main branches; use, methods, and valuing. Evaluation use has traditionally been regarded as the use of evaluation findings (in the evaluation report) for 1) *instrumental use* – findings lead to immediate actions for example program change or termination 2) *conceptual use* - or enlightenment, refers to the general learning that takes place by taking part of the evaluation findings 3) *symbolic use* – the justification of the purported rationality of an agency (Mark and Henry 2004). More recently *process use* has been added to the uses of evaluation (Patton 1997; Russ-Eft *et al.* 2002). Process use differs from the use of findings in that it refers to uses that arise from the participation in the process of evaluation (Mark and Henry 2004). Process use also indicates the perception of evaluation as an intervention with its own set of processes, outputs, and outcomes.

The instrumental use of evaluations, or the implementation of evaluation results, may not follow a straight path forward to change and betterment. "Most studies that examine the consequences of evaluation find the same thing: that decision makers seldom use evaluation evidence as the basis of immediate decisions" (Weiss 2004). Weiss continues with saying that the times when evaluations tend to influence is often due to that the evaluation evidence strengthens already hold beliefs of decision makers or legitimises prior opinions. Sometimes evaluations can give directions in situations when the organisation is facing a crisis and no one is sure how to proceed. Occasionally new administers comes in from outside and is receptive to negative findings and new ideas.

We think that the perception of evaluation as an intervention with its own procedures, results and effects will help us to better locate and understand the way evaluations can produce change. When we perceive evaluation as intervention we take into account the influences that the evaluation activities has on people in the organisation. In section 4 we present our process model of evaluation, in line with the interventionist view, with four interrelated phases: initiate, arrange, evaluate, change & develop. These phases are processed by people participating in evaluation activities and conversation around the object of evaluation. While the evaluation precedes different kinds of results steam out from the conversation involving actors in the organisation; insights are given, understanding is raised, concepts are defined, situations are identified, misconceptions are articulated, agreements are held, purposes and objectives are negotiated, conclusions are drawn, actions are planned and taken, language and grammar for the conversation is developed. The evaluative conversation influence peoples thinking and actions and produce change on different levels in the organisational practice. Henry and Mark (2004) have developed a framework (Table 1), based on empirical investigations, of the mechanisms through which evaluation may achieve influence and changes. It includes three levels of analysis, individual, interpersonal and collective; the levels indicate the locus of the change mechanisms.

The mechanisms are classified into four processes. General influence processes are fundamental architecture of change, likely to set into motion some change into the cognitive/affective, motivational or behavioural processes. Such processes can occur at all three levels, they are not likely to be important as change mechanisms in isolation but are of interest because the may stimulate outcomes of greater practical interest such as changes in beliefs and feelings, motivations and actions. Mark and Henry mean that the processes lead to one another and could trigger a cascade of changes in the organisation. Evaluators can, for example, benefit from the framework to better capture and plan for the consequences of an evaluation by identifying pathways of socially mediated changes that the evaluation process and findings set into motion.

Table 1: The mechanisms and outcomes of evaluation influence (Mark and Henry 2004).

Type of process/outcome	Level of analysis		
	Individual	Interpersonal	Collective
General influence	Elaboration Heuristics Priming Skill acquisition	Justification Persuasion Change agent Minority-opinion influence	Ritualism Legislative hearings Coalition formation Drafting legislation Standard setting
Cognitive and affective	Salience Opinion/attitude valence	Local descriptive norms	Agenda setting Policy-oriented learning
Motivational	Personal goals and aspirations	Injunctive norms Social reward Exchange	Structural incentives Market forces
Behavioural	New skill performance Individual change in practice	Collaborative change in practice	Program continuation, cessation, or change Policy change Diffusion

The individual level refers to change in the thoughts or actions of one or more individuals, when a difference in question takes place in one individual. The source of a change in attitude could be the elaboration that is done by reading an evaluation report carefully or by participating in dialogue about criteria for the evaluation object. This change in attitude could emphasize individual aspirations and trigger behavioural changes in practice.

The interpersonal level refers to change brought about in interactions between individuals. Evaluation findings could work as authoritative arguments in persuasion processes when trying to change attitudes and behaviours of others or justifying held positions. Evaluation findings or processes can stimulate individuals to rise to action as change agents.

The collective level refers to the direct or indirect influence on the decisions and practices of organisations. This level is involved when a change process or outcome operates in the aggregate social organisational body as a formal policy change.

4. The evaluation study

Our study concerns the design of methodology for interpretive evaluation of information systems. The emerging methodology is called VISU (Swedish acronym for IS evaluation for workpractice development).

4.1. Study procedure

In our action research study (Susman and Evered 1978) a methodology for interpretive IS evaluation has been designed and tested during several cycles of use. VISU has been refined in several stages (Lagsten 2005) and built originally on constructivist evaluation (Guba and Lincoln 1989), Change Analysis (Goldkuhl and Röstlinger 2005) and an explicit pragmatic knowledge perspective. Constructivist evaluation contributes with principles on stakeholder perspective, dialectic process and stakeholder generated criteria. Change analysis contributes with methods and modelling techniques for capturing, modelling and analysing problems, strengths, goals and change requirements as well as guiding principles on participation. The pragmatic perspective emphasises that the evaluation knowledge created during the process is intended to be used for transformation of the studied problematic situation. Confer the notion of inquiry in Dewey (1938).

VISU is designed for taking into account, and make use of, process results of an evaluation. The principal approach is to ensemble concerns of all stakeholders of the information system in systematic dialogues. This is done by the use of dialogue-seminars. A dialogue-seminar can be compared to a focus group were a special set of questions are addressed and examined by a stakeholder group. The principles of interpretive IS evaluation (section 2) are incorporated in VISU through various components. Figure 2 presents the process model of VISU.

The VISU approach originally emerged in a study of project evaluation at the Swedish employment agency (Lagsten, 2005). Later it was transformed into an explicit IS evaluation approach (ibid). VISU has been tested through the use of the methodology in performing evaluation of the information system Procapita (supporting social welfare services) in a municipality in Sweden.

INITIATE	ARRANGE	EVALUATE	CHANGE & DEVELOP
Identify preconditions	Make entrance Understand the practice Create a model of the evaluation object Identify stakeholder groups Identify possible uses	Carry out dialogue-seminars with different stakeholder groups Analyse activities, problems, strengths and goals Identify change needs Shape change measures Joint valuation Make completions	Use evaluation results Report and inform

Figure 2: Process model of VISU (Swedish acronym for IS evaluation for workpractice development).

Procapita is an off-the-shelf system from a large Swedish ERP vendor and is in use by approximately 150 municipalities in Sweden. In this studied municipality the system is used by 350 social workers (case handlers) in their daily workpractice with case handling. The clients of the service are adults or children who have difficulties in organising a normal life (due to drug-abuse, violent behaviour, insufficient provision etc.). Case handling includes writing field notes, document investigations, take decisions on measures, assess measures and take decisions on placements in institutions and residential care. The social workers carry out 40%-60% of their working hours throughout Procapita. The system has been in use in this authority since 1999.

One of the authors has had the role of the evaluator in the study. Techniques used to capture results and uses are questionnaires to participants in the evaluation, interviews and participative observations.

4.2. The evaluation

In the initiation phase the evaluator, the IS manager (assigner) and the IS operations manager together identified and defined the situation. A preconditions document were formulated and worked as a mutual commitment for the evaluation. The precondition document defined the evaluation object, the aim of the evaluation, the questions that the municipality wanted to resolve through the evaluation and the evaluation method. The main question for the IS manager was if it was about time to terminate Procapita or if the current system satisfied the organisational needs.

In the arrangement phase an inventory of stakeholders were done. The evaluator put an effort in understanding the practice supported by the system by participating in regular meetings with the maintenance personnel and the social welfare committee, participating in Procapita education, and reading central documents. A theory based model of the case handling practice was created in interaction social workers. The evaluator contacted administrative personnel and managers in order to inform about evaluation activities and organise stakeholder participation in the forthcoming dialogue-seminars. An evaluation board was set up consisting of the IS manager, the IS operations manager and maintenance people. Stakeholders were chosen to participate in the seminars; the choice was based on their crucial interests in Procapita and on the possibility to get answers to the evaluation questions.

In the evaluation phase 16 dialogue-seminars were held. The stakeholders represented were users (five different user groups), unit managers, maintenance, and IS management. Each group (3-7 individuals) had two seminars taking two hours in general. Central organisers of stakeholder concerns are four specific VISU-questions elaborated in the seminars: What do you do while using Procapita? What problems do you perceive? What good does the system do for you? What are the goals you try to achieve? The VISU-questions are other than the evaluation questions and worked as tools for gathering information to answer those.

Every seminar was documented in a working report articulating stakeholder concerns and issues arranged by activities, problems, strengths and goals. In between the first and second seminar every participator got the report by e-mail, in the second seminar the group made refinements and validated the report. All reports were successively published on the intranet. Altogether there were about 70 individuals participating in the evaluation process. Paralleled with the ongoing dialogue-seminars the evaluation board interpreted the reports and transformed them into change requirements.

After the dialogue-seminars were carried out the evaluator analysed the working reports according to statements on activities, problems (400), strengths (50) and goals (70). The analysis was done, to a large degree, with the use of analytical tools from Grounded Theory (GT) (Strauss and Corbin 1998). For each stakeholder group an account was written. After having identified change needs for the different stakeholder groups, the thorny task of identifying and formulating change measures weighted together and aggregated for all stakeholder groups were conducted. A range of change measures were identified and described under following labels: 1) Wash away usability problems from the interface 2) Develop adjusted education 3) Develop conceptual models for cases and registration 4) Demand bug-free versions and fixes from the vendor 5) Establish an arena for communication between practice and maintenance 6) Explicate the interface between practice and maintenance 7) Assess and evaluate continuously. An evaluation report were written, the report contained a comprehensive model of the system from a multiple-stakeholder perspective, descriptions and analyses of problems, strengths and goals for the different stakeholder groups. The report concluded with the identified measures and a discussion on the initial evaluation questions. Seminars were held to discuss the findings. The IS manager has got the assignment from the social welfare committee to write a detailed plan on how to act upon the findings and the knowledge produced in the evaluation.

5. Analysis

In this section we employ the influence framework to analyse the results and uses that were identified during and a short time after the evaluation. The purpose here is to illustrate different influences from the performed evaluation on an individual, interpersonal and organisational level. The analysis is based on statements from participants (via a questionnaire), and on interviews and observations during the process. Figures 3, 4 and 5 illustrate the framework.

General influence	"It has contributed to reflective thinking about Procapita." (User) "You learn new ways and shortcuts on how to handle Procapita." (User) "I think we shall benefit from this way of working in our practice" (Manager) *Commentary:* The dialogue-seminar joins stakeholders in reflective thinking and elaboration on Procapita. Due to the evaluative dialogues users get more aware of the system and their perception of system features in the work practices as well. Participants develop new knowledge and skills through sharing experiences on handling Procapita. The way of working in the seminar becomes as well new skills for evaluative inquiry.
Cognitive and affective	"It becomes an opportunity to stop and reflect about strengths and betterment issues." (User) "It's more obvious now which problems that are general in Procapita." (User) "It has been a long journey and I have struggled back and fourth with my opinion but now I feel satisfied with the system. It's a good system." (Maintenance) *Commentary:* Participation develops personal standpoints and attitudes on what is god or bad about the system and related routines relative to what stakeholders do and try to achieve in their workpractice. The conversation explicates tacit heuristics when participants explain their standpoints to each other.
Motivational	"It makes clear what issues it is important to go on with. "(User) "A forum for discussion on measures to make it work." (User) "Necessary with more education." (User) "Has the side effect that we discuss case handling in the group." (User) "It's also fun and educating." (Unit manager) *Commentary:* The evaluative conversation shapes personal goals and aspirations and motivates individuals to go on with specific issues revealed in the process.

Leading Issues in IS Evaluation Research

Behavioural	*Commentary*: In the second of the two seminars some users reported that they have started to use the system differently due to what they learnt in the first seminar.

Figure 3: Results and uses, individual level.

General influence	"Shortcomings and strengths become more evident in discussions with others." (User) "Someone in the group says something that leads to that someone else thinks of a second/third issue and so on." (User) "Everybody has the right to put forth their opinion." (User) *Commentary*: Stakeholders shape more precise accounts of the system in interaction. Minority-opinions are included.
Cognitive and affective	"Gets a joint and overall picture of the system." (User) "The maintenance personnel has adopted a new approach – they have taken on a user perspective." (IS manager) *Commentary*: Stakeholder groups develop local descriptive norms based on a larger picture and mutual understanding. Understanding of other stakeholder perspectives start to influence.
Motivational	
Behavioural	*Commentary*: The evaluation process, and the reading of working reports from the dialogue-seminars, had strong influence on the maintenance personnel who made changes during the process. The maintenance people took on a new role in working groups and started to hand over responsibility (for registry maintenance, corrections, user knowledge) to the case handling practice. Maintenance also made an assessment of a system from another vendor but that system was judged to not have enough support for "heavy operations". Several projects were formulated, some were started during evaluation process: New user roles with routine support Templates New organisation of education Log project Investigation of new module for text editing The maintenance people put forward more precise demands on the vendor and did more careful investigations in ongoing projects. Some fixes were also made in Procapita. It seems like they, through participating in the evaluation process, understood the importance of those needs and changes and got the final motives that made up their minds on which changes to go on and work with.

Figure 4: Results and uses, interpersonal level.

General in-	*Commentary*: The social welfare committee has decided that a

fluence	detailed plan shall be drawn up on how to take care of the findings from the evaluation. The development committee is analysing the evaluation report in order to tighter anchor the evaluation findings to other change measures in the organisation. The IS manager has introduced the evaluation to the vendor; the evaluator is vited to give a seminar on the evaluation with vendor.
Cognitive and affective	*Commentary*: The evaluation has been presented to 10-15 of the largest municipalities that uses the same system. Evaluation of Procapita has become an issue in other organisations.
Motivational	*Commentary*: A month after the evaluation report were delivered the IS manager stated that "we are already in action, the benefits are concrete and the thoughts are used". The evaluation has activated different organisational structures and motivates to go on and make betterments.
Behavioural	Commentary: The IS manager has decided not to terminate the system but to renegotiate the contract with the vendor. The renegotiation has started. The evaluation process gives rise to diffusion in other areas than the focal matters of the evaluation. An information security education for 250 managers within the municipality has been held; conceptualisations produced in the evaluation are used in the education. The IS-manager explained that "the insights from the evaluation gave me the extra strength to negotiate the funding for the education that was not planned for in this budget". Another example is that a new element, evaluation, is now incorporated in the business plan.

Figure 5: Results and uses, collective level.

6. A model of interpretive evaluation results and uses

We found the influence framework to be a useful instrument in order to locate and elaborate on the results and uses of the evaluation. The framework helped us recognise influences from the evaluation on different levels and via different mechanisms. The analysis also brings an understanding on how socially mediated changes set into motion a cascade of changes in the organisation. The framework represents influences from evaluation by starting within the individual body of knowledge and feelings – we recognise this as an important acknowledgement both from this study and from other similar studies that we have performed.

It was sometimes thorny to categorise observations into entrances in the framework, especially to differentiate between cognitive/affective and motivational processes. Maybe the framework is too fine-grained for our purpose. That is why we used the dashed lines to separate between the processes.

As a contribution from our study we have created a model depicting results and uses from an interpretive IS evaluation (figure 6).

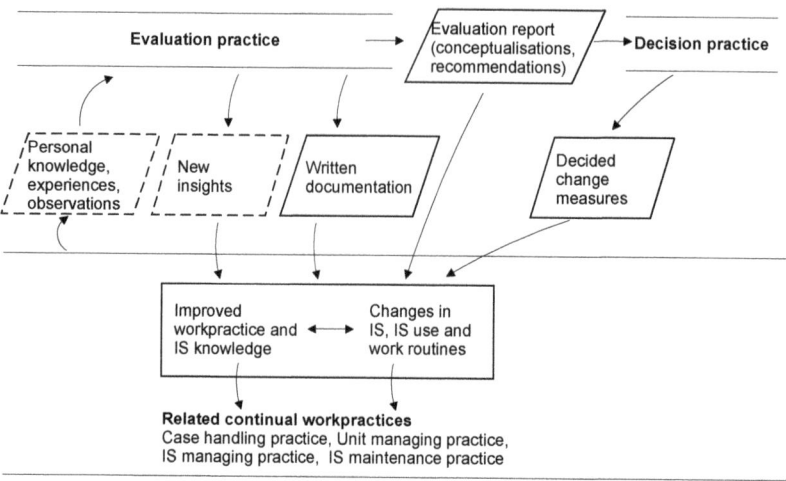

Figure 6: Evaluation results and uses.

The evaluation process is a temporary practice related to ordinary continual work practices. In this case we distinguish several related work practices as case handling (involves IS use), unit managing practice (includes governance of case handling), IS managing practice and IS maintenance practice. The evaluation practice is concerned with these continual practices and is furnished with knowledge from them through the participating stakeholders. Stakeholders/participants go back and forth between the temporary evaluation practice and their respective ordinary work practice. They bring experiences from their practices to the evaluation and they gain insights from the evaluation dialogue-seminars which they bring back to their work practices. The evaluation produces gradually written documentation which the participants also can bring back.

Participation in the evaluation yields learning about their work practice. These new insights may be turned into changed behaviour in work practices and even in immediate changes in routines, IS uses and sometimes in

IS changes. There is a flow of knowledge from the evaluation process to the ordinary work practices during the conduct of evaluation. People may do not wait until the evaluation process has come to an end and a formal report is written, and formal decisions are taken, to start changing their work practices. New insights are often imperative to action. People may also bring back parts of the emerging written documentation from the evaluation arena. They may show them to their colleagues and together reflect on possible interventions. What is described here are process uses in the continual work practices during the evaluation process.

One essential result from the evaluation practice is of course the written evaluation report which comprises documented learnings about the evaluation object and recommendations for future actions. Such report is often handled in some official decision context; we call it a decision practice. Decision makers make deliberations based on the report and produce some formal decisions, which often will be change measures to be implemented in the ordinary work practices. The decision practice and the continual workpractices are different workpractices, which may explain why not always the decided changes correspond to the implemented ones. Implementers (from outside and inside the continual workpractices) usually make adaptations of the stated decisions during the implementation process.

In our model we recognise the different types of uses (process, instrumental, conceptual and symbolic) that are represented in the evaluation research literature. Process use is characterised in the flow of knowledge between the temporary evaluation practice and the related continual workpractices and in the transformation of thinking and doing in these practices due to the knowledge that is produced in the process. Conceptual use, that usually refers to that general learning that takes place from reading the evaluation report, is represented both in the learnings due to participation in the evaluative dialogues and due to the reading of documents produced in the process. Instrumental use is represented in the model by the decision practice and the flow of decided change measures into the continual work practices. The symbolic use that refers to the "evaluation ritual behaviour" of decision makers in order to justify the rationality of an agency could be more of an aspect of using the model itself and is not an aspect within the model.

In our model there is a distinction between result and effect. This is an important pragmatic insight made by for example von Wright (1971); confer also Goldkuhl (2005). The result is what is produced through an action and this is what is within the range of the actor. Effects are what arise as consequences through the use and influence of the action results. This distinction can be used to make a "macroscopic" clarification. The evaluation process will create an evaluation report as a primary result for instrumental use. It is important to conceive that uses and effects of this report may be different from what is stated within it. Suggested change measures may be rejected by the decision makers or they may be transformed in the implementation process. However, "microscopic" effects arise already in the evaluation process. Evaluation statements are interpreted by the participants and they bring this knowledge back to their continual workpractices, as described above, and process uses occur.

This distinction between results and effects must also be complemented by the pragmatic insight of action reflexivity (e.g. Mead, 1938; Giddens, 1984; Goldkuhl, 2005). The actions conducted always act back on the actors themselves. There is a natural learning inherited in all action. The actor perceives the result of her action and possible effects of it. Knowledge evolves through action (Kolb, 1984). People learn through participating in evaluation. There are not only external results as produced evaluation statements. Insights among participants arise through the process; both as consequences from listening to the evaluation dialogues and as reflections from their own active participation. As said above, these insights produce process uses.

7. Conclusions

In order to understand the consequences of interpretative evaluation processes we need conceptions on how such processes produces results and how these results are used to be transformed into effects. Conceptions, in the shape of models, frameworks and illustrations help us to recognise how evaluation outputs proceeds into evaluation outcomes. We also need vocabulary and grammar for the consequences of evaluation so that we can talk about those in a comprehensive manner.

We have suggested a model of interpretive evaluation results and uses. The model uncovers the process where evaluation outputs transforms into outcomes. The results and use model is anchored in empirical findings from interpretive evaluation processes and in literature on evaluation, knowledge and change. In our case there is gradual use of insights and documentation during the evaluation process. This may not be the result of any formal decision process. Stakeholders, participating in the evaluation, just start adjusting their behaviour according to their improved knowledge. This new behaviour may imply changes in work routines, in IS use and in the actual information system. There is also a more formal chain of actions; from evaluation to evaluation report and further to a decision practice resulting in formal decisions which can lead to implementation of planned changes in workpractices and information systems.

We think it is important to include awareness and logic about the different type of results and the different type of uses into the design of evaluations, as well as into the design of evaluation methodology. We need evaluation methodology that guides and supports an interpretive evaluation process, that recognises the process as an intervention within its own procedures and results, and that especially acknowledges the process use that take place during the ongoing evaluation. This will help us to better understand and appreciate such evaluation processes for its capability to generate change and betterment. Then, we think, we have improved the opportunities for better use and usefulness of interpretive IS evaluations in practice.

References

Alkin Marvin and Christie Christina (2004) "An Evaluation Theory Tree", In *Evaluation Roots - Tracing Theorists' Views and Influences* (Ed, Alkin M) Sage, Thousand Oaks.

Avgerou Chrisanth (1995) "Evaluating Information Systems by Consultation and Negotiation", *International Journal of Information Management,* 15(6), 427-436.

Dewey John (1938) *Logic: The theory of inquiry*, Henry Holt, New York

Farbey Barbara, Land Frank and Targett David (1999a) "The Moving Staircase Problems of Appraisal and Evaluation in a Turbulent Environment", *Information Technology&People,* 12(3), 238-252.

Farbey Barbara, Land Frank and Targett David (1999b) "Moving IS Evaluation Forward: Learning Themes and Research Issues", *Journal of Strategic Information Systems,* 8189-207.

Giddens Anthony (1984) The constitution of society. Outline of the theory of structuration, Polity Press, Cambridge

Goldkuhl Göran and Röstlinger Annie (2005) "Change Analysis – Innovation and Evolution", *Invited paper, 14th International Conference on Information Systems Development (ISD)*, Karlstad, Sweden.

Goldkuhl Göran (2005) "Socio-Instrumental Pragmatism: A Theoretical Synthesis for Pragmatic Conceptualisation in Information Systems", in *Proceedings of the 3rd Intl Conf on Action in Language, Organisations and Information Systems (ALOIS)*, University of Limerick

Goles Tim and Hirschheim Rudy (2000) "The Paradigm Is Dead, the Paradigm Is Dead...Long Live the Paradigm: The Legacy of Burell and Morgan", *The International Journal of Management Science, OMEGA*, 28249-268.

Guba Egon and Lincoln Yvonna (1989) *Fourth Generation Evaluation*, SAGE, Newbury Park.

Henry Gary and Mark Melvin (2003) "Beyond Use: Understanding Evaluation's Influence on Attitudes and Actions", *American Journal of Evaluation*, 24(3), 293-314.

Hirschheim Rudy and Smithson Steve (1999) "Evaluation of Information Systems: A Critical Assessment", In *Beyond the It Productivity Paradox*, (Eds, Willcocks and Lester) John Wiley&Sons, Chichester.

Introna Lucas D. and Whittaker Louise (2002) "The Phenomenology of Information Systems

Evaluation: Overcoming the Subject/Object Dualism", In *Global and Organizational Discourse about

Information Technology*, IFIP TC8/ WG8.2, (Eds, Wynn E, et al.), Barcelona, Spain, pp. 155-175.

Jones Steve and Hughes Jim (2001) "Understanding Is Evaluation as a Complex Social Process: A Case Study of a UK Local Authority", *European Journal of Information Systems*, 10 189-203.

Kolb David A (1984) Experiential learning. Experience as the source of learning and development, Prentice Hall, Englewood Cliffs, NJ

Lagsten Jenny (2005) Verksamhetsutvecklande Utvärdering I Informationssystemprojekt. (In Swedish; Evaluation in Information Systems Projects, for Business Development), Licentiate Thesis, Department of computer and information science, University of Linköping, Linköping.

Lagsten Jenny and Karlsson Fredrik (2006) "Multiparadigm Analysis - Clarity into Information Systems Evaluation", *European Conference on Information Technology Evaluation (ECITE)*,Genoa, Italy.

Mark Melvin and Henry Gary (2004) "The Mechanisms and Outcomes of Evaluation Influence", *Evaluation*, 10(1), 25-57.

Mead George H (1938) *Philosophy of the act*, University of Chicago Press

Patton Michael Quinn (1997) *Utilization-Focused Evaluation the New Century Text*, 3rd ed., SAGE, Thousand Oaks.

Russ-Eft Darlene, Atwood Regina and Egherman Tori (2002) "Use and Non-Use of Evaluation Results: Case Study of Environmental Influences in the Private Sector", *American Journal of Evaluation*, 23(1), 19-31.

Serafeimidis, V. & Smithson, S. (1996) "The Management of Change for Information Systems Evaluation Practice: Experience from a Case Study", *International Journal of Information Management*, Vol. 16, No. 3, pp205 - 217.

Serafeimidis, V. & Smithson, S. (2000) "Information systems evaluation in practice: A case study of organizational change", *Journal of Information Technology*, Vol. 15, No. 2, pp93-105.

Strauss Anselm and Corbin Juliet (1998) Basics of Qualitative Research. Techniques and Procedures for Developing Grounded Theory, SAGE, Thousand Oaks.

Stufflebeam Daniel (2001) "Evaluation Models", *New Directions for Evaluation*, Spring 2001(89), 7-98.

Susman Gerald and Evered Roger (1978) "An Assessment of the Scientific Merits of Action Research", *Administrative Science Quarterly*, 23(4), 582-603.

Symons Veronica (1991) "A Review of Information Systems Evaluation: Content, Context, Process", *European Journal of Information Systems*, 1(3), 205-212.

Symons Veronica and Walsham Geoff (1988) "The Evaluation of Information Systems: A Critique", *Journal of Applied Systems Analysis*, 15.

Walsham Geoff (1999) "Interpretive Evaluation Design for Information Systems", In *Beyond the It Productivity Paradox*, (Eds, Willcocks and Lester) John Wiley&Sons, Chichester.

Weiss Carol (2004) "Rooting for evaluation: A cliff Notes Version of My Work", In *Evaluation Roots - Tracing Theorists' Views and Influences* (Ed, Alkin M) Sage, Thousand Oaks.

Von Wright Georg Henrik (1971) *Explanation and understanding*, Routledge & Kegan Paul, London.

Proposal of a Compact IT Value Assessment Method

Przemysław Lech
Faculty of Management, University of Gdańsk, Poland
Originally Published in EJISE (2007) Volume 10: issue 2

Editor's Comment

This is an ambitions paper. Author Lech takes on the subject from the level of defining value to addressing issues of strategy. Nor is he afraid of being controversial.

After an extensive but interesting literature review the paper reports on a short empirical study which allow the reader to see some of the ideas discussed in action.

Given its practical nature, IT Evaluation research is often focused on developing methodologies and this paper is an excellent example of a successful approach in this area. On top of this the combination of the views of the theoretical and philosophical background supported by the empirical study make this paper even more valuable.

Abstract: This paper contains a proposal of a compact IT value assessment method. It follows the assumption that most methods available for the public are either described in a very general manner or concentrate on one of the evaluation aspects only. The proposed method relates the evaluation approach to the main IT initiative characteristics, such as the investment purpose and IT element to be implemented. Based on these criteria, the evaluation process is shaped by putting emphasis on the relevant evaluation aspects and choosing the relevant evaluation methods. The method design is focused on the ease of use and practical relevance so it can be used by IT practitioners to assess IT initiatives in their organisations. The paper finishes with the case study of the method usage in a mid-sized production enterprise.

Keywords: IT value assessment, IT evaluation, practical method, case study

1. Introduction

Although a large number of IT value assessment methods is available (Renkema and Berghout 1997), still, many enterprises do not use any structured evaluation approach while judging their IT investments (Love and Irani 2004) and if they do, the selection of methods is often limited to the simple cost – benefit analysis tools (Bannister and Remenyi, 2000). Discussing this phenomenon, Bannister and Remenyi (2000, p. 232) conclude that "theory has completely lost touch with reality, the theoreticians have failed to get their message across to practitioners, or the body of theory is still very immature and in all probability far from complete." While these authors have stressed the second possibility, it seems that the first statement is also at least partially true. This paper will try to respond to this statement by introducing a simple and ready to use framework for assessing the most important economical aspects of IT initiatives. The aim of this framework is to help enterprises in conscious decision-making concerning IT initiatives. To meet the requirements of practical relevance and ease of use, it concentrates on the most important IT value aspects and intentionally ignores the others.

2. Practical relevance as a critical success factor

Academic researchers in the IT field are beginning to understand that their work is far away from business practice. Practitioners do not read academic journals and do not attend academic conferences. This is surely not because practitioners neglect the necessity of learning and acquiring new knowledge. The IT world is changing so rapidly that every reasonable practitioner in this field understands the importance of constant learning. If someone needs proof, it is enough to visit a good seminar or congress dedicated to practice. If the practitioners search for new sources of knowledge, want to learn, and still are not present at the academic conferences and are not academic journals' readers, the only conclusion might be that Bannister and Remenyi (2000) were right saying that theoreticians have lost touch with reality. Benbasat and Zmud (1999) have also noticed this fact while analysing the MISQ audience. There is absolutely no doubt about the need of theory building research which might not be directly practice-relevant but then there should be a lot of practical research done based on that theory as well. Davenport and Markus (1999) have concluded that the research in the IT field should contain high science, applied theory and practical research in equal proportions. To answer the question on how to increase the practical relevance of the study, it might be beneficial to examine the theoretical concepts successfully incorporated into the practice. Two examples may be Business Process Reengineering (Davenport 1993, Hammer and Champy 1993) and Balanced Scorecard (Kaplan and Norton 1996). Those examples have several common characteristics which are absent in many other academic books and papers:

- The ideas are based on field experiments – the authors were actually doing the exercise in living companies before describing it in a book or article (it is worth mentioning that at least one of the authors in both cases had a consulting background),
- The ideas are ready to use – with enough time and energy, one can take the book and introduce the idea described in it into her/his organisation.

Complying with those two rules should significantly increase the practical relevance of the research. Examining the existing books and papers on IT evaluation, one can come to the conclusion that it is difficult to find examples of ready-to-use methods suitable for evaluating a wide range of IT investment economic aspects. The indications are either very general (Irani 2002, Renkema 2000, Remenyi et. al. 2000, Willcocks and Graeser 2001) or concentrated only on one specific IT evaluation aspect (Dos Santos 1991, Kaplan and Norton 2004 , Schell 1999). The multi-criteria methods (Parker and Benson 1988, Murphy 2002) are exceptions, but the need to supply more ready-to-use evaluation approaches to the practitioners has already been noticed (Lech 2005, Videira and Rupino da Cunha 2005). This paper is a continuation of the work presented in (Lech 2005) to supply a practically relevant, easy to use evaluation tool.

3. Definition of IT value

As Bannister and Remenyi (2000) pointed out, to be able to assess value, one has to clearly define it. Those authors have discussed the notion of value in detail, citing many definitions, from which the most straightforward one is given by Parker and Benson (1988), stating that IT value is the ability of IT to enhance the business performance of the enterprise. Generalising this definition, one could say that IT value is the ability of IT to support the enterprises' business goals. The business goals will vary from enterprise to enterprise and so the value definition presented here will also be flexible. Of course for most profit oriented enterprises the main goal is to grow and sustain long-term value for the shareholders (Read et. al.

2001, p.11). This value is achieved by the application of a suitable strategy which delivers the answers to the question what tangible and intangible assets should be combined with what processes to create value for a customer (the amount that a customer is willing to pay) that is higher than the cost of creating it (Porter and Millar 1985). If one accepts this definition of value, based on Porter's value chain (1985), it becomes fairly easy to determine the way IT can support the value creation process:

- It can support the strategic and operational goals and thus create value indirectly by allowing the enterprise to act according to the strategy,
- It can generate positive or reduce negative cash flows by decreasing costs, increasing revenues or shortening the operational cycles (from cash to cash) and thus create value directly.
- The weights assigned to those two aspects of value and the way they should be evaluated depend on the characteristics of the IT initiative to be evaluated, such as the investment purpose, the IT element to be implemented and the benefit/cost types.

4. Evaluation method formulation

4.1. What and how to evaluate – the general approach

The two factors constituting the IT business value identified above are:
- Support of the enterprise's business goals,
- Direct return on IT investment.

Those two aspects of IT value are certainly present in the existing evaluation methods. Multi-criteria methods, like Information Economics (Parker and Benson 1988) or '5 pillars method' (Murphy 2002) include the 'strategic match' and 'direct return' as the evaluation parameters. Treating strategy as the 'black box' and assigning one rank only, which states whether the IT initiative supports the strategy or not, seems strongly insufficient. Neither of these methods give indications on how to calculate the direct return. If the evaluation method is to be used in practice, both aspects should be explored in far more detail. The evaluation should answer the detailed questions about what business goals, related to which business processes are supported by the IT solution, how important these goals and processes are in the value creation and to what extent the IT solution is necessary to achieve them. Information Economics evaluates some other

IT initiative characteristics from the business and technology domain. All the characteristics from the business domain, except for risk, should be reflected by the company's goals' analysis. Enterprises may undertake IT initiatives for many strategic, as well as operational reasons. Moreover, usually one initiative would be undertaken for more than one reason and the list of possible IT initiative goals is infinite. By limiting the number of evaluated factors 'ex definitione', one can thus miss the important information. The only characteristic from the business domain that would not come out of the IT initiative goals is the risk. Risk, defined as the uncertainty of achieving the desired goals, has to be incorporated into the evaluation model.

The technology evaluation of business-oriented IT initiatives seems to be less important now than it was in the early 1990's, when multi-criteria evaluation methods were designed. This is because of two main reasons:
- Most IT packages are now available for all leading technology platforms,
- The technology is changing so fast that most enterprises do not treat technology as a fixed, strategic choice

The technology in my opinion should be evaluated mostly from two perspectives:
- Risk factors, which should be added to the risk evaluation,
- As the helping, additional factor while choosing the specific system.

Reassuming, the three main aspects that must be considered during IT business value evaluation are:
- Support of the enterprise's business goals,
- Direct return on IT investment,
- Risk (organisational and technological).

This answers the question of what to evaluate. Then it is necessary to determine how to perform the evaluation of each of the aspects. As it was already stated, the plethora of situations in which IT investment decisions are made virtually exclude the possibility of designing one, rigid evaluation approach. This fact was recognised by some groups of researchers (Bannister and Remenyi 2000, Deschoolmeester et. al. 2004, Farbey et al. 1992, Willcocks and Graeser 2001) who postulate to relate the evaluation methodology to the characteristics of the IT initiative. Such an approach to the evaluation is called the 'meta approach' (Bannister and Remenyi 2000) or 'contingency model' (Serafeimidis and Smithson 1999). In the next section, the indications for creating the evaluation model, based on the main IT initiative characteristics, will be presented.

4.2. Determination of evaluation strategy

The summary of the IT initiative characteristics to which the evaluation method is related in literature is available in (Lech 2005). From the analysis of those characteristics it becomes clear that the main one is the reason for IT investment. The purpose of implementation determines the general evaluation strategy and strongly affects the next steps. The proposal of the purpose – evaluation technique mix is available in (Remenyi et. al. 2000, p. 66). Those general indications must be converted into the more detailed rules of evaluating each of the IT initiative's aspects listed in the previous section. The proposal of a relation between investment purpose and the way those aspects should be evaluated is presented in Table 1.

Table 1: Investment purpose – evaluation strategy own elaboration, based on: Remenyi et al. (2000)

Investment purpose/type	Goal measurement	Direct cost/revenue measurement	Key success indicator
business survival (must-do investments)	IT initiative functional goals (goal achievement)	costs	achievement of the functional costs at the expected cost level
business improvement (operational investments)	operational business goals (goal dependency on the IT initiative, goal achievement)	revenues/costs	operational goals achievement, revenue/cost ratio >1
competitive advantage (strategic investments)	strategic business goals (goal dependency on the IT initiative, goal achievement)	costs or revenues/costs	strategic goal achievement
capacity improvement (infrastructure)	IT initiative functional goals (goal achievement)	revenues/costs	functional goals achievement

The investment purpose is the general factor determining what should be measured. If the investment is a must-do – which means that it is either required by law or is an industry standard, then the main strategic goal lying behind is clear and fixed: 'staying on board'. This business goal is achieved when the functional requirements of the IT initiative itself are fulfilled. The achievement of the IT functional goals (meaning: achievement of the desired functionality of the IT system) is the first evaluation criterion. The business survival investment does not have to be directly profitable as the main benefit from this kind of IT initiatives is the possibility to continue the (possibly profitable) business activity. The cost revenue optimising criterion for such investment should thus be to obtain the desired goal at minimum costs. Direct profitability evaluation can be therefore made for costs only.

The business improvement IT investments are undertaken to achieve operational business goals, which may or may not be directly related to the main strategy of the enterprise. If they are, the IT initiative should be evaluated in the same way as the one that helps to gain competitive advantage. If they are not, the effect of the IT initiative should provide direct benefits that exceed costs. Direct profitability will be the central aspect of the evaluation. Of course, the IT initiative will provide the desired direct benefits only when the operational goals are achieved, so this aspect has to be measured too. Moreover, the role of IT in the achievement of the operational goals may differ from case to case. If the achievement of these goals is not possible without the evaluated IT initiative, its importance will be greater than when it plays only the supportive role and the business goal could be achieved without the IT project. The goal dependency on the IT project will be the third aspect of the evaluation. Strategic investments are undertaken to enable or support the realisation of the enterprise's strategy. Therefore most business benefits come from the strategy, not from the initiative itself. The main evaluation effort should thus be put into assessing the dependency of the strategic goals on the IT project and the degree to which the strategic goals have been achieved. Direct benefits from IT are less important here and in many cases it seems reasonable to track the project costs only.

If the investment has the purpose of increasing the technical capacity, then the achievement of the functional goals (technical specification) will be the main success and thus also evaluation criterion. Achieving these goals may cause some direct benefits (like IT infrastructure maintenance cost reduction) so the cost/benefit analysis should also be performed. An additional benefit will be the option for further development and this may also be assessed in the extended evaluation process. The investment purpose analysis answers the question to what aspects of the IT initiative the main focus of the evaluation should be set. In the next section, the evaluation framework will be presented together with the indications as to what elements of this framework should be used depending on the investment purpose.

4.3. Goal support measurement

The main value of IT comes from creating the possibility of doing the business in a way, which would be impossible without it. Therefore in that case, IT does not create the value directly but acts as an enabler for value-creating business actions. What should be thus measured, from the IT perspective, is:

- The degree to which business goals are dependent on the IT solution (goals' IT dependency),
- The degree to which business goals are achieved (goals' achievement).

The first aspect can be evaluated both before (ex-ante) and after the IT investment (ex post). The business goals achievement can be assessed only during the ex-post evaluation.

4.3.1. IT initiative goals' identification

The first step here is the identification of all business goals related to the evaluated IT initiative. If the business need for IT investment comes from the enterprise's strategy, there is a tool available, allowing to identify and initially evaluate IT initiatives that satisfy this need: the 'strategic readiness report' by Kaplan and Norton (2004). It provides a list of IT applications needed to accomplish the strategic business goals coming from the balanced scorecard, together with the overall rating, stating whether the application is already in place, under construction, needs to be enhanced or developed from scratch. Those applications which have been identified as new or requiring major enhancements constitute a list of strategic IT investments. The main strategic goals which should be achieved with the help of those IT initiatives are also available from the strategic readiness report. However, to be complete, the list has to be worked out in more detail. The strategic goals rarely happen to be achieved directly: more often they would be a result of achieving a set of operational goals. If this is the case, the list of IT initiative business goals should be expanded with these operational goals. The operational goals should be then related to the functional goals of the IT project, stating how the business goals will be realised in the information system. The procedure of converting the strategic business report into the IT initiative goals list is illustrated by figure 1:

The goals above the dotted line come directly from the strategic readiness report, whilst the ones below were added during the IT initiative evaluation process. If the enterprise does not use a balanced scorecard to illustrate its strategy, the list of the IT initiative goals would have to be made independently. For strategic IT projects it will look exactly the same as the one presented on the right-hand side of figure 1 below.

For business improvement initiatives, the list will usually contain only operational business goals and functional goals of the IT project. For business survival and capacity improvement projects, the list might contain only functional goals.

4.3.1. Evaluation of business goals' IT dependency

Having the list of business goals related to the IT initiative, one can start to evaluate the dependency of these goals on IT. This evaluation will be performed mostly for strategic and business improvement investments. The evaluated IT project can play different roles in the achievement of business goals: it can be indispensable for the business goals to be achieved, can play only supportive role, be neutral or even may hinder their achievement. There seems to be no other way of evaluating this aspect than by ranking. The proposition of the ranks is presented in table 2:

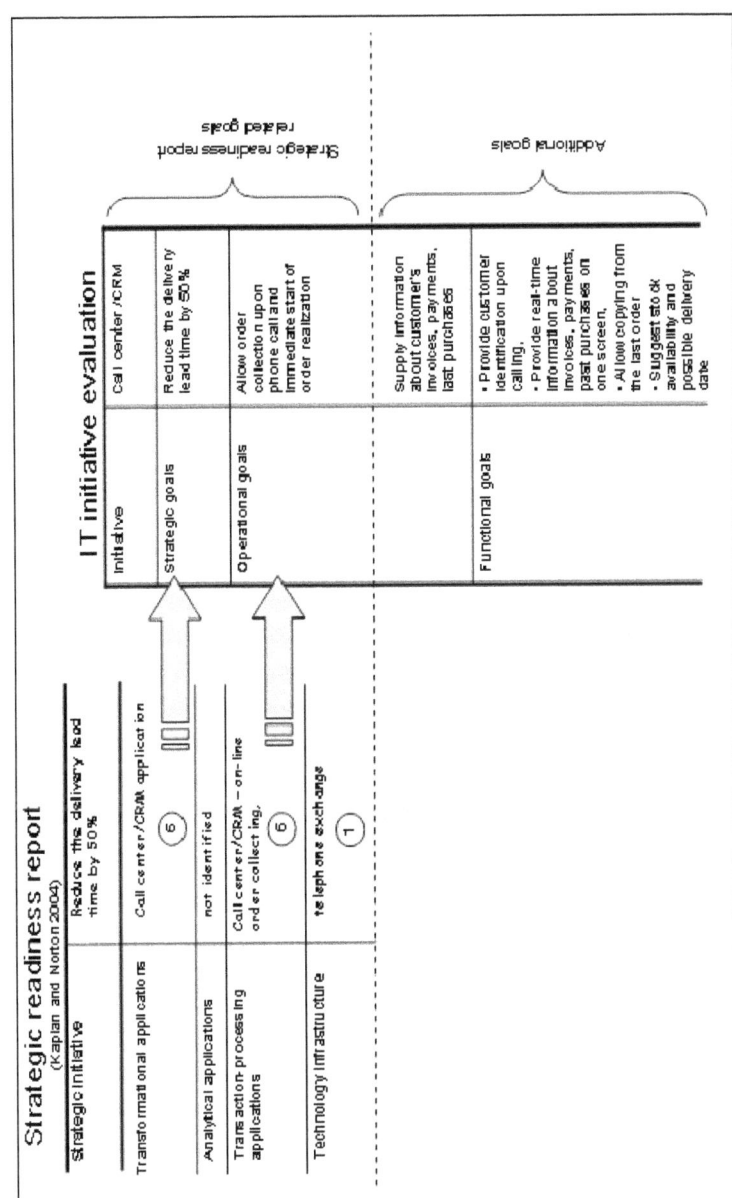

Figure 1. Preparation of the IT initiative goals list elaboration, based on Kaplan and Norton (2004)

Table 2: Ranks for dependency of business goals on IT initiative

Rank	Meaning
3	A goal cannot be achieved without the IT initiative.
2	IT initiative will strongly facilitate the achievement of the business goal. Goal achievement without the IT initiative is theoretically possible but there is strong probability that the result will be weaker.
1	IT initiative has supportive role in the achievement of the business goal. There is a way of achieving the goal without IT.
0	IT initiative has no impact on the possibility of achieving the business goal.
-1	IT initiative may hinder the realisation of the business goal. It may lengthen the time or increase the budget by less than 50%
-2	IT initiative may strongly hinder the realisation of the business goal. If the initiative is undertaken, it may preclude the achievement of the business goal in 100%, lengthen the time or increase the budget by more than 50%
-3	IT initiative makes the achievement of the business goal impossible.

The overall rank will be calculated as the mean of the ranks for business goals related to the IT initiative. If the overall rank for the initiative considered to be strategic is 2 or more, this means that its role in accomplishing the strategy is high and the business value should appear primarily as a result of the strategic initiatives. The evaluation should focus on goal achievement and cost control. If the rank is less than 2, it means that the initiative has only a supportive role for strategy attainment and should rather be treated as a business improvement initiative. Further evaluation should concentrate on direct profitability and business goal achievement. For IT initiatives considered to be operational (business improvement), the overall rank shows its significance in accomplishing the desired goals. If the rank is 2 or more, the initiative should be undertaken. If the rank is less than 2 it is necessary to study carefully all the other options of achieving the desired goals and choose the one with the optimal efficiency.

4.3.2. Evaluation of IT initiative goals' achievement
The next step during ex-post evaluation is the evaluation of the goals' achievement. This evaluation concerns both business and functional goals.

If the business goals' list is prepared based on the strategic readiness report, then each of the goals has some kind of measure assigned to it in the balanced scorecard. If the goals do not come out of the strategic readiness report, then the measures should be assigned to them during the IT initiative goals identification. During ex-ante evaluation, it is necessary to examine each of the goals separately and design the measurement system for each of them. If the enterprise is using some kind of performance measurement system, then this system should be used to evaluate business goals. Functional goals are usually described during the requirements gathering process (which is part of the software engineering that is not the subject of this paper) in such a way, that it is relatively easy to determine, whether the goal is achieved or not.

4.4. Cost, revenue and risk measurement

A lot of work has been already done to identify and classify the IT costs and benefits (Irani 2002, Lucas 1999, Murphy 2002; Remenyi et. al. 2000; Renkema 2000). The list of benefits and costs varies from case to case and must be determined for each IT investment individually. Following Zuboff's (1988) classification of IT benefits, to identify possible benefits one has to formulate and answer the questions like:

- What processes will be automated?
- What will the process cost reduction be?
- Will there be any process error reduction and what is the average cost of an error?
- Will it shorten the process time and what will be the value of finishing the process sooner?
- What new, currently unavailable information will be provided by the IT initiative and what is its value for decision making?
- What information will be available in a shorter time than now and how will it affect the decision making (and the expected value of these decisions)?
- What resources will be released due to the process automatisation and new information?
- What new products and services will be available thanks to IT and what is their value?
- How will IT affect the quality of service, customer care, contacts with customers and how could those be valued?

A good way of structuring the benefit search is to perform the business process analysis workshop, during which each process is analysed with the use of the questions listed above. The list of the questions is of course open and has to be modified during the workshop, according to the current life scenario. Activity-based costing can be a helpful tool in searching for business process cost reduction as well (Roztocki and Weistroffer 2004). Cost identification seems to be an easier task although it is not necessarily the truth (Maanen and Berghout 2002). At least main costs, like licence fee, hardware cost, implementation fee, maintenance cost are in most cases direct, simple costs, easy to identify and value. After the preparation of the benefits and costs list, it is necessary to choose the appropriate measurement method. The description of the commonly used evaluation methods and the process of assigning the method to each cost and benefit is described in (Lech 2005).The last issue is the risk. From the practical point of view, it is more important to identify and manage the risk than to assess its value. The easiest way of incorporating the risk factor into the evaluation model is to reflect each of the benefits and costs as a range with assigned probabilities rather than a fixed value.

5. Field study

The methodology of evaluating IT investments presented above will be illustrated by a field study, performed in a medium-sized production company. The information for this field study was gathered during the life project, carried out according to the methodology presented above in which I was a project leader and leading consultant.

5.1. Description of the company

The company is the country leader in the production of external identification systems. The company produces and installs signing systems for petrol stations, shops, banks etc. Most of the production is made to order and the orders are usually short and non-repetitive. Being the technological leader in the country, the company does not have problems with sales of its products. The main problem that the company faces is the lack of production capacity not allowing it to accept all the orders. Due to this fact, the company has come to the conclusion that implementing a new ERP system would be the solution to this problem. The evaluation has been performed to find out if the implementation of the ERP system would add value to the company.

5.2. Evaluation process description

The evaluation has been performed in the following steps:
- Workshop with the CEO to determine the business goals of the enterprise.
- Preliminary analysis of the existing IT environment
- Business process modelling workshop (direct benefits search)
- Analysis of the:
    - Support of the business goals by the currently performed business processes – proposal of the process change,
    - Support of the processes by the current IT environment,
    - Possibility of supporting the processes with the ERP system.
- Value analysis:
    - Goals achievement,
    - Direct payback.

During the business goals' workshop the following main goals have been identified:
- Increase the production capacity usage by better organisation of the production process (benchmark from a similar company in another EU country stated that there is a possibility to increase the capacity usage by 40 %),
- Keep the currently applied short lead times,
- Keep the possibility to accept orders for non-standard products and offer short lead times for them,
- Eliminate delivery delays,
- Allow the company to analyse the profitability of each order.

The analysis of the currently used IT systems has revealed that the enterprise is using a homemade solution that has most of the functionality needed for production and material planning. Thus a workshop has been performed to find out, how this system is used to support the business processes. The business process-modelling workshop gathered key people from all departments. Each process was examined from the following perspectives:

Process improvement:
- How is the process performed now?
- What could be changed in the process itself to make it better?

- What inputs from the other processes are necessary to make the analysed process better?
- What information is necessary to make the process better?

Process support by IT:

- How is the process supported in the current system?
- What is the reason for not using the available system functionality?
- How should the system be supported by IT (model approach)
- How could the current system be improved to support the process better?

Process value:

- What is the process value for the customer and how will it be improved if the process is changed and properly supported by IT?
- What is the process cost and how can it be reduced?
- What resources do the process use and how these can be reduced?

The data gathered during the workshop has formed the basis for the next analytical steps. It became clear that the problem with low production capacity usage emerges not from the lack of IT support but from organisational problems. IT tools allowing proper material and capacity planning were available in the currently used system but they were omitted by the employees. The ERP system would not solve the problem as it could be omitted as well. It became clear that to support business goals, it is necessary to implement organisational procedures that will force people to input the information about the production process into the system. The value analysis of the two IT variants (enhancements to the current system and implementation of ERP) has been done based on the information gathered during the workshops.

5.3. Results of IT value analysis

The summary of the value analysis is given below. As the IT investment is clearly a business improvement one, it should be performed only if the revenue/cost ratio is more than 1. The aspects to be evaluated are:

- Operational business goals support,
- Direct payback.

Business goals support was evaluated with the use of the ranks presented in Table 3:

Table 3: Evaluation of business goals support

No	Business goal	Current system	ERP	Remarks
1	Increase of the capacity usage	2	3	The use of ERP might lead to the capacity usage increase up to 40% but can cause longer lead times (detailed BOM-s needed) and decrease elasticity in accepting non-standard orders. The use of the simplified production planning in the current system should cause the capacity usage increase by 20%.
2	Keep short lead times	2	-1	The usage of MRP procedure will lengthen the lead times as the detailed BOM and work routings is needed for the new products before the production start.
3	Accept non-standard orders	2	-1	as above
4	Eliminate delays	2	2	
5	Enable profitability analysis	3	3	
	Mean rank	2,2	1,2	

The current system supports the business goals better than ERP.

Possible direct benefits were identified and those, for which it was feasible, were assigned a monetary value. The expected value of the revenue increase due to better capacity usage was estimated as 1 200 000 EUR per year. The reduction of non-rotating stock was estimated as 40 000 EUR per year. Some other possible benefits like transport cost optimisation, better assembly and post sales service planning were identified but it was impossible to assign a value to them. Thus the measurable benefits were estimated to be *1240 000 EUR* per year. The cost analysis of the two variants gave the following results:

Table 4: Estimated costs related to the usage of the current system

Activity	Cost
Prepare and input BOMs and routings for each new product – simplified version (1 employee)	15 000/year
Real time input of all information concerning production	15 000/year

Activity	Cost
(material issues, material returns) (1 employee)	
Necessary enhancements in the current system (internal IT department) 3 months	4 000
TOTAL	34 000

Table 5: Estimated costs related to the ERP implementation

Activity	Cost
Prepare and input BOMs and routings for each new product – full version (2 employees)	30 000/year
License	180 000
Maintenance	25 000
Implementation	240 000
TOTAL	475 000

Providing a similar level of benefits, the usage of the current system is less costly than implementation of ERP. The overall recommendation is to enhance the currently used system as it supports the business goals better and provides better ROI than the ERP suite.

6. Summary

The main aim of this paper was to propose a framework for creating practically relevant, easy to use evaluating methods that would help enterprise managers in taking reasonable decisions concerning IT investments. To keep it as simple as possible, the framework concentrates on the two aspects which seem to be the most important in creating business value of IT: support of the enterprise's goals and direct payback. It relates the IT initiative aspects that should be the subject of evaluation as well as the success criteria, to the investment purpose. It then gives the indications on how to determine the business goals related to the IT initiative and evaluate the support of these business goals with IT. It provides some fingertips for the search of direct benefits as well. The use of the method was illustrated by the field study, which proved its usability for decision making at least in the case being the subject of this study. Of course the method presented here would not solve all real-life IT investment decision problems but it supplies the framework for further development and research

References

Bannister F., Remenyi D. (2000) *Acts of faith: instinct, value and IT investment decisions*, Journal of Information Technology, 2000/15, pp. 231-241

Benbasat I., Zmud R. (1999) Empirical Research in Information Systems: The Practice of Relevance, MISQ, vol 23, no 1, pp 3-16

Davenport T (1993) Process Innovation. Reengineering Work through Information Technology, Harvard Business School Press, Boston

Davenport T., Markus M. (1999) Rigor vs. Relevance Revisited: Response to Benbasat and Zmud, MISQ, vol 23, no 1, pp 19-23

Deschoolmeester D., Braet O., Willaert P. (2004) *On a Balanced Methodology to Evaluate a portfolio of ICT Investments*, in: Proceedings of the 11th European Conference on Information Technology Evaluation, Royal Netherlands Academy of Arts and Sciences, Amsterdam 2004, pp 115-126

Dos Santos (1991) *Justifying Investments in New Information Technologies*, Journal of Management Information Systems, 1991, Spring, vol 7/4, pp 71-90

Engelbert A. (1991) *Scientific information as an economic category,* in: The Economics of Information Systems and Software, Veryard R. (ed), Butterworth – Heinemann, Oxford, pp. 31-43

Farbey B., Land F., Targett D. (1992) *Evaluating investments in IT,* Journal of Information Technology, 1992/7, pp. 109-122

Hammer M., Champy J. (1993) Reengineering the Corporation. A Manifesto for Business Revolution, Harper Business

Irani Z. (2002) Information systems evaluation: navigating through the problem domain, Information and Management, 2002/40, pp. 11-24

Kaplan S., Norton D. (1996) *The Balanced Scorecard: Translating Strategy into Action*, Harvard Business School Press

Kaplan R., Norton D.(2004) *Measuring the Strategic Readiness of Intangible Assets*, HBR, February 2004, pp 53-63

Lech P. (2005) *Evaluation Methods' Matrix – A Tool for Customised IT Investment Evaluation,* Proceedings of the 12th European Conference on Information Technology Evaluation, Turku, pp. 297-306

Love P., Irani Z. (2004) An exploratory study of information technology evaluation and benefits management practices of SMEs in the construction industry, Information and Management, 42, pp. 227-242

Lucas H. (1999) Information Technology and the Productivity Paradox, Oxford University Press, Oxford

Maanen H., Berghout E. (2002) Cost management of IT beyond cost of ownership models: a state of the art overview of the Dutch financial services industry, Evaluation and Program Planning, vol 25, pp. 167-173

Murphy T. (2002) *Achieving Business Value from Technology*, John Wiley and Sons, Chichester

Parker M., Benson J. (1988) *Information Economics*, Prentice Hall, Upper Saddle River

Porter M., Millar V., (1985) *How information gives you competitive advantage,* HBR, July – August, pp. 149-174

Porter M. (1985) *Competitive Advantage,* The Free Press, New York

Read C., Ross J., Dunleavy J., Schuman D., Bramante J., eCFO: Sustaining Value In The New Corporation, John Wiley and Sons, Chichester 2001

Renkema T.(2000) *The IT Value Quest*, John Wiley and Sons, Chichester

Remenyi D., Money A., Sherwood-Smith M. (2000) *The effective measurement and management of IT costs and benefits,* Butterworth-Heinemann, Oxford

Roztocki N., Weistroffer H. (2004) *Using Activity-Based Costing for Evaluating Information Technology Related Investments in Emerging Economies: A Framework*, Proceedings of the Tenth Americas Conference on Information Systems, New York, pp.642-645

Serafeimidis V., Smithson S. (1999) *Rethinking the Approaches to Information Systems Investment Evaluation*, Journal of Enterprise Information Management, January 1999, vol. 12, no. 1-2, pp. 94-107

Schell G. (1999) *Evidence of Information System Value,* [online], EJISE, http://www.ejise.com/volume-3/volume3-issue1/issue1-art2.htm

Videira A., Rupino da Cunha P. (2005), *Evaluating IT Investments: A Manager-Friendly Roadmap,* Proceedings of the 12th European Conference on Information Technology Evaluation, Turku 2005, pp. 501-509

Willcocks L., Graeser V. (2001) *Delivering IT and e-business value,* Butterworth-Heineman

Zuboff S. (1988) In the Age of the Smart Machine: The Future of Work and Power, Basic Books, New York

When Paradigms Shift: IT Evaluation in a Brave New World

Frank Bannister
Trinity College, Dublin

> **Editor's Comment**
> This is a speculative paper which peers into the future. The author, Bannister is an accomplished story teller and he demonstrates his skill in this paper. It is an excellent read whether or not you agree with the vision of the future and all the arguments.

Abstract: Over the years, there have been many avenues explored in the search for ways to measure ICT value. One area where evaluators have sometimes struggled is where new technologies shift paradigms or change the ground rules. When this happens, the concept of value itself can change, making existing methods of evaluation redundant or at least suspect. A further problem is that the impact of the shift itself can be misjudged. This has sometimes resulted in over- and (occasionally) underestimation of the impact of new technology. The irrational value placed on the Internet and Web for e-business during the dot.com boom is a good example of such misjudgement, but it is by no means unique.

An intriguing question is, therefore, how to evaluate ICT when a technological development changes the nature of the problem entirely. The is particularly important at the moment because it is arguable that such a point has now been reached and that the speed and nature of pending technology change presents enormous conceptual and even philosophical challenges for IS evaluation research. In this paper, it is argued that there is a rapidly diminishing window of opportunity in which to get our values and value systems clear before a combination of technological advance and market forces overwhelms our ability to make value choices. This paper explores some potential developments in IT, the difficulties posed for IT evaluation in this context, the risks in this situation and some issues that need to be further explored.

1. Introduction: Thinking outside the box

1.1. A Short Parable

Consider for a moment the electric motor. The electric motor was invented in 1834 by Thomas Davenport, an impoverished, but self-taught, Vermont blacksmith (Wicks, 1999). At the time, the new invention was seen as a possible replacement for other forms of rotational power delivery. Davenport himself saw it as a way of powering the machines in his workshop. Later he came to view it as a possible form of engine for locomotives. Unfortunately for Thomas Davenport, despite patenting his brilliant invention, it did not become commercially successful in his lifetime. In fact its first major commercial success came when somebody had the idea of inverting an electric motor and turning it into a generator. Alas, Davenport never saw this possibility and consequently missed out on making a fortune. He died in 1849, still of modest means.

The relevance of this story in this context is that it illustrates the problem of paradigm limited vision, i.e. people's tendency to overlook the transforming possibilities of new technology. For a long time, the electric motor's potential was considered only in terms of those current technologies that it might replace, i.e. steam, wind and water. Apart from not seeing the potential for electricity generation, nobody at that time dreamed of refrigeration or vacuum cleaners or DVD players. Yet these technologies utterly depend on Davenport's invention. The electric motor was going to change the world – but it was a generation or more before just how much it was going to change things became evident.

This salutary tale informs much of what follows.

1.2. Three categories of evaluation

The time horizons within which IT evaluations are generally discussed, whether this be in the most abstract of theoretical expositions or in the most pragmatic of case studies, fall into three distinct categories:
- First there are studies that focus on the long term historical economic impact of investments in IT. Brynjolfsson (with Hitt and others) have spent many years exploring the so-called productivity paradox and the cumulative effect of investments in IT on organisa-

tions. Brynjolfsson (Brynjolfsson and Hitt 2003) is now sufficiently confident of his findings to pronounce the so-called productivity paradox as near dead as matters and assert that it is now beyond dispute that almost all of the increase in US productivity in the past 20 years is due to IT. Other long term thinkers such as Strassmann (1985) have argued for many years that such effects are only really assessable over even longer periods, maybe as long as half a century.

- Secondly, on a less ambitious scale, there are studies of whether specific investments made over shorter periods have yielded value (or of ways of doing this). Usually such research is in the form of case studies and retrospective analyses. These vary from application of innovative methods to measure value realised to use of well established methodologies such as return on investment, comparison of how different metrics report or combinations of measures (such as the balanced scorecard (adapted from Kaplan and Norton 1992) or the Prudential Appraisal Method (Coleman and Jamieson 1994). Methods can be quite complex as theorists try to distil out the effects of IT from those of other factors and identify the variables that determine the degree of value received. Value for money studies fall into this category.
- Thirdly there is the forward looking segment of the field. This is concerned with ways of assessing whether or not a potential investment in IT is worthwhile. This is probably the most voluminous part of the literature with, by this stage, dozens of techniques for such evaluations being proposed (and sometimes disposed). In the nature of the task, the horizon here is typically fairly short, usually five to ten years though from time to time studies will contemplate a more distant time horizon. Almost all such studies are at the level of the organisation, be it a firm or a public sector body. Evaluation of impacts at the personal or societal level are relatively rare.

All of these analyses have at least one important thing in common; they are all about *existing* information and communications technologies. These technologies[1] may be well established or they may be cutting edge, but in each case the evaluators or researchers are concerned with either

---

[1] The word 'technologies' is used here and elsewhere to mean information technologies unless explicitly stated to the contrary.

the detectable impact of a known technology or the potential impact of a known, albeit sometimes an emergent technology. Such assessments may be of organisations or, as already noted, less commonly of individuals or economies. In all instances, the technology itself, if not its impact, is understood.

1.3. Time for a re-think?

Ironically, the much debated article *IT Doesn't Matter* (now a book less confrontationally entitled *Does IT Matter?*) by Carr (2003, 2004) reflects this same mode of thought. Carr argues that, from a business perspective, there is not much exciting left to come from information technology. It may be possible to build more efficient supply chains, make processes even faster, improve customer relationship management or even find out how to manage knowledge better using machines rather than people or organisations, but if everybody is doing these things, where is the strategic advantage? Carr's thesis *per se* is not the issue in this paper. What is of interest is the nature of some of the attacks on it from scholars and professionals. Several of these argue that Carr's vision is hopelessly limited; that he does not understand the nature of technology nor does he take sufficient account of what is to come (see Stewart *et al*, 2003). An uncomfortable question that might also be asked is can the same criticism be made of IT evaluation? Is it time for IT evaluation researchers to start thinking about what is to come, i.e. outside the box?

It is, of course, well established that technology can have unexpected effects on both individuals and organisations. The way people use a technology may not be that for which it was designed, even where the mechanics of the technology itself are known and well understood. A simple example is the explosion in the use of mobile telephones for text messaging – something not anticipated by the telecoms companies. Another example comes from the early 1980s when there was great excitement about the 'home' PC and all the wonderful things for which people would use them. In practice, those that did not end up gathering dust, ended up being used for playing computer games. The ability of pundits, be they academics or business gurus, to forecast the impact of a technology is far from infallible. If this is true of established technology, how much more true it is likely to be of technology that is not yet with us? It is the conjecture of this paper that there are impending developments in technology for which the weapons currently stockpiled in the arsenal of evaluation techniques are not only inadequate, but are quite inappropriate. This is a bold conjecture and not easy to establish. Nonetheless, this paper will at least try to make the case that there may be a case. In so doing, it will ask some fundamental questions about the nature of evaluation itself in the context of paradigm shifts.

This will be done in two steps. First, although to support the argument it is not necessary to speculate on exactly what the future will be, it is necessary to look at some of the ways that potential developments in information technology could change individuals, organisations and societies over the next few decades. Five probable (or at least possible) developments will be considered. Secondly, it will be argued that contemporary evaluation tools either do not work at all with such developments, or at least do not work very well. Finally there are some reflections on what this might mean in terms of new opportunities for IT evaluation.

2. Brave New Worlds

2.1. Knee Points

"Prediction", said Yogi Berra, *"is very hard, particularly when it's about the future"*. When surveying the world of IT futures, it is not practical to pursue every possible avenue, so what follows is necessarily selective. There are many technologies which have the ability to radically alter the way people live and work, organisations operate and societies function. Many of these are closely interrelated; indeed all are interrelated at some point and it is frequently at the intersection of technologies that the most challenging issues arise. This section describes some of the more immanent possibilities.

An important point to bear in mind is that some of these technologies are approaching what Kurtzweil (1999) calls the 'knee of the curve'. By this he means that point on an exponential growth curve at which a technology which has been growing slowly for some time suddenly takes off. The concept is illustrated in figure 1.

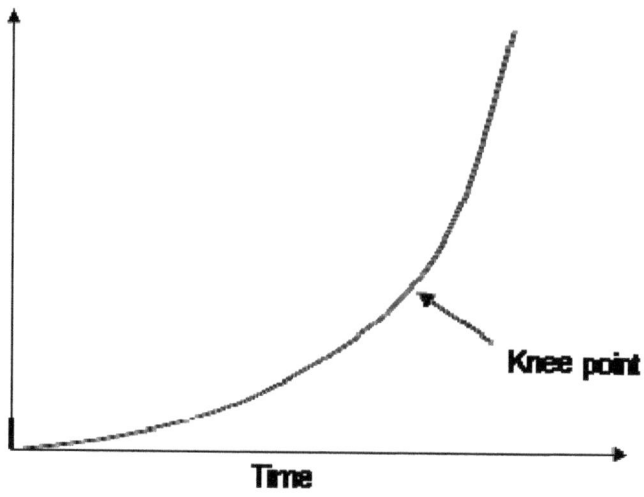

Figure 1: Knee point of a curve

One of the characteristics of a knee point is that once a technology passes it, it becomes exceedingly difficult to control it thereafter. The technology takes on a life of its own and subsequent social or even legal constraint may be impossible. Beyond this point the technology tends, as it were, to find its own level[2]. Whether social control is necessary or even desirable is a debate for another day (for those interested, McKibben (2004) discusses this issue at some length). The point to note here is that the IT/IS evaluation community may be faced with tricky questions about several of these technologies sooner rather than later.

2.2. Artificial Intelligence

Artificial intelligence is a broad church, encompassing technologies from rule based programming to image recognition. Some of these technologies are now at the knee of the curve. Some are still some distance away and yet others would still appear to be in the realms of science fiction though the latter have an increasingly disconcerting habit of become fact. While the areas in which AI is likely to have a radical impact over the next decade are robotics, control systems and localised intelligence/interfaces, the more remote possibilities of consciousness and self awareness need to be

---

[2] It is easy to think of examples of this phenomenon. A pertinent one is the use of performance enhancing drugs in the Olympics. Another example is peer-to-peer sharing of music files.

considered. A key step up on the AI tree is the adapting/learning system. At the most basic of levels this is now commonplace. Contemporary developments in robotics are one aspect of this. Anybody who has used a voice recognition system will be familiar with the concept.

For the purposes of this discussion, robots will be defined as differing from (mere) automation in two ways. First, within limits, they are capable of being programmed to do a wide range of *non predetermined* tasks. Secondly, robot systems have a capability to learn and more advanced systems can adapt to the problems they face and/or the environment that they are in. As a technology, robotics (as opposed to automation) has been slower to take off than many of its more misty eyed advocates anticipated although the market for robotics is forecast to rise to $16 billion by 2007 (Quality 2003). Despite major investments in robotics, today's factories are still extensively dependent on human labour. Where humans have been displaced in the workplace or in the home it has tended to be by automation rather than by adaptive machines. Nonetheless the prognosis must be that robots will eventually be able to do many of the repetitive manual tasks currently done by humans. This may range from fitting a door on a car to serving a burger and fries.

Localised intelligence/interfaces are a more visible (or audible) development in AI. Such systems are already partially embedded in applications such as directory enquiries systems and help lines. When a customer dials a directory enquiry number today, there is a reasonable probability that she will be answered by a computer. Already experiments have taken place with fully automated telephone booking systems and help desks. Current research in Interactive Voice Recognition (IVR) includes emotion recognition so that machines can respond to users more appropriately (Yacoub et al 2003). Such systems try to solve the problem themselves and only pass it to a human operator if they cannot resolve it or for the key decision(s). There is no reason why such systems should not be widespread by the end of the decade even at the level of domestic appliances or office equipment.

The ultimate goal of AI is the self aware or conscious machine. Currently this is still science fiction, the world of the film *The Terminator* or HAL in *2001*. Whether a self aware, thinking computer is possible is hotly debated. Popular authors such a Kurzweil (1999) have long forecast this development. The late Nobel laureate, Francis Crick spent much of his later life trying to establish that the brain was nothing more than a biological machine (Crick and Koch 2003) and many of his fellow life-scientists hold similar views. One of the most noted proponents of this theory in the IT world is Marvin Minsky (1988). Philosophers and others have challenged the concept, one of the most forceful being Penrose (1989, 1995). However, if such a development were to be possible, the evaluation of the consequences would raise profound issues including, *inter alia*, for evaluation.

2.3. Cyborg Technology

If AI is about machines behaving like humans, cyborg technology is about machines merging with humans[3]. This is the world of film *The Matrix* and the television series *The Six Million Dollar Man*. One of the most passionate advocates of this type of technology is Warwick (2003) who has gone so far as to have a chip implanted in his arm[4]. This chip enabled devices in Professor Warwick's laboratory to detect his presence. Doors would open on his approach and greet him. Chip and bolus technology has been the subject of experiments with animals for tracing purposes (where it causes problems, not least from the tendency of such chips to migrate within the animal). In the Netherlands, customers at the Baja Beech club in Rotterdam have chips embedded in their upper arm in order to get automatic access to the VIP area of the club[5]. Humans already walk around with artificial limbs and pacemakers; having intelligent devices on board is only the next logical step.

Putting Radio Frequency Identification (RFID) chips into one's upper arm is one the simplest applications for this type of technology. The ultimate goal is to link the body's own central processing unit, the brain, to the computer. In theory, there are many ways in which this can be done. A crude method is to provide a link to external machines via electrodes attached to the skull. As fiction, this was the theme of Craig Thomas' book *Firefox* (1990) in which the Russians had supposedly developed a fighter aircraft where the pilot's brain was directly connected (via external electrodes in his helmet) into the aircraft's control system. To fire a weapon, for example, the pilot merely needed to think of the required action.

---

[3] Also a common theme in science fiction (e.g. the Borg in the *Star Trek* series or the film *Demon Seed*).
[4] www.wordiq.com/definition/Kevin_Warwick
[5] The author thanks Professor Egon Berghout for drawing his attention to this interesting example.

Enormous research is going into making this particular piece of fiction into fact. With fighter aircraft the race may be between this technology and aircraft that have no pilot at all. Warwick (2004b) describes just such an experiment. A further stage would be to implant such a communications system *within* the brain so that people could connect to a control system or the Internet via (say) WiFi anytime they desired. Imagine a house that responded automatically to one's wishes, that would sense one was cold and turn up the central heating or automatically find the TV programme you wanted to watch or music you wanted to hear. In a business context, such a system would enable employees in an organisation to be in constant contact with each other without the hassle of bulky laptops or vulnerable mobile phones. In the longer term there is the possibility of clustering human brains in the way computers are clustered today. It would certainly give a whole new meaning to the concept of teleconferencing.

The ultimate development of cyborg technology would be with the implantation of enhancing technology within the body itself. To take a silly, but not entirely implausible' example many people are poor at mental arithmetic. Suppose a company developed an arithmetic processor that could be connected to the brain in such a way that the user could pass any arithmetic problem to it and get an answer[6]. Such an enhancement could even be biological in nature (see below). Or what about the ability, as in the film *The Matrix*, to program in any mental skill[7]? Or how about a memory enhancing device? Many of the science fiction features first seen in the television series, *The Six Million Dollar Man* in 1975 are today close to becoming realities. However even the bionic man was confined to increased physical powers; increased mental powers are a different matter entirely.

2.4. Miniaturisation

Another potential source of change, or it may be more accurate to say a catalyst for change, comes from developments in areas such as nanotechnology, biotechnology and quantum computing. At the moment, the first of these is nearer to large scale practical application (for IT) than either of the latter. Nonetheless the possibilities for radical change here are formidable. Biologically based computing, for example, offers the potential to put vast amounts of processing power into the tiniest spaces – a few

---

[6] Readers who think this is far-fetched might wish to look at Warwick (2004a).
7 Programming in physical skills presents more fundamental problems!

spoonfuls of water according to one group of Israeli researchers[8]. Quantum computing offers even more staggering possibilities in terms of power per cubic nanometre. As a result, the potential exists to build in, say, a high level of intelligence into any machine or device not to mention into humans. There are also implications in, for example, cryptography where quantum computing could lead to unbreakable codes (Singh 1999).

Miniaturisation is not, in itself, that significant from an evaluation perspective. After all, the world has lived with Moore's law for three decades now. It is when miniaturisation is combined with developments in AI and cyborg technology that is acquires critical significance. To take but one aspect of this, contemporary surveillance systems still have a limited ability to process the amount of information they gather. The ECHELON system may be able to monitor most of the world e-mail, but it relies on slow and unreliable keyword searching to deduce information (Bamford 2001, Levy 2001). A quantum computing system could read every e-mail, listen to every mobile telephone conversation and digest the contents from every CCTV camera on the planet – a thought that gives a whole new meaning to the concept of a surveillance society. A particular case of miniaturisation is the concept of nanobots. Applications for nanobots are legion from cleaning up waste to keyhole surgery. Most of these applications are benign, but there are risks of undesirable consequences, in particular in control of such technology and in undesirable uses.

2.5. Networking

In many ways, networking is the most prosaic of trends. Unlike some of the technologies discussed in the preceding sections, this is a here and now. The means to connect and collect is already developed if not yet widely deployed. Although, unlike some of the other technologies discussed, the impact of networks is moderated by basic logistical constraints, when combined with artificial intelligence and miniaturisation then the potential effects are profound.

For example, in theory networks could connect everybody in the world or in a state to a central 'nervous system' of some sort. A crude version of this already occurs with the telephone system. Mobile phone systems mean that people can be contacted any time and (provided they leave their phone on) their movements traced. Already some nervous wealthy

---

[8] http://search.eurekalert.org/e3/query.html?col=ev3rel&qc=ev3rel&qt=drop+of+water

parents are putting RFID chips into their children so that they can trace them if they get lost or are kidnapped. Tagging of criminals is common. It is not difficult to envisage a world where the whereabouts of anybody is knowable at any time, and where everybody who does not make energetic efforts to avoid it is linked into some soft of universal communications matrix. There are considerable attractions in this for some people. The fact that people are prepared to leave their mobile phones on in place as diverse as bathrooms and lecture theatres suggests that many of us are all too willing to be on-call 24 hours a day. From an evaluation perspective, this presents quite complex challenges. What of the risks? What if a virus got into such a network, a possibility explored in fiction by Stephenson (1993). Like the other technologies, networks present opportunities and risks and it is this that causes problems for evaluators.

2.6. Electronic Identification

A related issue electronic identification. Reference has already been made to the surveillance society. However there is a broader issue here than a simple fear of big brother looking over everybody's shoulder. It is will shortly be within the reach of technology to issue a citizen identity card with unique identifying information such as a person's DNA or retina pattern to all citizens. Identity cards have been a fact of life in many countries democratic as well as undemocratic for decades. Some countries, including the UK and Ireland do not have a citizen identity card although the UK government is keen to introduce one (Stephens 2004).

There are obvious benefits from a universal identification system from countering terrorism to preventing fraud. Apart from the implications for privacy and civil liberties, there are also risks from identity theft. These risks differ by an order of magnitude when an identity system become electronic. In a society that is ever more dependent on carrying an increasing volume of personal identification, the downside risks to both citizens and society increase. To make matters more complicated, questions of freedom and the nature belonging to a society means are made more complicated. Can somebody remain a citizen without having a card? What is the position of those who refuse to comply? For evaluators, these questions raise difficult issues with soft benefits and disbenefits which have, to date, seen little discussion within the community.

3. Some Problems in Evaluation

3.1. Conventional Methods

Traditional or conventional evaluation of IT assumes that IT has a cost (which may or may not be exclusively financial) and benefit(s). The central question in most of the literature is how to measure these benefits (although as Bannister *et al* (2003) have argued, measuring the cost is not that straightforward either). Benefits can be individual, organisational, economic or social or any combination of these, but, and it is an important 'but', the nature of the change wrought neither threatens the whole basis of society nor our social understanding nor our understanding of ourselves. Each of these is relevant in the context of potential future developments. If the evaluation community has struggled with valuing the impact of current systems and technologies, then the problems in evaluation discontinuous technologies are likely to present an even more formidable challenge.

3.2. Buying some brainpower

To illustrate the problems it is easiest to use examples. Taking cyborg technology as an example, consider the following thought experiment.

A computer company produces an electronic device which can be connected directly to a human brain in order to enhance a person's mathematical ability. John, a dealer in the financial services industry, is contemplating having such a device installed. It is quite expensive, costing, say, €100,000 including implantation and after sales support. There are no known risks from this technology and running costs are minimal although its estimated working life is 20 years. How might this be evaluated?

In this instance, the financial cost is clear. What about the benefits? A crude approach might to be assess the increase in John's lifetime earning power or by (say) his ability to make a killing on the futures exchange through a capacity to compute arbitrage rates faster than the market. Adopting this worldview, standard return on investment techniques can be used and value can be quickly assessed. There might also be slightly more subtle benefits from enhancements to John's lifestyle. He may be able to impress his friends with his mathematical skill or keep track of what he spends in a supermarket as he fills up his trolley. The feeling of well-being from this might be worth something although adaptation (Schwartz 2004) makes it likely that this effect will sooner or later wear off. Furthermore, the pleasure might be diluted by the vague feeling that he is cheating, that this ability is not really 'his', but that of a device to which he has access.

Another question is who pays the €100,000? If John pays it from his own resources, then there is one kind of evaluation problem. If his employer pays it, then the issues are different[9].

3.3. On being human

All of the above questions are easily to deal with when compared to the problems raised by the following awkward question: *is John the same person that he was before the implant?*

It could be argued 'yes he is' if one follows the line that John's improved ability is not really 'his' at all. Apart from integration and speed, there is no essential difference between John and somebody with a good laptop and fast fingers. John's integrity as an individual is not therefore compromised. On the other hand, it can also be argued that there *is* a difference between such an implant and a laptop. The laptop is out there. Anybody can use it. It can be switched off. The implant is uniquely attached to John, it may even be personalised or tailored to his physiology, and the question *'does John still exist apart from the implant?'*, especially if the implant were biological, is a valid one. Furthermore, would John be able to differentiate between the implant and his 'normal' brain. And if one answers no to that question, then some part of John has changed: certainly his ability has been enhanced, but his integrity as an individual has been diminished or at least altered by the fact that he is now partially constructed. The question then is, what is the value of this change/loss?

To make this case more vivid, suppose that instead of a computational implant, John has a memory implant. As the computational implant contains powers John does not have, so the memory implant can contain information that John has not 'learned'. It might contain a dictionary or an encyclopaedia or two or a language module. And how about some pre-programmed happy memories? It is alleged (it is a much debated topic) that the brain can generate its own false memory (Stanton 1997); imagine what it could do with a little technical help. This raises uncomfortable

---

[9] In answer to the obvious question why would an employer pay for such a device, the short answer is that employers currently pay to improve their employees in various ways from putting them on training courses to giving them free medical check-ups.

questions about the meaning of reality, at least from John's perspective. He may be unable to distinguish his real past from an artificial past created for him. Again this issue has been explored in science fiction. One of the most famous examples is by Dick (2002)[10]. It needs to be explored in the evaluation community.

The question that arises in both these scenarios of what it means to be human? Is John more or less human because of these enhancements, or is the nature of his humanity unaffected. He now has increased powers, but less integrity, because he is now, in part, designed by somebody else. However John also has an artificial hip and two dental crowns. Is the brain implant qualitatively different? Furthermore, his perception of reality is in part constructed by outsiders and is not part of his authentic experience. Pushing this to extremes, it is possible to envisage a whole range of IT-powered enhancements that might improve John's 'performance' at the progressive expensive of altering who John is. Is this a cost and if so should it be added to the financial cost of the implant? Even the counter argument that as long as his personality is unchanged, John is unchanged, does not stand up to close scrutiny. How is it possible to disconnect personality or behaviour from memory for example? Finally, how are such benefits and 'costs' to be evaluated?

3.4. What is a Life?

Another type of problem (if not several such problems) is/are posed by AI. To take an extreme case, suppose that a self-aware, conscious machine is developed. By any definition this would be a new life form. Furthermore, given the dynamics of the situation, unless its design specifically inhibited it, it is likely to be a form of intelligence that will rapidly surpass the mental capacity of its inventors (provided that is they keep supplying it with the extra processing power and memory it needs) [11]. The impact of such a development on humanity, not to mention business, is hard to assess. Like cloning and genetic engineering, a conscious machine may subtly (or maybe not so subtly) change the meaning of what it is to be human or at least our understanding of ourselves. This poses major problems for evaluation of such technology. How would one value such a creation? Philosophers, politicians and insurance companies debate the value of a

---

[10] This short story was the basis of the film 'Total Recall'.

[11] Dick (1968) also wrote a famous book on this subject. It was made into the film 'Blade Runner'. In the story, the lifespan of androids is deliberately kept short.

human life. What value would one put on such a machine life (even if it did not have any feelings)? Even avoiding this question, what are the business implications? Such a machine might soon make most managers redundant. This may be cost effective, but the implications for those making the investment could be redundancy and given that many large corporations these days seem to be run mostly for the benefit of managers (Galbraith 2004), who would want to make such a decision?

3.5. Joining the matrix

Another example is the potential of new technologies to disrupt society in too short a time for humanity, be it individuals, organisations or societies to react, is the ability of computers to intrude into people lives. One of the most difficult of evaluations is the trade off between personal security and privacy. With modern technology, it is possible to make people's lives more secure in a variety of ways. Identity cards with biometric information, closed circuit television, RFID tagging, mobile phone tracking and other technologies can be employed to ensure that citizens are not defrauded, mugged, kidnapped or lost. But this is achieve at a price to privacy and a risk of misuse by private organisation or by the state.

Balancing risks in this situation is not simple and again represents a challenge to the evaluation community. A large part of the problem in evaluation is the asymmetry in risk perception. People perceive the risks from, say, injury in a terrorist attack to be much higher than it is in practice. In parallel, they fail to perceive potential risks to freedom, privacy and even democracy from technologies ostensibly designed to prevent terrorist attacks. Recently two US commentators, Dash (2004) and Rosen (2004) have looked at this problem from a broad perspective. However it is also an IT evaluation problem and one which, to date, the evaluation community has given little or no attention.

3.6. Problems for evaluators

The problem for the evaluator of the type of technological developments outlined above is which evaluation techniques are appropriate? Financial and economic methods hardly seem appropriate. Consumer satisfaction, organisational improvement, information economics, balanced scorecards; none of these seem adequate to cope with the philosophical problems raised. Questions of risk, judgement, bias, uncertainty, humanity, meaning and society are all impacted by these developments. The English poet John Donne once wrote that *'no man is an island entire of itselfe'* and this has never been more true than it is today. An investment by any business in these technologies affects far more than the business. Evaluation cannot be ring fenced in these circumstances.

The more transformative an IT induced change, the more difficult is can be to evaluate. There are several reasons for this. First, as was pointed out above, the metrics applicable in the before and after situation may not be the same because, to use a well known phrase, apples are not being compared with apples. This may not be a problem when looking at the investment in retrospect, but it is a definite difficulty in *ex ante* evaluation. The problem here is that the type of change that might happen with these technologies is more than merely transformative, it is discontinuous. It represents a potential radical departure from the known.

Secondly, the more transformative the change, the more likely it is that evaluation will depend on subjective metrics, i.e. metrics which depend on the views or judgments of actors and in particular 'experts' and so-called gurus. It is clear that such views and judgments are not just problematic from a psychological and judgemental perspective, but are time dependent, so the impact may depend on when the measurement is taken (Schwartz 2004, Myers 2002).

Thirdly, the more transformative a technology, the greater the degree of uncertainty about the outcome and the greater the scope for errors of judgment. The law of unintended consequences will inevitably apply. There are many cases of IT investments where the result has not been quite what was expected[12]. In evaluating technologies such as AI and cyborg technology, IT evaluation may therefore have to make much more extensive use than heretofore of general risk evaluation tools such as scenario analysis (see, for example, Wright 2001) and sophisticated risk analyses methods.

In summary, the challenge presented by some of the technologies now evolving is that they are more than radically transformative, they are discontinuous technologies. The evaluation toolset currently available is not capable of providing meaningful assessments of such technologies. It is

---

[12] For an amusing, but insightful, collection of examples see O'Boyle (2000) or Harvey-Jones and Tibballs (1999)

necessary to reach not just for new methods, but for deeper philosophical tools.

4. Some Reflections

In his keynote speech at the 10th European Conference on IT Evaluation (ECITE) in Madrid in 2003, John Ward, reviewing the state of IS evaluation ten years after the first ECITE, suggested that maybe after three decades of academic attention, the topic of IT evaluation was running out of steam. There were many hundreds of papers, books and articles now in print on the topic, but there was still no one agreed approach or agenda. Instead there was a large toolkit of techniques, none of which was entirely satisfactory and which users therefore mixed and matched as the circumstances required.

A more accurate reflection (as a glance of the proceedings of that particular conference shows) would have been that there is no shortage of new ideas, interesting case studies, new applications and new ways of combining techniques around. Research and thinking in the field remains healthy and active; special issues of journals on the topic of IS evaluation are still being published. But it is probably accurate to say that there have been no big conceptual breakthroughs in quite some time (although there are some approaches that may hold promise, for example Halpin and Stapleton's (2003) application of complexity theory to post implementation evaluation). Pluralism is increasingly the name of the game. Approaches to evaluation tend to be holistic and reflective (Cronk's (1999) concept of 'holistic construal' is a good example of this school of though) of the complex realities that are involved in all but the most simple of situations. A good example of this type of rounded approach can be found in Curley (2004).

This paper proposes a radical new line of enquiry for evaluation of IT, one that looks beyond the known and the short term future and contemplates the impacts of discontinuous technology. In so doing, this paper has raised questions rather than attempt to provide answers. One possible way forward is for the world of IT evaluation to engage much more with current thinking in decision sciences and in risk analysis. Nonetheless there remains a major intellectual challenge in evaluating discontinuous developments. Evaluation here has to move beyond the financial and economic, beyond the conceptual toolkit of the current literature and even beyond questions of risk and uncertainly into fundamental questions about the nature of organisations, humanity, meaning and society. For a subject that is engaged with technology, IT evaluation has tended to be fairly tame in its remit[13]. Dealing with the types of challenge and potential for discontinuous change which IT may present over the next few decades will require new tools and engagement with philosophers from Wittgenstein to Midgley who have wrestled with this problem. What may emerge from this may be quite different from the type of discourse that has dominated the field since these issues were first broached in the 1960s.. To paraphrase another piece of science fiction, it may be evaluation Jim, but not as we know it.

References

Bamford, J. (2001) Body of Secrets: How America's NSA and the UK's GCHQ eavesdrop on the world, Century Books, London.

Bannister, F., McCabe P. and Remenyi, D. (2003) "IS costing: the case for a reference model", Southern African Business Review, 7, 1, 1-16.

Brynjolfsson, E. and Hitt, L. (2003) "Computing Productivity: Firm-Level Evidence", MIT Sloan Working Paper No. 4210-01, June 2003.

Carr, N. (2003) "IT Doesn't Matter", Harvard Business Review, May 2003, 41-49

Carr, N. (2004) Does IT Matter?, HBS Press, USA.

Coleman, T. and M. Jamieson (1994) "Beyond return on investment: evaluating ALL the benefits of information technology" in Willcocks, L. (Ed.), Information Management, The evaluation of information systems investments, Chapman Hall, London, pp 189-206.

Crick, F and Koch, C. (2003) "A Framework for Consciousness", Nature Neuroscience, 6. 2, February 119-126.

Cronk, M. (1999) "Understanding Complex Information System Constructs through Holistic Construal" in Brown A. and D. Remenyi (Eds.), Proceedings of ECITE 1999, Trinity College, Dublin, pp 69-76.

Curley, M. (2004) Managing Information Technology for Business Value: Practical Strategies for It and Business Managers, Intel Press.

Dash, S. (2004) The Intruders: Unreasonable Searches and Seizures from King John to John Ashcroft, Rutgers University Press, New Jersey.

---

[13] There are, of course, some exceptions to this general rule!

Dick, P.K. (1968) Do Androids Dream of Electric Sheep?, Del Ray Books

Dick, P.K. (2002) "We can remember it for you wholesale", in Selected Stories of Philip K. Dick - Volume 2, Pantheon Books.

Galbraith, J.K. (2004) The Economics of Innocent Fraud, Houghton Miflin, Boston, MA.

Halpin, L. and Stapleton, L. (2003) "A theoretical framework based on complexity theory for evaluation of large-scale Information Systems Development projects", in Remenyi, D. (Ed.), Proceedings of the 10th European Conference on IT Evaluation, MCIL, Reading, UK, 297-306.

Harvey-Jones, J. and Tibballs, G. (1999) Business Blunders, Constable and Robinson, London.

Kaplan, R.S and D.P. Norton (1992) "The balanced scorecard - measures that drive performance", Harvard Business Review, Jan-Feb, 70, pp 71-19.

Kurzweil, R. (1999) The Age of Spiritual Machines: When Computers Exceed Human Intelligence, Penguin Books, New York.

Levy, S. (2001) Crypto, Viking (Penguin books), Harmondsworth, UK.

McKibben, B. (2004) Enough, Staying human in an engineered age, Owl Books, New York.

Minsky, M. (1988) Society of Mind, Simon and Schuster, New York.

Myers, D. (2002), Intuition: Its powers and perils, Yale University Press, New Haven, CT.

O'Boyle, J. (2000) Wrong: The biggest mistakes and miscalculations made by people who should have known better, O'Mara Books, London

Penrose, R. (1989) The Emperor's New Mind, Oxford University Press, Oxford.

Penrose, R. (1995) Shadows of the Mind, Oxford University Press, Oxford.

Quality (2003) Robotics Market to Double by 2007, 42, 9, p15.

Rosen, J. (2004) The Naked Crowd: Reclaiming Security and Freedom in an Anxious Age, Random House, New York.

Schwartz, B. (2004) The Paradox of Choice, Harpur Collins, New York.

Singh, S. (1999) The Code Book: The science of secrecy from ancient Egypt to quantum cryptography, Fourth Estate, London.

Stanton, M. (1997) "U-Turn on Memory Lane", Columbia Journalism Review, July/August, 36,2, 44-49.

Strassmann, P. (1985) Information Payoff: the Transformation of work in an electronic age, Free Press, New York.

Stephens, P. (2004), " A prime minister with no regard for liberty", Financial Times, December 21st 2004.

Stephenson, N. (1993) Snowcrash, Penguin Books, New York.

Stewart, T. and others (2003) Do IT Matter? An HBR Debate. Letters to the Editor, Harvard Business Review, June, 1-17.

Thomas, C. (1990) Firefox, Harper Paperbacks, UK.

Warwick, K. (2004a) "Linking Human and Machine Brains - Why you should volunteer", Proceedings of the 5th International Conference on Creative Thinking, ed. S.Dingli, Malta University Press, to appear (2004)

Warwick, K. (2004b) "Mind Blending", People Management, 10, 7, 32-33.

Warwick, K. (2003) "Cyborg morals, cyborg values, cyborg ethics", Ethics and Information Technology, 5, 3, 131-137.

Wicks, F. (1999) "The Blacksmith's Motor", Mechanical Engineering, July.

Wright, G. (2001) Strategic Decision Making: A Best Practice Blueprint, John Wiley & Son, UK.

Yacoub, S., S. Simske, X. Lin and J. Burns (2003) "Recognition of Emotions in Interactive Voice Response Systems" paper presented at Eurospeech 2003, 8th European Conference on Speech Communication and Technology, 1-4 September 2003, Geneva, Switzerland.

Available at *www.hpl.hp.com/techreports/2003/HPL-2003-136.pdf*.

The Eleven Years of the European Conference on IT Evaluation: Retrospectives and Perspectives for Possible Future Research

Egon Berghout[1] and Dan Remenyi[2]
[1]University of Groningen, The Netherlands
[2]Trinity College Dublin, Ireland
Originally Published in EJISE (2005) Volume 8: issue 2

Editor's Comment

Is it not true that research is supposed to answer a question? If this is so why have we not been able to answer the question of IT evaluation. There are hundreds of academics around the world and maybe as many consultants working on this subject. Thousands of papers have been published. Maybe IT evaluation is not a question after all. Maybe it's a journey and a journey whose destination can and does shift with new developments on technology. And there are also new developments in our knowledge of how to use the technology.

This paper reports on 11 years of this journey as seen through the papers presented at the European Conference on IT Evaluation. Authors Berghout and Remenyi provide an excellent introduction into IT Evaluation research.

Abstract: This paper provides an overview of the papers that have been presented at the European Conference on IT Evaluation during the past eleven years. It considers the main issues, and learning themes addressed in papers presented to these Conferences. The paper also reflects on the possible future direction, which this research may take and three major research themes are suggested. Some 356 papers have been presented at ECITE. Over the eleven year period it is clear that the level of understanding as reflected in the papers has significantly increased. Themes, which were particularly well addressed, include IT and IS value, the multidisciplinary nature of evaluation, the Importance of stakeholder analysis, organisational learning and life cycle management. Three issues are identified as particularly important for further research. These are, the theoretical underpinning of IT evaluation, improving the data sets for research and establishing a more common core of concepts.

Keywords: IT, IS, Evaluation, Theoretical frameworks, empirical research, case studies, questionnaires, core concepts, corporate politics, data sets, research maturity.

1. Introduction

This paper describes the research conducted by those who have presented papers at the European Conferences on IT Evaluation (ECITE). It is a high level overview of the proceedings of these Conferences and is based on the papers published during the first eleven proceedings. The purpose of this paper is to facilitate an understanding of the thrust of research in this field of study and to reflect on its possible future direction.

The objective of ECITE, which has remained constant throughout the eleven-year period, is to provide a platform for academics and professionals to join together and discuss the theory and practice of the evaluation of information technology. The first ECITE was held at Henley Management College on the 13th-14th of September 1994.

The first paper in the first issue of the conference proceedings concludes by stating: '…. *IT costs have been growing by rates of about 15% p.a. over the last decade.' 'This rate of growth is far in excess of the growth in the underlying businesses and cannot be sustained into the next century*' (Dier and Mooney, 1994, p.11). This statement, although perhaps a little naïve, clearly indicated the relevance of the research. Considering the current state of the IT industry it also illustrates that evaluation research may be thought of as being unable to achieve a soft landing. This overview of the 10 conferences, therefore, addresses what might be regarded as research highlights in terms of vision and practical relevance and at the same time it also considers problems such as industry impact.

Questions addressed in this paper are:
- What type of researchers contributed to the IT evaluation conferences?
- What type of research questions were addressed?
- What were the most prominent research findings?
- What other interesting research questions are suggested?

2. Background of participating researchers

ECITE has always been a small specialist Conference. It was never intended that it should attract large numbers of papers or attendees and thus the focus of the Conference has been retained. During the eleven years 513 authors contributed to the conference. Of this group 458 were academics and 55 authors had an industry background (11%). A number of authors contributed on multiple occasions to the conference. In the second and third conference 30% of the authors had also contributed to previous ones. As the conference grew so this ratio changed. For the last three years this number was 9%.

The conference has been held in the UK, in the Netherlands, in Ireland, in France and Spain.

Although the conference is referred to as a European conference, ECITE has always welcomed contributions from authors around the globe and there have been papers presented from 38 different countries. Of these 38 there have been 17 different European countries as well as the USA, Australia, South Africa, New Zealand and several Asian counties. The largest number of contributions to the conference have come from the UK (34,9%), Australia (9,4%) and Netherlands (9,4%) as shown in Figure 1.

Country of origin	Quantity	%
Australia	48	9.4%
Austria	5	1.0%
Bangladesh	1	0.2%
Belgium	12	2.3%
Brazil	2	0.4%
Canada	6	1.2%
Chile	1	0.2%

Leading Issues in IS Evaluation Research

Country of origin	Quantity	%
Denmark	5	1.0%
Estonia	1	0.2%
Finland	32	6.2%
France	12	2.3%
Germany	15	2.9%
Greece	5	1.0%
India	1	0.2%
Indonesia	1	0.2%
Ireland	30	5.8%
Italy	9	1.8%
Korea	3	0.6%
Latvia	1	0.2%
Luxemburg	3	0.6%
Mexico	3	0.6%
Netherlands	48	9.4%
New Zealand	3	0.6%
Norway	2	0.4%
Poland	1	0.2%
Portugal	2	0.4%
Romania	1	0.2%
Saudi Arabia	1	0.2%
Seychelles	1	0.2%
Slovakia	2	0.4%
South Africa	17	3.3%
Spain	9	1.8%
Sweden	21	4.1%
Switzerland	4	0.8%
Tunisia	1	0.2%
Turkey	2	0.4%
UK	179	34.9%
USA	23	4.5%

Figure 1: Nationality of researchers

With only 11% of conference attendees coming from industry it is clear that this combination of academics and practitioners could be improved. For two of the years the conference supported a doctoral colloquium.

3. How the research papers were focused

The evaluation of IT encompasses many topics and this diversity is reflected in the papers. A total of 356 papers were published in the proceedings. It is interesting to note that the majority of the papers are based on case study research, representing 52,7%.

There was a diverse range of topics and this paper considers the research under the following categories:
- Types of information systems;
- Industry sectors;
- Geographical areas;
- Organisation of the overall information function;
- Development of particular evaluation methods;
- Theoretical foundation of evaluation.

3.1. Types of Information Systems researched

A plethora of information system types have been investigated. Examples are:
- Executive information systems (ElKordy, et al., 1997; Carlsson, 1998).
- Strategic information systems (Spil, 1995; Deitz, 1995; Savolainen, 2000).
- Electronic data interchange (EDI), (Hoogeweegen, et al., 1994).
- Manufacturing information systems (Wheeler and Chang, 1994; Bonner, 1995; Ezingeard, 1998; Coronado, 1999).
- Knowledge based systems (Clark and Soliman, 1996; Poon, 1999; Savory, 2001; Tyndale 2002).
- Workflow (Kueng, 1998; Grunden, 2002).
- Intranets (Magrill and Brown, 1997).
- Electronic commerce (Miller, et al., 1999; Stamoulis, 1999; Lee, 1999; Cherian, 2001; Al-Mashari and Al-Samad, 2002; Beyno-Davies, 2002;).
- Groupware (Josefsson and Nilsson, 1999).

- Enterprise systems (Ezingeard and Chandler-Wilde, 1999; Stefanou, 2000; Stafyla and Stefanou, 2000; Al-Mudimigh, et al., 2001; Hillam and Edwards, 2001; Al- Mudimigh and Al-Mashari, 2002).
- Customer relationship management systems (CRM) (Ezingeard, et al., 2001; McCalla, et al., 2002).
- Infrastructures (Renkema, 1997).
- Development tools (Addison and Sutherland, 1995).
- Evaluation of Transhuman technology (Bannister 2004)

These papers typically addressed ex ante assessments of the above systems investigating the potential value of investment in these areas. In general the researchers are quite successful in this type of investigations. However, it is clear from the analysis of these papers that the authors are also often uncertain about the correctness or validity of their outcomes. This is probably caused by the fact that the researchers are not often able to study the actual realisation and outcome of the projects researched. However, most of these information system based papers also lack a theoretical underpinning of their methodology, which results in additional uncertainty about their measurement instrument. Due to the labour intensiveness of case study research the number of involved organisations was also limited.

3.2. Industries researched

Many papers refer to particular industry sectors. Examples are:
- Healthcare, which is also the most often researched topic overall (Kaplan, 1995; Lock, 1996; Murray and Dhillon, 1996; Peterson and de Wit, 1997; Salmela and Turunen, 1997; Vlug and Lei, 1999; Niss, 1999; Orr et al., 1999; Protti, et al., 2000; Suomi and Tahkapaa, 2001; Bergamaschi and Ongaro, 2001; Turunen, 2001; Ammenwerth, et al., 2002;Carson et al, 2004
- Telecom industry (Peterson and de Wit, 1997; Demkes, 1997; Lampikoski and Rusi, 2002; Cheverst et al, 2004).
- Small and medium sized enterprises (SME), McNutt and O'Donnell, 1997; Hillam and Edwards, 1999; Dans, 2000; Dans, 2001; Johansson and Carlsson, 2002).
- Public sector (Newton, 1995; Worrall, et al., 1998; Oliver, 2000).
- Financial services industry (Nijland and Berghout, 2000; Maimbo and Pervan, 2002; Diniz et al, 2004).

It is clear that evaluation research requires insight into specific industry practice. Without this contextual knowledge the assessment of competitive advantage or organisational improvements is extremely difficult. Through focusing on a particular industry sector, researchers are better able to understand industry contexts and validate elements of the evaluation framework. However it is interesting to note that authors frequently do not retain the industry specific focus when discussing their conclusions. And thus too much is sometimes made of the finding from what is essentially a narrow focused study.

3.3. National focus

Many studies have referred to a particular geographical area. Examples are:

- United Kingdom (Miller and Dunn, 1997; Stansfield, et al., 2000).
- The Netherlands (Nijland and Berghout, 2000; Stansfield, et al., 2000).
- Spain (Arribas, 1996; Arribas and Ingusta, 1997).
- South Africa (Hart, 1999; Sutherland, 1994, Pather et al, 2004).
- Australia (Cronk, 1999; Myles, et al., 2000; Singh and Byrne, 2004).
- Belgium (Deschoolmeester and Braet, 2000).
- Romania (Avram, 1999; 2000).
- Greece (Mitris and Serafeimidis, 1994).
- Denmark (Andersen, 1999).
- Ireland (O'Donnell and O'Regan, 2000).
- Saudi Arabia (Al-Turki, 2000)
- Sweden (Frisk and Planten, 2004)
- Finland (Kontio, 2004)

These papers often suggest that they provide state-of-the-art overviews of IT evaluation in a particular country and thus these studies do include regional specific elements of evaluation. The way groups or cultures deal with corporate dimensions such as power, user participation and risk are major influences on the evaluation. Country studies typically include representative data sets.

3.4. Organisation of the IT function

Besides evaluation of IT projects or operational information systems, the evaluation may also refer to the overall IT function (see, Watad, 1995; Shin, 1997). In particular, issues relating to outsourcing is an object of study (Willcocks and Fitzgerald, 1994; Currie and Irani, 1999; Khalfan, Gough, 2000; Lin and Pervan, 2001).

Papers in this area all refer to measurement problems and evaluation i.e. the evaluation of an outsourcing decision requires some form of measurable objectives and processes. These papers also typically address the boundaries of measurement (not everything is measurable) and also consider some of the arguments related to the nature of the measurement activity (every measurement potentially raises another measurement problem).

3.5. Evaluation methods

A number of evaluation methods are especially noteworthy. Those that received more attention then others include:

- The Balanced Scorecard (Grembergen and Bruggen, 1997; Hillam and Edwards, 2001; Deschoolmeester and Braet, 2000).
- Simulation as analysis tools for examining the effects of an envisioned information system (Jong, 1999; 2000; Anderson, 2000).
- DSDM (dynamic systems development method), as an approach to enhancing a system development methodology with an evaluation approach (Barrow and Maylew, 2001).

Given the focus of the conference, the number of papers that actually develop evaluation methods is modest. The discussion about evaluation methods has primarily been taken place outside the conference (Parker and Benson 1988; Remenyi and Sherwood-Smith, 1997; Thorp, 1998; GAO, 2000) and was published in book form. Perhaps this is due to the fact that any discussion on the development of evaluation methods requires much more detail than can be reduced to approximately 5,000 words.

These methods are all of a multidisciplinary nature. Financial approaches receive relatively little attention except for the option theory approach (see next Section for references).

3.6. Evaluation theory

Evaluation is a multidisciplinary topic and many theoretical approaches have been applied to study evaluation practices and explain the various phenomena. Examples of theory-based approaches are:

- Economics/accounting theory (Dier and Mooney, 1994; Dirks and Lent, 1997; Bannister and McCabe, 1999; Maanen and Berghout, 2001; Svavarsson, 2002;);

- Interpretative approach (Serafeimidis and Smithson, 1994; McBride and Fidler, 1994; Abu-Samaha, 2000);
- Critical approach (Nijland, 2001; O'Donnell and Hendriksen, 2001; Jones and Basden, 2002);
- Structuration theory (Vaujany, 2001, Jansen and Nes (2004));
- Grounded theory (Jones and Hughes, 2001);
- Contingency approach (Turk, 2000);
- Soft Systems Methodology and process theory (Kefi, 2002; Stansfield et al., 2000).
- Cognitive mapping (Newman and Hang, 2002);
- Option theory (Jong, et al., 1997; Clare and Lichtenstein, 2000; Mehler-Bicher, 2001; Svavarsson, 2002;);
- Social theory (Berghout et al., 1996);
- Post-modernism (Remenyi and Sherwood-Smith, 1996).

Theoretical underpinning of IT evaluation research is a major issue, because this very well demonstrates the level of understanding of the topic. The variety of approaches already illustrates that there is little consensus in this area. It is even extremely complex to make a statement about more or less promising approaches. Option theory has not been very successful from a practical point of view. However, it remains noteworthy from a theoretical perspective explaining the economical aspects of evaluation. The interpretative approach such as that advocated by Walsham, (1993) received the widest attention. Elaborating upon a theoretical foundation of IT evaluation research is certainly an urgent issue.

4. Research results

In this section the conclusions of the 298 papers are summarised into four main research findings as follows:
- The untangling of IT value;
- The multidisciplinary nature of evaluation;
- The importance of stakeholder analysis;
- The importance of organisational learning and life cycle management.

4.1. The untangling of IT value

The untangling of IT value is discussed, first, through elaboration on IT cost, second, through elaboration on IT benefits, and third, through elaboration on IT value creation.

4.1.1. Untangling IT cost

Many of the 298 papers deal with the notion of cost as a resolved issue. However, a number of papers illustrate that this is perhaps not the case (Bannister and McCabe, 1999; Maanen and Berghout, 2001; Dirks and Lent, 1997; Dier and Mooney, 1994). Costs associated with developing or operating information systems are primarily of a fixed and indirect nature. Calculating IS cost, therefore, always implies the allocation of cost and there are many unresolved issues regarding such allocation. Bannister and McCabe present a list of difficulties associated with understanding IT related costs (Bannister and McCabe, 1999):

- Identification problems. IT is always part of something else, being a project or departmental unit. For example, to what extent are user-cost included in IT costs?
- Data capture problems. Besides general accounting failures, there are typical non-recorded costs, such as, implementation cost.
- Overhead allocation problems. Cost accounting of IT includes many charging issues making this a personal and political problem.
- Accounting conventions. Different standards regarding amortisation and capitalisation are applied between and within countries.
- Disbenefits. This typically refers to the negative consequences of introducing IT, such as, increased risk of fraud and decreased flexibility of operations.

A cost-based approach also seems to be more adequate for investment analysis than cash flows. Examples of cost that would be unaccounted for using a cash flow analysis could be hardware cost, when the IT investment would not directly result in a purchase of additional hardware.

In contrast to what is suggested in many of the conference papers, there are many issues still unresolved regarding IT cost. There is little knowledge of the cost behaviour of information systems and few, if any tested methodologies or even theories to manage and control IT cost. IT costing is a complex issue, which is well suited for further research.

4.1.2. Untangling IT benefits

Most of the papers deal with the complex issue of untangling IT benefits. Sometimes this is done in great detail (Bannister, 1998; Remenyi, 1999; Bannister, 2000; Lillrank, et al., 2000; Remenyi, 2002). Remenyi identifies four major problems with IT benefits measurement and management (Remenyi, 1999):

- Benefits such as intangible performance improvements. Unlike cost, such benefits primarily impact processes inside an organization and seldomly associated to goods or services sold on an outside market. Their value is, therefore, predominantly dependent on individual judgement and not on market prices.
- The issue of information reach. Even for the most straightforward application it is never simple to understand exactly what the results will be of bringing together information about different business issues. There will nearly always be knock-on effects, especially when such a system results in integrating business processes.
- Tangible and intangible benefits. Some aspects of an information system may produce hard or tangible benefits which will directly improve the performance of the firm, such as reducing cost and will therefore be seen in the accounting numbers of the organisation as an improvement in profit and perhaps in return on investment. However, other aspects of this system will only create soft or intangible benefits, which will make life easier in the organisation, however, will not directly lead to identifiable performance improvements. In a competitive market cost reductions are primarily transferred to customers and the associated prevented competitive loss may also not show up in the accounting numbers of the firm.
- Benefit evolution. Many information systems will have some easy to identify or obvious benefits which will be sustainable over a period of time. However, as the development of the project proceeds and the ramifications of the system more fully understood, new ideas about potential benefits will also become apparent. This will have been due to the process of creative dialogue between the principal stakeholders, which will bring to light new business processes and practices. In short, potential benefits should not be seen as being static, but rather evolve as a greater understanding is gained of the organisation and the role which the system will play in this. Given this observation, some researchers developed techniques to actively manage benefits (Lillrank et al., 2000; Remenyi and Sherwood-Smith, 1997).

Notable is that most researchers define value in a multidisciplinary perspective and very few restrict themselves to a purely financial analysis. There is, however, no consensus about the operationalisation of the measurement and management of benefits.

4.1.3. Untangling IT value creation

Given the problems encountered with untangling IT cost and benefits, it may be expected that there will also be difficulties with untangling the notion of IT value, and this is certainly the case. However, some common understanding has also developed in this area.

Process models have been developed to illustrate the process of value creation at a higher level of detail. Well-known examples of such models from outside the conference are Trice and Treacy, (1986), Weill (1990), Soh and Markus (1993). Conference papers regarding process models include McKeen et al. (1996), Jurison (1999), McAuley (2000), Remenyi (2002).

Similar to the discussion around benefits there is a prominent role for individual perspectives and the multidisciplinary nature of value.

Almost all studies presented at the conference evaluate the value of IT on an organisational level and, remarkably, few on higher levels, such as, governments or countries (Shu, 2001, Bannister and Remenyi 2003). There are also few publications regarding the lower individual level (exceptions are Bannister, 2002 and Hughes, et al., 2002). The country studies that have been presented focus on the use of evaluation techniques in a particular industry or organisation and not on the effects of its impact upon the country or the society. Although, the mission of the conference explicitly includes macro economic studies, these papers still have to find their way to the conference.

4.2. The multidisciplinary nature of evaluation

There has been a special interest in the multidisciplinary nature of evaluation since the first conference, see for example the papers McBride and Fidler (1994), Serafeimidis and Smithson (1994), Brown (1994), Jurison (1994). Section 3.6 already provided an overview of the various theories that have been suggested or used. However, there is no common understanding regarding the methodology necessary to understand a multidisciplinary field of study. Difficulties with finding appropriate data sets and issues related to how handle these have yet to be resolved.

4.3. The importance of stakeholder analysis

Regardless of the research approach or theoretical underpinning, an analysis of the objectives and influence of the various stakeholders has become a common part of evaluation studies (see for instance Serafeimidis (1999), Hughes and Jones (1999), Jones and Hughes (1999), Khalifa, et al. (2000), McAuley and Doherty (2001). Although a stakeholder analysis appears to be an essential element of an evaluation study, the methodological consequences remain relatively unexplored (Grembergen and Bruggen, 1997; Deschoolmeester and Braet, 2000; Hillam and Edwards, 2001). First studies that contain a methodology to include stakeholder perspectives are Jones and Hughes (1999), Barrow and Mayhew (2001), Remenyi (2002). These approaches all focus on a continuous value management: the more traditional accounting viewpoint of pre and post implementation studies is abandoned. These types of continuous management are typically suited to managing scope dynamics of projects and emergent values (Remenyi, 2002). These approaches seem to be, however, far from robust.

4.4. The importance of organisational learning and life cycle management

In line with the multidisciplinary nature of evaluation and stakeholder analysis is the importance of organisational learning and life cycle management. The organisational and strategic impact of IT primarily depends on organisational and market characteristics, such as the ability to adapt new working methods, as well as, the willingness to pay for additional product information. Information about already completed projects is, therefore, essential to improve ex-ante or up-front assessments (Alsen and Linde, 1994; Kaplan, 1995; Ward, et al., 1995; Serafeimidis and Smithson, 1995; Swinkels, 1997; Nijland and Berghout, 2000).

Many researchers observe problems in this learning process (see Nijland and Berghout, 2000). Several reasons are given:
- The project objectives were defined in an uncontrollable fashion.
- The priorities of other tasks are higher.
- The outcome differs from the initial perspective and the various stakeholders try to avoid discussing who is to blame for this.

As a consequence evaluation researchers are confronted with the situation that evaluation practice is relatively poorly developed, case studies are unable to validate the more advanced elements of evaluation methods and practitioners are reluctant to use untested methods.

There is also the issue of diminishing value of additional evaluations. Although continuous evaluation and life cycle management do seem to be an obvious route for the development of evaluation methods, there is always the risk over 'over-measuring'. This issue has, so far, not been explored at the conference.

5. Perspectives

In this Section three issues are presented that we consider particularly interesting for further study. Given the complex nature of this field of study and the relatively short time it has been of interest to academic researchers the number of topics that could be explored is, of course, almost endless. However, based on the observations in the previous Sections we conclude that some issues might have a higher priority than others. These issues are:

- Theoretical underpinning of IT evaluation.
- Improved methodological understanding of which data sets are appropriate and how they may be used in this type of research.
- Establishing a more common core of concepts.

5.1. Theories used to underpin IT evaluation

As presented in Section 3, the number of different theories used in the studies of the past nine years is significant and there is certainly no commonly accepted understanding of which of these might be most appropriate.

Accounting theory and interpretive analysis are most frequently applied. Interpretive analysis has been supported since the first days of the conference (Serafeimidis and Smithson, 1994). In this case IT evaluation is viewed as a socially embedded process including formal and informal procedures and where actors try to make some sense of their situation. Other researchers encouraging this approach are (Abu-Samaha, 2000; Jones, 2001; Agerfalk et al., 2002; Kefi, 2002).

Several researchers refer to Habermas' theory of social action, where the "world" is explained as a whole (Jones and Basden, 2002). Habermas' theory is centred on communication and seeks to clarify the conditions, means, content, constraints and objectives of socially organised human behaviour (Habermas, 1984). Researchers that encourage this approach are O'Donnell and Hendriksen (2001) and Jones and Basden (2002).

Glaser and Strauss's Grounded Theory is referred to by Jones and Hughes (2001) as a more structured approach that provides some form of synergy between the more quantitative interpretive research and more qualitative positivistic research.

Other noteworthy frameworks include critical theory, referred to by Nijland (2001) and Giddens' structuration theory, referred to by Vaujany (2001). Furthermore, option theory is another referred to quantitative approach (Jong, 1997; Clare and Lichtenstein, 2000; Meher-Bicher, 2001; Svavarsson et al., 2002).

Clearly there is no single, superior, theoretical underpinning for research in this field of study. And this issue in itself is a major problem which deserves much attention.

5.2. Improved data sets

Business research is primarily built on empirical data and often in the form of case studies and questionnaires. This is a logical situation given the relative immaturity of this research. Comparable with medical sciences, most medical breakthroughs historically originated from observations of initially successful patients and were not the result of double blind testing. However, the internal and external validity of some case studies is a matter of concern to the rigorous researcher.

The issue of what data is appropriate and how to use it in reaching conclusions is by no means agreed and needs much more attention.

5.3. Common concepts

IT evaluation researchers are still far away from a generally agreed and accepted use of common concepts. This is a major problem and can cause substantial misunderstanding and disagreement. For example, costs and cash flows are sometimes confused. Putting more effort in the creation of more commonly accepted concepts will probably also reveal that we left many issues unattended in the scientific rush forwards.

Particularly noteworthy papers in the area of concept development are those of Bannister and McCabe (1999) on cost, Remenyi (1999) on benefits and Remenyi (2000) on value.

6. Summary and conclusions

The purpose of this paper is to present an overview of eleven years of an IT evaluation conference. In these conferences 407 authors contributed to 298 papers. The number of different approaches to IT evaluation was considerable and this diversity of the papers reflected the complexity of this field of study.

One of the most obvious conclusions, which may be reached from this analysis, is that this field of study is still active across a wide range of issues and that there has not been any major attempt to focus the breath of topics researched. This eclectic approach to the research may reflect the fact that there has been only a marginal improvement in the maturity in this field of study over the past eleven years. On the other hand the view can be taken that although a substantial amount of research has been conducted in IT evaluation there are still many problems to be addressed and many of the problems, which have been addressed as yet are still to be fully resolved.

However before sharpening pencils and diving into more case studies or surveys it is important to reflect at a more fundamental level on what is being done in the field of IT evaluation. So far the energy expanded on research in this field has not produced much insight into the core problems.

Three suggestions are made:- firstly, it would be useful to focus more research on the reasons why IT evaluation is important and also on why it is not conducted by practitioners as much as perhaps the academic community feels it should. The fact that there is a political dimension of evaluation is well known but more work needs to be undertaken in this direction. Corporate politics and power relationships within organisations are not a well researched area perhaps because of the difficulties of getting to the root of the problems. But this should not discourage academic researchers. This research into power relationships should include careful study of how investment analysis both ex ante and ex post is performed for other functions in business or in government and if it is correct that IT projects are regularly singled out for more sever scrutiny and more thorough analysis than other similarly sized investments.

Secondly, research attention needs to be focused on the question of data or evidence. Are case studies and questionnaires really relevant to researchers in this field of study? Do these research techniques really lend themselves to the delivery of useful insights in this field of study? Should for example action research not become the main paradigm in the field of IT evaluation? Clearly in the light of our first suggestion concerning power relationships there would appear to be a need for more research employing a critical theory perspective. Furthermore given the availability of certain data sets then what are the implications for the academic researchers' ability to analyse it and which are the most effective tools.

Finally, the question of trying to define the core of this field of study and in so doing create some degree of understanding and perhaps even consensus as to the important concepts which are required to be able to evaluate IT investment, needs to be addressed. This amounts to developing a theory of IT evaluation. This is not a simple matter as this field of study is intrinsically eclectic and thus draws on a wide range of theoretical and practical thinking. To integrate this so that IT evaluation could be regarded as having its own theoretical foundation is a major challenge. As it stands IT evaluation is very fragmented and to the outsider it looks quite disjointed. As mentioned above it is clear that misunderstandings creep into research because of this lack of consensus. Also there is a tendency for many novice researchers to try to reinvent or define basic concepts again and again. The notions of value and benefits to mention only two ideas are churned over again and again with virtually no progress to should for this debate. This need for theoretical underpinning is perhaps the most difficult area of IT evaluation research to tackle and one which needs the most philosophical and theory building attention.

In general there is no doubt that IT evaluation is a field of study, which very is complex. Its scope is exceptionally wide ranging. There are still many challenges and it is perhaps for this reason that it is so attractive to some researchers. However there are other fields of study which are complex and which have been able to arrive at a higher degree of maturity. In this respect is it not now time for IT evaluation research to catch up?

References

Addison, T., Sutherland, F. (1995). Development tools and the productivity payoff, Proceedings of the Second European Conference on Information Technology Evaluation, D. Remenyi and A. Brown (eds.), MCIL (Reading).

Abu-Samaha, A. (2000). Product, project and programme evaluation: the need to address the wider context of IT evaluation, Proceedings of the Seventh European Conference on Information Technology Evaluation, A. Brown and D. Remenyi (eds.), MCIL (Reading).

Agerfalk, P., Eliason, E., Sjostrom, J., Cronholm, S., Goldkuhl, G. (2002). Setting the scene for actability evaluation: understanding information systems in context, Proceedings of the Ninth European Conference on Information Technology Evaluation, A. Brown and D. Remenyi (eds.), MCIL (Reading).

Al-Masharis, M., Al-Samad, A. (2002). A best-practices model for measuring readiness levels for e-commerce, e-business and e-government applications, Proceedings of the Ninth European Conference on Information Technology Evaluation, A. Brown and D. Remenyi (eds.), MCIL (Reading).

Al-Mudimigh, A, Jarrar, Y., Zairi, M. (2001). An integrating approach to ERP-implementation: a proposed methodology, Proceedings of the Eighth European Conference on Information Technology Evaluation, D. Remenyi and A. Brown (eds.), MCIL (Reading).

Al- Mudimigh, A., Al-Mashari, M. (2002). A global survey of holistic enterprise resource planning implementation, Proceedings of the Ninth European Conference on Information Technology Evaluation, A. Brown and D. Remenyi (eds.), MCIL (Reading).

Al-Turki, S. (2000). The Saudi management style and its influence on information technology implementation: an academic review, Proceedings of the Seventh European Conference on Information Technology Evaluation, A. Brown and D. Remenyi (eds.), MCIL (Reading).

Alsen, R., Linde, G. van der (1994). Evaluation of investments in information technology: policy and practice at PTT Telecom, Proceedings of the First European Conference on Information Technology Evaluation, A. Brown and D. Remenyi (eds.), Operational Research Society (Birmingham).

Ammenwerth, E., Kaiser, F., Buerkly, T., Graber, S., Herrmenn, G., Wilhelmy, I. (2002). Evaluation of user acceptance of data management systems in hospitals, Proceedings of the Ninth European Conference on

Information Technology Evaluation, A. Brown and D. Remenyi (eds.), MCIL (Reading).

Andersen, J. (1999). Evaluation of IT in the Danish construction industry, Proceedings of the Sixth European Conference on Information Technology Evaluation, A. Brown and D. Remenyi (eds.), MCIL (Reading).

Anderson, J. (2000). Evaluation of information technology in the delivery of health care using computer simulation, Proceedings of the Seventh European Conference on Information Technology Evaluation, A. Brown and D. Remenyi (eds.), MCIL (Reading).

Arribas, H., Sanchez, P. (1996). A quantitative model for technological risk assessment in the process of information technology transfer, Proceedings of the Third European Conference on Information Technology Evaluation, A. Brown and D. Remenyi (eds.), MCIL (Reading).

Arribas, H., Ingusta, P. (1997). Development levels and IT evaluation models in Spanish companies: a cluster analyis, Proceedings of the Fourth European Conference on Information Technology Evaluation, E. Berghout and D. Remenyi (eds.), Delft University Press (Delft).

Avram, G. (1999). Considerations on the evaluation of IS in Romanian SMEs, Proceedings of the Sixth European Conference on Information Technology Evaluation, A. Brown and D. Remenyi (eds.), MCIL (Reading).

Avram, G. (2000). Evaluation of investments in e-commerce in the Romanian business environment, Proceedings of the Seventh European Conference on Information Technology Evaluation, A. Brown and D. Remenyi (eds.), MCIL (Reading).

Bannister, F. (1998). In defence of instinct: IT value and investment decisions, Proceedings of the Fifth European Conference on Information Technology Evaluation, A. Brown and D. Remenyi (eds.), MCIL (Reading).

Bannister, F. (2000). Marching a different drum: citizen centricity and the changing perception of IT value in public administration, Proceedings of the Seventh European Conference on Information Technology Evaluation, A. Brown and D. Remenyi (eds.), MCIL (Reading).

Bannister, F. (2002). Presenting productivity: a personal odyssey, Proceedings of the Ninth European Conference on Information Technology Evaluation, A. Brown and D. Remenyi (eds.), MCIL (Reading).

Bannister, F (2004) IT Value, Meaning and Identity: An Exploration of Things to Come, Proceedings of the Eleventh European Conference on Information Technology Evaluation, D Remenyi (Ed.), ACI, (Reading)

Bannister, F., McCabe, P. (1999). How much did we pay for that? The awkward problem of IT costs, Proceedings of the Sixth European Conference on Information Technology Evaluation, A. Brown and D. Remenyi (eds.), MCIL (Reading).

Bannister, F and Remenyi D, (2003). Evaluating the Information Society: Some conceptual issues, Proceedings of the Tenth European Conference on Information Technology Evaluation, Madrid, Berghout E and D. Remenyi (eds.), MCIL (Reading).

Barrow, P., Mayhew, P. (2001). Consensus building in formative and participative IS evaluation approaches, Proceedings of the Eighth European Conference on Information Technology Evaluation, D. Remenyi and A. Brown (eds.), MCIL (Reading).

Benson, R., Parker, M., Trainor, H. (1988). Information economics, Prentice-Hall (Englewood Cliffs).

Bergamaschi, W., Ongaro, E. (2001). Evaluation of the organizational impact of ICT as an instrument for the development of information systems in hospitals, Proceedings of the Eighth European Conference on Information Technology Evaluation, D. Remenyi and A. Brown (eds.), MCIL (Reading).

Berghout, E., Klompe, R., Vries, M. de (1996). Towards enhancing investment evaluation methods with behavioral theory, Proceedings of the Third European Conference on Information Technology Evaluation, A. Brown and D. Remenyi (eds.), MCIL (Reading).

Beynom-Davies, P. (2002). Evaluating the experience of e-business amongst SME's, Proceedings of the Ninth European Conference on Information Technology Evaluation, A. Brown and D. Remenyi (eds.), MCIL (Reading).

Bonner, M. (1995). DeLone and McLean's model for judging information systems success: a retrospective application in manufacturing, Proceedings of the Second European Conference on Information Technology Evaluation, D. Remenyi and A. Brown (eds.), MCIL (Reading).

Brown, A. (1994). Appraising intangible benefits from information technology investments, Proceedings of the First European Conference on Information Technology Evaluation, A. Brown and D. Remenyi (eds.), Operational Research Society (Birmingham).

Calla, R, Ezingeard, J., Money, A. (2002). IT-enabled customer relationship management: an exploratory construct development from content analysis of vendor claims, Proceedings of the Ninth European Conference on Information Technology Evaluation, A. Brown and D. Remenyi (eds.), MCIL (Reading).

Carlsson, S. (1998). Appraising executive support systems: a competing values based approach, Proceedings of the Fifth European Conference on Information Technology Evaluation, A. Brown and D. Remenyi (eds.), MCIL (Reading).

Carson E, Cramp D, Leicester H and Roudsari A (2004). Building Evaluation Into REALITY Telecare, Proceedings of the Eleventh European Conference on Information Technology Evaluation, D Remenyi (Ed.), ACI, (Reading).

Cherian, E. (2001). Electronic business: the business model makes the difference, Proceedings of the Eighth European Conference on Information Technology Evaluation, D. Remenyi and A. Brown (eds.), MCIL (Reading).

Cheverst, K, Fitton D, Rouncefield M and Graham C (2004). 'Smart Mobs' and Technology Probes: Evaluating Texting at Work, Proceedings of the Eleventh European Conference on Information Technology Evaluation, D Remenyi (Ed.), ACI, (Reading)

Clare, R., Lichtenstein, Y. (2000). Real options analysis of an electronic-auction infrastructure for the Irish fishing industry, Proceedings of the Seventh European Conference on Information Technology Evaluation, A. Brown and D. Remenyi (eds.), MCIL (Reading).

Clark, J., Soliman, F. (1996). Appraising knowledge based systems investments, Proceedings of the Third European Conference on Information Technology Evaluation, A. Brown and D. Remenyi (eds.), MCIL (Reading).

Coronado, A., Sarhadi, M., Millar, C. (1999). An evaluation model of IS for agile manufacturing, Proceedings of the Sixth European Conference on Information Technology Evaluation, A. Brown and D. Remenyi (eds.), MCIL (Reading).

Cronk, M. (1999). IS value alignment in Australian organisations, Proceedings of the Sixth European Conference on Information Technology Evaluation, A. Brown and D. Remenyi (eds.), MCIL (Reading).

Currie, W., Irani, Z., (1999). Assessing the benefits, costs and risks of IT/IS outsourcing, Proceedings of the Sixth European Conference on Information Technology Evaluation, A. Brown and D. Remenyi (eds.), MCIL (Reading).

Dans, E. (2000). IT investment in small and medium enterprises: paradoxically productive?, Proceedings of the Seventh European Conference on

Information Technology Evaluation, A. Brown and D. Remenyi (eds.), MCIL (Reading).

Dans, E. (2001). IT responsiveness in small and medium enterprises: it pays to be on top of IT, Proceedings of the Eighth European Conference on Information Technology Evaluation, D. Remenyi and A. Brown (eds.), MCIL (Reading).

Deitz, R. (1995). Investing in SIS: on the roleof selection in decision-making, Proceedings of the Second European Conference on Information Technology Evaluation, D. Remenyi and A. Brown (eds.), MCIL (Reading).

Demkes, R. (1997). Deciding on inter-organizational telemetics investments: the use of IT evaluation methods, Proceedings of the Fourth European Conference on Information Technology Evaluation, E. Berghout and D. Remenyi (eds.), Delft University Press (Delft).

Deschoolmeester, D., Braet, O. (2000). Evaluation of ERP investments in the Belgium assembly industry, Proceedings of the Seventh European Conference on Information Technology Evaluation, A. Brown and D. Remenyi (eds.), MCIL (Reading).

Dier, D., Mooney, J. (1994). Enhancing the evaluation of IT investments through comprehensive cost analysis, Proceedings of the First European Conference on Information Technology Evaluation, A. Brown and D. Remenyi (eds.), Operational Research Society (Birmingham).

Diniz E, Moreno Porto R and Adachi T (2004). Evaluating Internet Banking Web Sites in Brazil, Proceedings of the Eleventh European Conference on Information Technology Evaluation, D Remenyi (Ed.), ACI, (Reading)

Dirks, P., Lent, L. van (1997). Control of the information systems function: the role of cost allocation, Proceedings of the Fourth European Conference on Information Technology Evaluation, E. Berghout and D. Remenyi (eds.), Delft University Press (Delft).

ElKordy, M., Leeming, A., Khalil, O. (1997). EIS usage: a cross-cultural study, Proceedings of the Fourth European Conference on Information Technology Evaluation, E. Berghout and D. Remenyi (eds.), Delft University Press (Delft).

Enzingeard, J. (1998). Towards performance measurement processes for manufacturing information systems, Proceedings of the Fifth European Conference on Information Technology Evaluation, A. Brown and D. Remenyi (eds.), MCIL (Reading).

Ezingeard, J., Chandler-Wilde, R. (1999). Evaluating how ERP can provide competitive advantage: a bais for a research framework, Proceedings of the Sixth European Conference on Information Technology Evaluation, A. Brown and D. Remenyi (eds.), MCIL (Reading).

Ezingeard, J., Nolan, R., Money, A. (2001). A taxonomy of objectives of IT-enabled customer relationship management as a basis of evaluation of CRM success, Proceedings of the Eighth European Conference on Information Technology Evaluation, D. Remenyi and A. Brown (eds.), MCIL (Reading).

Frisk E and Plantén A (2004) IT Investment Evaluation – A Survey of Perceptions Among Managers in Sweden, Proceedings of the Eleventh European Conference on Information Technology Evaluation, D Remenyi (Ed.), ACI, (Reading)

GAO (2000). Information technology investment management: a framwork for assessing and improving process maturity, Report GAO/AIMD-10.1.23, United States General Accounting Office (Washington).

Grembergen, W. van, Bruggen, R. (1997). Measuring and improving corporate information technology through the balanced scorecard technique, Proceedings of the Fourth European Conference on Information Technology Evaluation, E. Berghout and D. Remenyi (eds.), Delft University Press (Delft).

Grunden, K. (2002). An evaluation model for CSCW systems, Proceedings of the Ninth European Conference on Information Technology Evaluation, A. Brown and D. Remenyi (eds.), MCIL (Reading).

Habermas, J. (1984). The theory of communicative action. Volume 1: Reason and rationalisation in society, T. McCarthy (trans). Polity Press (Oxford).

Hart, M., (1999). IT in the South African retailing industry, Proceedings of the Sixth European Conference on Information Technology Evaluation, A. Brown and D. Remenyi (eds.), MCIL (Reading).

Hillam, C., Edwards, H. (1999). A case study approach to evaluation of information technology/information systems investment evaluation processes within SMEs, Proceedings of the Sixth European Conference on Information Technology Evaluation, A. Brown and D. Remenyi (eds.), MCIL (Reading).

Hillam, C., Edwards, H. (2001). Applications and evaluations of enterprise resource planning, Proceedings of the Eighth European Conference on Information Technology Evaluation, D. Remenyi and A. Brown (eds.), MCIL (Reading).

Hoogeweegen, M., Nunen, J., Wagenaar, R. (1994). Edialysis: a decision support system for assessing costs and benefits of electronic data interchange, Proceedings of the First European Conference on Information Technology Evaluation, A. Brown and D. Remenyi (eds.), Operational Research Society (Birmingham).

Hughes, J., Jones, S. (1999). Situated plans: time to reassess IT/IS evaluation, Proceedings of the Sixth European Conference on Information Technology Evaluation, A. Brown and D. Remenyi (eds.), MCIL (Reading).

Hughes, R., Cooper, A., Crossey, A., Marshall, T. (2002). Models of user satisfaction with IT services: some preliminary findings, Proceedings of the Ninth European Conference on Information Technology Evaluation, A. Brown and D. Remenyi (eds.), MCIL (Reading).

Jansen A and Nes T. A Structurational Perspective on Technology: An Evaluation of why the same Technical Solution is Adopted Differently Across an Organisation Proceedings of the Eleventh European Conference on Information Technology Evaluation, D Remenyi (Ed.), ACI, (Reading)

Johansson, B., Carlsson, S. (2002). Application service providers and SMEs, Proceedings of the Ninth European Conference on Information Technology Evaluation, A. Brown and D. Remenyi (eds.), MCIL (Reading).

Jones, G., Basden, A. (2002). How Habermas action types can influence KBS design and use,

Jones, S., Hughes, J. (2001). An exploration of the use of grounded theory as an approach in the field of IS evaluation, Proceedings of the Eighth European Conference on Information Technology Evaluation, D. Remenyi and A. Brown (eds.), MCIL (Reading).

Jong, B., Ribbers, P., Zee, H. (1997). Option pricing for IT valuation: a dead end, Proceedings of the Fourth European Conference on Information Technology Evaluation, E. Berghout and D. Remenyi (eds.), Delft University Press (Delft).

Jong, W. de (1999). Simulation as evaluation tool in IT service management, Proceedings of the Sixth European Conference on Information Technology Evaluation, A. Brown and D. Remenyi (eds.), MCIL (Reading).

Jong, W. de (2000). Evaluation of IT service management using structured task analysis, Proceedings of the Seventh European Conference on Information Technology Evaluation, A. Brown and D. Remenyi (eds.), MCIL (Reading).

Josefsson, U., Nilsson, A. (1999). The progress of groupware use in local government, Proceedings of the Sixth European Conference on Information Technology Evaluation, A. Brown and D. Remenyi (eds.), MCIL (Reading).

Jurison, J. (1994). Measurement and evaluation of IT benefits: a stakeholder-based approach, Proceedings of the First European Conference on Information Technology Evaluation, A. Brown and D. Remenyi (eds.), Operational Research Society (Birmingham).

Jurison, J. (1999). Process-based measures for evaluating IT investments, Proceedings of the Sixth European Conference on Information Technology Evaluation, A. Brown and D. Remenyi (eds.), MCIL (Reading).

Kaplan, B. (1995). A model comprehensive evaluation plan for complex information systems: clinical imaging as an example, Proceedings of the Second European Conference on Information Technology Evaluation, D. Remenyi and A. Brown (eds.), MCIL (Reading).

Kefi, H. (2002). IS/IT evaluation: a process-oriented and context based approach, Proceedings of the Ninth European Conference on Information Technology Evaluation, A. Brown and D. Remenyi (eds.), MCIL (Reading).

Khalfan, A., Gough, T. (2000). Vendor selection criteria and post-implementation evaluation practices for IS/IT outsourcing: a case study of a developing country, Proceedings of the Seventh European Conference on Information Technology Evaluation, A. Brown and D. Remenyi (eds.), MCIL (Reading).

Khalifa, G., Irani, Z., Baldwin, L., Jones, S. (2000). Evaluating information technology with you in mind, Proceedings of the Seventh European Conference on Information Technology Evaluation, A. Brown and D. Remenyi (eds.), MCIL (Reading).

Kontio J (2004). Typical Problems in Information Systems – A Multiple Case Study in Six Finnish Organisations, Proceedings of the Eleventh European Conference on Information Technology Evaluation, D Remenyi (Ed.), ACI, (Reading)

Kueng, P. (1998). Impact of workflow systems on people, task and structure: a post-implementation evaluation, Proceedings of the Fifth European Conference on Information Technology Evaluation, A. Brown and D. Remenyi (eds.), MCIL (Reading).

Lampikoski, T, Rusi, T. (2002). Evaluating telecom operator's strategic technology assets, Proceedings of the Ninth European Conference on Information Technology Evaluation, A. Brown and D. Remenyi (eds.), MCIL (Reading).

Lee, M. (1999). A proposed business model for the electronic commerce: using resource based view to examine the strategic value of the web site, Proceedings of the Sixth European Conference on Information Technology Evaluation, A. Brown and D. Remenyi (eds.), MCIL (Reading).

Lillrank, P., Holopainen, S., Paavola, T. (2000). Catching intangible benefits, Proceedings of the Seventh European Conference on Information Technology Evaluation, A. Brown and D. Remenyi (eds.), MCIL (Reading).

Lin, C., Pervan, G. (2001). IS/IT investment evaluation, benefits management and oursourcing issues in an Australian Government Agency, Proceedings of the Eighth European Conference on Information Technology Evaluation, D. Remenyi and A. Brown (eds.), MCIL (Reading).

Lock, C. (1996). The assessment of IT in healthcare and the relevance of the private finance initiative, Proceedings of the Third European Conference on Information Technology Evaluation, A. Brown and D. Remenyi (eds.), MCIL (Reading).

Maanen, H., Berghout, E. (2001). Cost management of IT beyond cost of ownership models: a state-of-the-art overview of the Dutch financial services industry, Proceedings of the Eighth European Conference on Information Technology Evaluation, D. Remenyi and A. Brown (eds.), MCIL (Reading).

Maimbo, H., Pervan, G. (2002). A model for IS/IT investment and organisational performance in the banking industry, Proceedings of the Ninth European Conference on Information Technology Evaluation, A. Brown and D. Remenyi (eds.), MCIL (Reading).

Magrill and Brown, 1977

McAulay, L. (2000). Of clouds and clocks: the problem of IT evaluation and the freedom of the human being, Proceedings of the Seventh European Conference on Information Technology Evaluation, A. Brown and D. Remenyi (eds.), MCIL (Reading).

McAuley, L., Doherty, N. (2001). The stakeholder dimension in information systems evaluation, Proceedings of the Eighth European Conference on Information Technology Evaluation, D. Remenyi and A. Brown (eds.), MCIL (Reading).

McBride, N., Fidler, C. (1994). An interpretative approach to justification of investments in information systems, Proceedings of the First European Conference on Information Technology Evaluation, A. Brown and D. Remenyi (eds.), Operational Research Society (Birmingham).

McKeen, J., Smith, H., Parent, M. (1996). An integrative research approach to assess the business value of information technology, Proceedings of the Third European Conference on Information Technology Evaluation, A. Brown and D. Remenyi (eds.), MCIL (Reading).

McNutt, L., O'Donnell, G. (1997). Evaluating the needs and perceptions of small to medium sized enterprises in relation to emerging technologies: a qualitative exploratory research study, Proceedings of the Fourth European Conference on Information Technology Evaluation, E. Berghout and D. Remenyi (eds.), Delft University Press (Delft).

Mehler-Bicher, A. (2001). Questionnaire template for assessing e-business investments by applying an option pricing, Proceedings of the Eighth European Conference on Information Technology Evaluation, D. Remenyi and A. Brown (eds.), MCIL (Reading).

Miller, K., Dunn, D. (1997). Post-implementation evaluation of information system/technology: a survey of UK practice, Proceedings of the Fourth European Conference on Information Technology Evaluation, E. Berghout and D. Remenyi (eds.), Delft University Press (Delft).

Miller, K., Whiteley, D., Quick, P. (1999). A trade-based view of evaluating e-commerce, Proceedings of the Sixth European Conference on Information Technology Evaluation, A. Brown and D. Remenyi (eds.), MCIL (Reading).

Mitris, D., Serafeimidis, V. (1994). Evaluating information technology investments in Greece, Proceedings of the First European Conference on Information Technology Evaluation, A. Brown and D. Remenyi (eds.), Operational Research Society (Birmingham).

Murray, P., Dhillon, G. (1996). Management of benefits: interpreting IS/IT success in a National health service trust environment, Proceedings of the Third European Conference on Information Technology Evaluation, A. Brown and D. Remenyi (eds.), MCIL (Reading).

Myles, J., Terry, J., Cowan, E. (2000). Information technology investment and benefit realisation in the Austrian utility industry, Proceedings of the Seventh European Conference on Information Technology Evaluation, A. Brown and D. Remenyi (eds.), MCIL (Reading).

Newman, J., Hang, J. (2002). Mapping the IT evaluation domain, Proceedings of the Ninth European Conference on Information Technology Evaluation, A. Brown and D. Remenyi (eds.), MCIL (Reading).

Newton, K. (1995). Corporate versus business area benefits from IT: practical experiences from the public sector, Proceedings of the Second

European Conference on Information Technology Evaluation, D. Remenyi and A. Brown (eds.), MCIL (Reading).

Nijland, M. (2001). IT cost benefit management improvement from a critical perspective, Proceedings of the Eighth European Conference on Information Technology Evaluation, D. Remenyi and A. Brown (eds.), MCIL (Reading).

Nijland, M., Berghout, E. (2000). Management of IT costs and benefits: results of a quick scan at nine financial institutions, Proceedings of the Seventh European Conference on Information Technology Evaluation, A. Brown and D. Remenyi (eds.), MCIL (Reading).

Niss, K. (1999). Model for investment evaluation of medical information systems (MIEMIS), Proceedings of the Sixth European Conference on Information Technology Evaluation, A. Brown and D. Remenyi (eds.), MCIL (Reading).

O'Donnell, D., Hendriksen, L. (2001). In search of a critical theory of ICT evaluation: from Heidegger to Habermas, Proceedings of the Eighth European Conference on Information Technology Evaluation, D. Remenyi and A. Brown (eds.), MCIL (Reading).

O'Donnell, D., O'Regan, P. (2000). An exploration of the structural dimensions of intellectual capital: perceptions of CEO's indigenous Irish software companies, Proceedings of the Seventh European Conference on Information Technology Evaluation, A. Brown and D. Remenyi (eds.), MCIL (Reading).

Oliver, D., (2000). IT in public agencies: pressure generating investment, Proceedings of the Seventh European Conference on Information Technology Evaluation, A. Brown and D. Remenyi (eds.), MCIL (Reading).

Orr, S., Sohal, A., Gray, K., Harbrow, J., Harrison, D., Mennen, A.(1999). The impact of information technology on a section of the Australian health industry, Proceedings of the Sixth European Conference on Information Technology Evaluation, A. Brown and D. Remenyi (eds.), MCIL (Reading).

Pather S, Remeyi D and de la Harpe A. e-Commerce Success? – kalahari.net a South African Case Study, Proceedings of the Eleventh European Conference on Information Technology Evaluation, D Remenyi (Ed.), ACI, (Reading)

Peterson, R., Wit, D. de (1997). Telecare: on strategic assessment of telematics in healthcare, Proceedings of the Fourth European Conference on Information Technology Evaluation, E. Berghout and D. Remenyi (eds.), Delft University Press (Delft).

Poon, J., Potts, K., Cooper, P. (1999). Developing an expert system in order to improve efficiency and success of the construction process, Proceedings of the Sixth European Conference on Information Technology Evaluation, A. Brown and D. Remenyi (eds.), MCIL (Reading).

Pouloudi, A. Serafeimidis, V. (1999). Stakeholders of information systems evaluation: experience from a case study, Proceedings of the Sixth European Conference on Information Technology Evaluation, A. Brown and D. Remenyi (eds.), MCIL (Reading).

Protti, D., Freeman, M., Dyson, T., Drury, P., Farenden, J., England's National health information strategy: a two year status report, Proceedings of the Seventh Conference on IT Evaluation, MCIL (Reading).

Remenyi, D. (1999). The elusive nature of IS benefits, Proceedings of the Sixth European Conference on Information Technology Evaluation, A. Brown and D. Remenyi (eds.), MCIL (Reading).

Remenyi, D. (2002). The value scorecard: beyond the business case, Proceedings of the Ninth European Conference on Information Technology Evaluation, A. Brown and D. Remenyi (eds.), MCIL (Reading).

Remenyi, D., Sherwood-Smith, M., White, T. (1996). Information systems management: the need for a post-moderrn approach, Proceedings of the Third European Conference on Information Technology Evaluation, A. Brown and D. Remenyi (eds.), MCIL (Reading).

Remenyi, D., Sherwood-Smith, M. (1997). Achiving maximum value from information systems: a process approach, Wiley (Chichester).

Renkema, T. (1997). The four P's revisited: appraising and managing the infrastructure impact of IT investments, Proceedings of the Fourth European Conference on Information Technology Evaluation, E. Berghout and D. Remenyi (eds.), Delft University Press (Delft).

Salmela, H., Turunen, P. (1997). Evaluation of information systems in health care: a framework and its application, Proceedings of the Fourth European Conference on Information Technology Evaluation, E. Berghout and D. Remenyi (eds.), Delft University Press (Delft).

Savolainen, V. (2000). The task of evaluating strategic information systems planning, Proceedings of the Seventh European Conference on Information Technology Evaluation, A. Brown and D. Remenyi (eds.), MCIL (Reading).

Savory, C. (2001). Co-operative inquiry as a basis for evaluation of knowledge management tools, Proceedings of the Eighth European Conference on Information Technology Evaluation, D. Remenyi and A. Brown (eds.), MCIL (Reading).

Serafeimidis, V., Smithson, S. (1994). Evaluation of IS/IT investments: understanding and support, Proceedings of the First European Conference on Information Technology Evaluation, A. Brown and D. Remenyi (eds.), Operational Research Society (Birmingham).

Serafeimidis, V., Smithson, S. (1995). Requirements for an investment appraisal framework for the 1990s: towards a more rigorous solution, Proceedings of the Second European Conference on Information Technology Evaluation, D. Remenyi and A. Brown (eds.), MCIL (Reading).

Shin, N. (1997). The impact of information technology on vertical coordination structure and performance of firms, Proceedings of the Fourth European Conference on Information Technology Evaluation, E. Berghout and D. Remenyi (eds.), Delft University Press (Delft).

Shu, W. (2001). How industry drives productivity growth, Proceedings of the Eighth European Conference on Information Technology Evaluation, D. Remenyi and A. Brown (eds.), MCIL (Reading).

Singh M and Byrne J (2004). Evaluating e-Business in Australia: A Measure of Operational and Financial Improvements, Proceedings of the Eleventh European Conference on Information Technology Evaluation, D Remenyi (Ed.), ACI, (Reading)

Soh, C., Markus, M. (1993). How IT creates business value: a process theory synthesis, Proceedings of the 16th International Conference on Information Systems (ICIS), Amsterdam.

Spil, T. (1995). The evaluation of strategic information systems planning: from a quality undergrowth to a semiotic clearing, Proceedings of the Second European Conference on Information Technology Evaluation, D. Remenyi and A. Brown (eds.), MCIL (Reading).

Stamoulis, D. (1999). A multi-perspective evaluation of an electronic banking delivery channel: the case of AlphaLine, Proceedings of the Sixth European Conference on Information Technology Evaluation, A. Brown and D. Remenyi (eds.), MCIL (Reading).

Stansfield, M., Berghout, E, Grant, K. (2000). Problems and issues relating to IT investment evaluation: experiences from Scottish and Benelux studies, Proceedings of the Seventh European Conference on Information Technology Evaluation, A. Brown and D. Remenyi (eds.), MCIL (Reading).

Stafyla, A., Stefanou, C. (2000). ERP software selection: a study using cognitive maps, Proceedings of the Seventh European Conference on Information Technology Evaluation, A. Brown and D. Remenyi (eds.), MCIL (Reading).

Stefanou, C. (2000). The evaluation of ERP systems, Proceedings of the Seventh European Conference on Information Technology Evaluation, A. Brown and D. Remenyi (eds.), MCIL (Reading).

Suomi, R., Tahkapaa, J. (2001). Assessment of health-care project Primus: methodological lessons learned, Proceedings of the Eighth European Conference on Information Technology Evaluation, D. Remenyi and A. Brown (eds.), MCIL (Reading).

Sutherland, F. (1994). Some current practices in the evaluation of IT benefits in South African organizations, Proceedings of the First European Conference on Information Technology Evaluation, A. Brown and D. Remenyi (eds.), Operational Research Society (Birmingham).

Svavarsson, D. (2002). Evaluating IT investments in the AEC industry, Proceedings of the Ninth European Conference on Information Technology Evaluation, A. Brown and D. Remenyi (eds.), MCIL (Reading).

Swinkels, G. (1997). Managing the life cycle of information and communication technology investments for added value, Proceedings of the Fourth European Conference on Information Technology Evaluation, E. Berghout and D. Remenyi (eds.), Delft University Press (Delft).

Thorp, J. (1998). The information paradox, McGraw-Hill (Toronto).

Trice, A, M.E. Treacy (1986). Utilisation as a dependent variable in MIS research, Seventh Conference on Information Systems, San Diego (Ca.).

Turk, A. (2000). A contingency approach to designing usability evaluation procedures for WWW sites, Proceedings of the Seventh European Conference on Information Technology Evaluation, A. Brown and D. Remenyi (eds.), MCIL (Reading).

Turunen, P. (2001). A model for evaluation of health care information systems, Proceedings of the Eighth European Conference on Information Technology Evaluation, D. Remenyi and A. Brown (eds.), MCIL (Reading).

Tyndale, P. (2002). Evaluating knowledge strategy and knowledge management frameworks, Proceedings of the Ninth European Conference on Information Technology Evaluation, A. Brown and D. Remenyi (eds.), MCIL (Reading).

Vaujany, F. (2001). Grasping the social dynamics of IT use: illustrations of a structurational approach, Proceedings of the Eighth European Conference on Information Technology Evaluation, D. Remenyi and A. Brown (eds.), MCIL (Reading).

Vlug, A, Lei, J. van der (1999). Methodological evaluation of systems case study on a Dutch drug-safety system, Proceedings of the Sixth European Conference on Information Technology Evaluation, A. Brown and D. Remenyi (eds.), MCIL (Reading).

Walsham, G. (1993). Interpreting information systems in organizations, Wiley (Chichester).

Ward, J., Taylor, P., Bond, P. (1995). Identification, realisation and measurement of IS/IT benefits: an empirical study of current practice, Proceedings of the Second European Conference on Information Technology Evaluation, D. Remenyi and A. Brown (eds.), MCIL (Reading).

Watad, M. (1995). The application of content analysis in IT reach: measuring the organisational benefits of IT, Proceedings of the Second European Conference on Information Technology Evaluation, D. Remenyi and A. Brown (eds.), MCIL (Reading).

Weill, P. (1990). Do computers really pay off ? ICIT Press Washington D.C.

Wheeler, F., Chang, H. (1994). Examining the benefits of computerising manufacturing systems: a study of computer aided manufacturing management in Taiwan,

Worrall, L., Remenyi, D., Money, A. (1998). Evaluating IT service delivery from a user perspective: a comparison of six UK local authorities, Proceedings of the Fifth European Conference on Information Technology Evaluation, A. Brown and D. Remenyi (eds.), MCIL (Reading).

Willcocks, L., Fitzgerald, G. (1994). To outsource or not? Recent research on economics and evaluation practice, Proceedings of the First European Conference on Information Technology Evaluation, A. Brown and D. Remenyi (eds.), Operational Research Society (Birmingham).